THE COMPLAINER AND THE THINKER

Family Dynamics

James Jenkins

ISBN: 979-8-89979-972-3

Dedication

There are many people I would like to thank for their contributions and support. **To my family**, thank you for giving me the drive and encouragement to follow my dreams. When I look at the dynamics of family and values, I am grateful and thankful for being part of different diverse family structures.

To the Kropps, a family with well-rounded structural integrity, all of you played a valuable role in the development of my family and structured success. You supported me in several ways, for which I am grateful.

To the Paynes, I learned values beyond my expectations of life. I am very grateful and appreciative to have lived in a structured environment that taught me the real meaning of discipline and how to live within my means, the moral values of being a real man.

To the Lewis and Brown families, and many others, it took a township's commitment and the courage to make sacrifices beyond understanding. When the road got rough, home was always the backbone for moving forward.

To my family, thank you for giving me strength when I needed it and the ability to make it through diverse and challenging situations. I hope this book finds meaning for you all and serves as a resource you can keep for reference when the roads get rough.

Finally, to all those who supported me in establishing a presence in society and to all the readers who support and continue to contribute to bringing our youth's visions to light, I thank you.

Acknowledgment

First, I want to thank God for giving me the inspiration to write this book, to all who have supported my materials, much love and appreciation. To all my family members, friends, and colleagues, thank you. Special thanks to all the media outlets and platforms that showcase my work.

To my readers, I hope you continue to support and enjoy every novel we publish.

About the Author

James W. Jenkins, an American author and entrepreneur, is rapidly making a name for himself in the world of urban street fiction and gritty urban thrillers. Known for his unflinching portrayal of life's harsh realities, Jenkins writes novels that delve deep into the complexities of street life, focusing on the emotional journeys of individuals caught in challenging circumstances. His compelling storytelling resonates with readers who seek authenticity, emotional depth, and narratives rooted in survival, ambition, and hope.

James W. Jenkins is a bestselling author with a diverse portfolio spanning multiple genres. His critically acclaimed work is distinguished by a unique approach to narrative structure and character development, resonating deeply with contemporary readers. His novels have garnered significant recognition, achieving both critical success and commercial appeal, consistently placing him on bestseller lists including the New York Times and Wall Street Journal.

Today, James W. Jenkins channels his passion for storytelling into his writing, which serves as both entertainment and inspiration. His books shed light on real-world challenges, showing that even in the face of adversity, hope and transformation are possible. James believes that stories have the power to connect people and inspire change, a message evident in his work.

James is not only an author but also a symbol of perseverance, demonstrating that it is possible to overcome adversity and turn one's dreams into reality.

James W. Jenkins's work transcends fiction. It is a powerful reflection of the human experience, filled with ambition, struggle, and triumph. Through his novels and dedication to personal growth, James continues to inspire readers and future generations of authors alike.

Contents

Chapter 1
Meet the Complainer & the Thinker

They say it takes a village to raise a child, in retrospect. It takes organization to create a family structure that can withstand the test of time. Every single person within the family must take ownership of their role, their actions, and their responsibility to the whole. Building a solid foundation is not a one-person job; it's a collective effort. Understanding and respecting the principles that bind us together is crucial for survival. This book is about those principles and practices that teach us how families can stay together despite challenges.

The strength of a family lies not in perfection but in the mutual understanding of each person's role and the respect for the shared journey. It's in how we come together to face difficulties and how we support each other through them. When we understand one another, whether as children, parents, or extended family members, we are capable of creating bonds that are truly indestructible.

We will explore the contrasting dynamics between two key figures found in many families: the complainer and the thinker. These two types of individuals reflect two very different approaches to life, challenges, and responsibilities. Their mindsets and actions shape the environment of their families, and by understanding them, we can better comprehend how our own families function or, sometimes, struggle.

The Complainer

Underachieving Mindset

In many households, there exists a person who seems to always see the world through a lens of dissatisfaction. This individual finds fault in nearly every aspect of their life, never fully satisfied with what they have. They complain about their circumstances, their relationships, and their environment. In the face of challenges, the complainer rarely looks for solutions; instead, they dwell on the problems, intensifying them in their mind and allowing them to define their existence.

The complainer's mindset is deeply ingrained in their approach to life, and this mindset tends to filter into the way they manage both personal and professional affairs. One prime example of this mindset can be seen in the way the complainer runs their business or manages their assets. Let's take a man who owns several properties as an example, and we'll call him Sam. Sam is the type of person who believes that the world is working against him, and in his eyes, everyone has an agenda to make his life harder.

Despite being somewhat successful in property ownership, Sam is constantly looking for ways to save costs. However, his approach to saving money is not the most sustainable or intelligent. He often cuts corners to save a few bucks, ignoring the long-term consequences. In the world of real estate, for instance, Sam owns a few rental properties that generate a steady stream of income. To most, the dream of having passive income from properties sounds like an ideal situation. However, Sam is not the kind of person who invests in quality, nor does he focus on creating sustainable value. He is someone who focuses solely on saving money, often at the expense of long-term gain.

For example, when a pipe bursts in one of his properties, instead of hiring a licensed plumber, Sam will opt for a cheap, unlicensed repairman who will do the job quickly but without the proper care and attention. The repairman might slap some duct tape on the problem, ensuring the pipe works for a short time, but the issue will inevitably resurface later, leading to higher repair costs down the road. Sam's approach to this problem is rooted in his need for quick fixes, a mindset that often leads to long-term financial issues rather than solutions.

The same approach applies to other aspects of his properties. When a tenant complains about a broken window, rather than replacing it with a high-quality product, Sam will buy the cheapest replacement he can find, ensuring that the window looks fine for now but will likely break again within months. He does this because, in his mind, he's saving money. In the short term, his approach seems effective. He saves money on repairs and maintenance costs, allowing him to pocket more of the rent income.

However, Sam fails to realize that his cheap fixes are creating a cycle of repairs and dissatisfied tenants. As the window breaks again, tenants complain, leaving Sam to hire someone to fix it once more. The cycle continues, and his reputation as a landlord begins to deteriorate. He may think that saving money in the short term is clever, but in reality, he's hurting his long-term success. Tenants may eventually move out, unwilling to live in poorly maintained properties, which can result in lost rental income and further costs to fix the issues they neglected. In the end, the money Sam saved from cutting corners has been spent in a much worse way, and his bottom line suffers.

This pattern continues across other aspects of his properties. He doesn't invest in preventive maintenance, and when something breaks, he chooses the cheapest, quickest fix. His properties deteriorate over time, and while the immediate effect might not seem catastrophic, over the long haul, the costs add up. Sam's business isn't growing. It's barely staying afloat because he's more focused on short-term gains than on building a sustainable, profitable venture.

The attitude Sam exhibits isn't just confined to his properties or his professional life. It spreads into his personal life as well. The complainer constantly seeks the easy way out, avoiding hard work, difficult conversations, or deep introspection. In his mind, it's everyone else's fault when things go wrong, but rarely does he take responsibility for the choices he has made. This lack of personal accountability permeates his relationships, whether they're with his family, friends, or colleagues. He is unable to see the impact of his actions on others and is quick to blame external factors for his unhappiness. Whether it's his financial difficulties, relationship struggles, or work problems, Sam is never fully to blame for any of it.

When things go wrong, he complains about them endlessly. His life becomes one long string of grievances, from his broken properties to his personal shortcomings, and he takes no action to fix the root causes of the issues. He doesn't work toward building his knowledge, improving his skills, or even making basic adjustments to his behavior that could improve his life. The focus is always on how everything and everyone else is to blame, never on the ways he could change himself or his circumstances.

This mindset has consequences not only for Sam but also for those around him. In a family, the complainer's behavior can create an atmosphere of tension and frustration. Their constant complaints chip away at the morale of those they interact with. Family members may begin to feel drained by the complainer's negativity and inability to find solutions to their problems. The complainer's unwillingness to take responsibility for their actions, combined with their focus on external blame, creates a toxic environment where it's difficult for others to thrive.

Family members, especially children, learn from what they see. If a child grows up in a household where the primary example is one of complaining and shirking responsibility, that child may learn to mirror these behaviors. They may come to believe that the world owes them something, and they may also struggle to take accountability for their own actions, ultimately passing this cycle down to the next generation.

The complainer, in essence, is stuck in a loop of negativity, always looking for something or someone to blame but never willing to make the changes needed to break free. And while this attitude may not have an immediate impact, over time, it causes damage. Whether in business or in relationships, the complainer is always one step away from collapse simply because they refuse to look beyond their immediate circumstances and take responsibility for their own actions.

The Thinker

The Road to Success in America

In stark contrast to the complainer, the thinker is someone who approaches life with a mindset focused on growth, resilience, and opportunity. The thinker doesn't dwell on the obstacles that may come their way; they view them as stepping stones to greater achievements. They are constantly searching for ways to improve, adapt, and evolve. Where the complainer seeks shortcuts and quick fixes, the thinker focuses on building sustainable, long-term success. While the complainer may fall into a cycle of negative thinking and external blame, the thinker constantly seeks internal growth, responsibility, and accountability.

The thinker, however, is not immune to hardships. The journey to success is rarely smooth, especially when venturing into a competitive market like the United States. Let's take a closer look at the thinker's path through the lens of James, an ambitious entrepreneur who succeeded in

America by taking a calculated, strategic approach to building his business from the ground up.

The Birth of the Idea

James came to America with an ambitious idea. He wasn't interested in the average 9-to-5 job. He had big dreams and a belief that he could build something meaningful. Coming from humble beginnings, James knew that opportunity in America could lead to great things, but only if he was smart about it.

The idea he settled on was simple: start a small business that catered to the growing demand for food delivery services. At the time, the food delivery market was still in its infancy, but James could see that with the right vision, it could become an essential service for busy people. He saw a gap in the market: people were looking for convenience but didn't want to sacrifice quality. James knew that if he could provide high-quality meals with a fast and reliable delivery system, he could tap into this demand.

But he also knew that the road would not be easy. America's market was vast, and the competition was fierce. Many others had similar ideas, and countless businesses had already attempted to conquer the food delivery space. It would take more than just a good idea to stand out; it would take grit, resilience, and a willingness to adapt.

With limited resources and no guarantee of success, James started small. He put together a simple business plan, outlining his goals, target market, and delivery model. His idea was to offer a small but diverse menu of high-quality meals, with an emphasis on fresh ingredients and a commitment to excellent customer service. James understood that while food delivery was a growing trend, the customer experience would set him apart.

His first challenge was securing the necessary funds to launch his business. James didn't have access to large investors or loans. Instead, he turned to his savings and sought out small-scale investors who believed in his idea. His ability to pitch the business concept in a clear, concise manner was the turning point. He didn't just focus on the potential profits; he spoke to the bigger picture, how his business could provide a service that would enrich the lives of customers and make their busy lives easier.

The first year of James' business was full of ups and downs. As expected, the early days were incredibly challenging. James didn't have a luxurious startup; there was no office space, no big marketing campaigns, and no large staff. He did everything himself, from cooking the meals to delivering them. The business was small, and James was fully immersed in the day-to-day operations.

But even with his hard work, things didn't always go smoothly. Early on, James faced logistical challenges. He didn't have an efficient system in place for managing orders, deliveries, or inventory. Orders would often get mixed up, and customers sometimes received their meals late. There were moments when James felt like giving up, questioning whether he had made the right decision to start his business.

The pressure of juggling everything on his own was overwhelming.

But rather than succumbing to frustration, James took these challenges as learning experiences. He understood that setbacks were a natural part of the entrepreneurial journey. Rather than seeing these mistakes as failures, he used them to refine his systems and improve his service. For instance, when he received negative feedback about late deliveries, he realized that he needed a more reliable delivery system. He invested in technology that would help him manage his orders and track deliveries in real-time. By incorporating this technology, he was able to update his operations and ensure that customers received their meals on time.

Financial struggles were another major hurdle in the early stages of James's business. As a new entrepreneur, he didn't have a large budget to work with, and there were times when the business wasn't generating enough revenue to cover his expenses. James had to make difficult decisions, often choosing between paying his suppliers or keeping the lights on. He learned how to manage cash flow more effectively and prioritized essential expenses. He also sought out mentors and advisors who could offer him guidance on managing his finances, something he had never been taught before.

Despite these challenges, James never lost sight of his long-term goals. He knew that success would require patience and perseverance. He was willing to make short-term sacrifices for the long-term success of his business.

As time went on, James' business began to grow. Word of mouth spread, and his reputation for high-quality meals and reliable service began to attract more customers. The growth was slow at first, but James remained focused on improving every aspect of the business. He made strategic decisions that would allow him to scale his operation without sacrificing quality.

The first major step in expanding his business came when James hired his first employee. Initially, he had done everything on his own, but as demand increased, he realized that he needed help. Hiring the right people was critical. James was careful to select individuals who shared his vision and work ethic. He hired people who were passionate about the food industry and who believed in providing an excellent customer experience.

With a team in place, James was able to focus on growing the business. He began to experiment with new marketing strategies, using social media and local partnerships to attract more customers. He also expanded his menu, offering more options to cater to different tastes and dietary needs.

One of the biggest challenges James faced as he expanded was maintaining the quality of his service. As the business grew, it became more difficult to keep track of every detail. James knew that if he didn't keep a close eye on operations, his business could quickly become overrun with inefficiencies and mistakes. To address this, he implemented strict quality control procedures and ensured that his team was trained to meet the high standards he had set.

Despite his growing success, James continued to face obstacles. The food delivery market was becoming more competitive, with new companies popping up all the time. James knew that he had to stay ahead of the curve to maintain his edge. He invested in technology, improving his website and app to make it easier for customers to place orders. He also started offering promotions and discounts to attract new customers and retain existing ones.

Through it all, James never lost sight of the bigger picture. He understood that success wasn't just about making money, it was about building something sustainable and meaningful. He was willing to adapt, learn from his mistakes, and make the necessary changes to ensure his business continued to thrive.

James realized that the true measure of success wasn't just financial, it was about creating something that would have a lasting impact. He wasn't interested in a quick win; he wanted to build a legacy. As his business grew, he started to think about how he could give back to the community that had supported him. He partnered with local food banks and started donating a portion of his profits to charity. He also began mentoring other young entrepreneurs, sharing his knowledge and experiences to help them succeed.

The Sacrifices Made During Disturbances to Build an Atmosphere for Success

Success rarely comes without sacrifice, especially when one is committed to building something from the ground up.

It's not just about making financial investments or hiring the right people. The real sacrifices often involve time, energy, relationships, and mental fortitude. For someone like James, the thinker, the journey toward building a successful business was fraught with challenges and disturbances that required him to make difficult decisions that would test his commitment, his resilience, and his long-term vision.

One of the first and most significant sacrifices James had to make was personal time. In the early stages of his business, James worked around the clock. His business didn't just need his attention, it needed all of him. There were no luxuries like weekends off or taking vacations. His personal life, at least for a while, took a backseat to his professional ambitions. He knew this wasn't ideal, but he also understood that the foundation of his business needed to be solid before he could afford to relax or take time for himself.

James would often miss family events, birthdays, and celebrations. While his friends and family enjoyed time together, James was working, sometimes late into the night, preparing meals, updating his website, or managing customer orders. He made sure that his service was reliable, even if that meant sacrificing sleep or time spent with loved ones. These sacrifices weighed heavily on him. There were moments when he felt lonely, questioning whether it was worth it. Would his family still support him? Would his relationships remain intact if he kept prioritizing the business?

It wasn't just the personal sacrifices in terms of time; it was the emotional toll of watching his loved ones grow distant because they didn't understand the pressures he was facing. He had to make decisions that, at the time, felt selfish, deciding to invest more hours in his business rather than attending important events. But James knew that he couldn't build a successful business without giving it his full attention. He had to make the tough choice to sacrifice personal moments in the short term for the long-term gain of providing a better life for his family.

As the months passed, James' business began to take root. Slowly, he started seeing the fruits of his labor, an increase in customers, positive feedback, and steady profits. He knew he had to continue pushing through. It wasn't easy, but he kept reminding himself of his ultimate goal: to build something that could provide not just for him but for his family's future. The idea of creating a business that could one day be stable enough for him to step back and have time for his loved ones kept him motivated.

Another significant sacrifice James had to make was financial. Early on, James didn't have the capital to hire a large team or invest in fancy equipment. Instead, he spent most of his savings on the most essential parts of his business, such as sourcing ingredients and maintaining reliable delivery services. But as his business grew, the need for more capital became evident. He had to decide whether to invest heavily in upgrading his operations or cut back and risk stagnation.

James faced a particularly tough moment when he realized that his delivery system needed major improvement. The process was inefficient, and delays in deliveries were affecting his customer satisfaction. He needed to invest in better technology, something that would help streamline operations and improve the overall experience for customers. The cost of the new system was significant, and James didn't have the money to pay for it outright. But rather than waiting for funds to appear magically, he took a financial risk. He decided to take out a loan to upgrade the technology.

This decision wasn't easy. He had to sacrifice his financial security and take on more debt. The thought of borrowing money to fund his business was terrifying, but James knew that without this investment, his growth would plateau. The pressure of paying back the loan weighed heavily on him, and there were moments when he questioned whether he had made the right choice. Would the system work as he hoped? Would it be enough to bring in new customers and help him maintain current ones?

Despite the risk, James went ahead with the investment. It was a gamble, but it paid off. The new system allowed him to track orders more efficiently, reduce delays, and streamline communication with customers. As a result, his delivery times improved, and customer satisfaction reached new heights. This financial sacrifice not only improved his business but also allowed him to establish credibility in the competitive market. His reputation for being reliable and consistent attracted more customers, and soon, the debt he took on became manageable.

While physical and financial sacrifices are often visible, the mental and emotional toll that James endured is less talked about but equally significant. As his business grew, so did the pressure. James was constantly juggling multiple responsibilities, managing staff, ensuring quality control, overseeing logistics, and balancing the books. On top of that, he had to maintain relationships with customers, suppliers, and partners. The mental strain was overwhelming at times.

There were nights when James lay awake, his mind racing with thoughts of what could go wrong. He questioned his decisions, second-guessed his plans, and feared that one mistake could ruin everything he had worked for. Stress became a constant companion. He couldn't escape the mental weight of his responsibilities, and at times, it seemed impossible to find peace.

There were also emotional sacrifices. As a business owner, James often had to make decisions that affected the lives of his employees. Letting go of someone who wasn't a good fit, even when they were friendly and well-liked, was one of the hardest things James had to do. He had to remind himself that these decisions were not personal, they were about the long-term success of the business. But it didn't make it any easier to see the disappointment in the faces of employees who were let go.

James was also confronted with the emotional burden of watching other businesses succeed while he was still growing. He would see competitors expand quickly, attracting more attention and customers while he was still working to find his footing. These moments of comparison often led to feelings of inadequacy and frustration. It felt like no matter how hard he worked, someone else was always a step ahead.

But through it all, James learned the importance of managing his mental health. He began practicing mindfulness, taking time to meditate and clear his mind. He also leaned on his family for support, sharing his struggles with them and seeking their encouragement. James realized that taking care of his mental and emotional well-being wasn't just important for his personal happiness, it was essential for the long-term success of his business. If he couldn't manage his stress, his ability to make clear decisions would suffer.

The sacrifices James made during the disturbances of his journey weren't just about enduring hardship. They were about creating the right environment for success to flourish. He understood that building a business wasn't just about profits but about building a sustainable foundation where his business could thrive long after the initial challenges were overcome.

By sacrificing his time, finances, and emotional well-being, James was able to create a stable environment where his business could grow. The atmosphere he cultivated wasn't one of chaos and instability, but one of determination, perseverance, and a clear focus on long-term goals. He built a strong team that believed in the mission, maintained high standards of quality, and embraced the challenges that came their way.

Through these sacrifices, James demonstrated a critical principle of success: the willingness to do whatever it takes in the face of adversity. He knew that sacrifices weren't permanent; they were temporary investments in the future. In time, his sacrifices paid off, his business became more profitable, his family supported him, and his relationships grew stronger as he learned to balance his time more effectively. The disturbances he faced didn't break him, they helped him build a business that could withstand the test of time.

How a Thinker and Complainer Affect a Family

The dynamics within a family are shaped by the individuals who make it up. Each person brings their unique perspective, values, and behaviors to the table, and these elements interact in ways that can either strengthen or weaken the family bond. The thinker and the complainer, as discussed earlier, represent two opposing forces that can influence a family in profound ways. Their mindsets, behaviors, and approaches to life create distinct environments within the household, impacting everyone involved, from the parents to the children.

The thinker, with their proactive and solution-oriented mindset, often serves as the pillar of strength within the family. They provide stability, offer guidance, and foster an atmosphere of growth and resilience. In contrast, the complainer tends to create an atmosphere of negativity and frustration. Their constant focus on problems rather than solutions can erode the family structure and make it difficult for the household to thrive. Understanding how these two contrasting figures impact family dynamics is crucial for fostering a healthy and supportive home environment.

The Thinker: A Source of Stability and Growth

The thinker brings a level of calm and logic to the family dynamic. Unlike the complainer, who gets easily overwhelmed by challenges, the thinker takes a measured approach to problems. This ability to stay level-headed and solution-focused is invaluable in a family setting. Whether dealing with financial issues, relationship struggles, or daily life challenges, the thinker can navigate these obstacles with patience and foresight, providing the necessary guidance to help the family move forward.

One of the most significant ways a thinker influences a family is by offering emotional stability. In times of distress, whether caused by external factors or internal family issues, the thinker is often the one who can keep their cool and help others do the same. Their ability to remain calm under pressure and approach problems with a logical mindset provides a sense of security for the family. This stability encourages others to stay grounded and focus on practical solutions rather than being swept away by emotions.

Moreover, the thinker instills a growth-oriented mindset within the family. They are often the ones who encourage others to learn from their mistakes and seek out opportunities for self-improvement. For example, when children face challenges at school or in their personal lives, the thinker provides them with the tools to overcome these difficulties, whether through offering advice, sharing their experiences, or guiding them toward resources that can help. The thinker is not just focused on surviving difficulties but on using those difficulties as opportunities to grow.

The thinker's influence also extends to fostering healthy communication within the family. They understand the importance of listening and seeking understanding rather than jumping to conclusions or blaming others. This open, empathetic communication style allows family members to express their concerns and frustrations without fear of judgment, creating a supportive environment where everyone feels heard. The thinker encourages constructive dialogue, which is essential for resolving conflicts and building stronger relationships.

Finally, the thinker sets an example of personal accountability. They take responsibility for their actions and decisions, demonstrating that growth requires self-awareness and a willingness to learn. This sense of responsibility encourages others in the family to do the same, creating a culture of accountability that strengthens the family unit as a whole.

The Complainer: A Source of Negativity and Frustration

The complainer, on the other hand, can have a deeply negative impact on the family dynamic. Their constant focus on problems rather than solutions can create an environment where negativity thrives. In contrast to the thinker, who seeks to address challenges head-on, the complainer tends to dwell on their misfortunes and struggles. This focus on the negative can be draining for others, leading to frustration, resentment, and emotional exhaustion within the family.

One of the most obvious ways the complainer affects the family is through their emotional impact. Constant complaining creates an atmosphere of pessimism, where it becomes difficult to maintain a positive outlook on life. Family members, particularly children, can be affected by this negativity. They may begin to mirror the complainer's behavior, adopting a mindset that focuses on what's wrong rather than what's right. This can hinder personal growth and lead to a sense of helplessness and defeatism.

The complainer also tends to create an environment of blame and finger-pointing. Rather than taking responsibility for their actions or trying to find solutions to their problems, the complainer often blames others for their misfortunes. This constant externalization of blame can cause tension within the family, as family members become frustrated with the complainer's unwillingness to take ownership of their actions. The complainer's behavior can lead to a breakdown in trust as others begin to feel that they are unfairly targeted or criticized for things beyond their control.

Moreover, the complainer's tendency to focus on problems rather than solutions can lead to a lack of progress within the family. Instead of working together to overcome challenges, the family becomes stuck in a cycle of negativity. The complainer may spend hours venting about issues without offering any practical solutions, leaving the rest of the family feeling helpless and discouraged. This lack of action can prevent the family from moving forward and achieving its goals.

The complainer's behavior can also affect the family's ability to handle stress. Rather than facing difficult situations with resilience and problem-solving skills, the complainer reacts with frustration and defeat. This emotional reaction can escalate conflicts and make it difficult for the family to work together during times of hardship. As a result, the family's ability to cope with challenges becomes compromised, and they may find themselves in a constant state of turmoil.

Lastly, the complainer's refusal to acknowledge their role in the family's difficulties can lead to a lack of personal growth within the household. When the complainer refuses to take responsibility for their actions, they fail to set an example for others. This lack of accountability can create a culture of avoidance and irresponsibility within the family, where problems are ignored or denied rather than addressed and resolved.

The Combined Effect

When the thinker and the complainer coexist within a family, the dynamics become increasingly complex. The thinker provides stability and growth, but the complainer's negativity can undermine those efforts. In some cases, the thinker may be able to counterbalance the complainer's negativity, but over time, the complainer's influence can take a toll. The family becomes a battleground between two opposing forces: one that seeks solutions and growth, and another that dwells on problems and complaints.

In these families, children may find themselves torn between two different models of behavior. On one hand, they see the thinker who demonstrates responsibility, resilience, and positivity. On the other hand, they know the complainer, who offers a more reactive and defeatist approach to life. This dichotomy can create confusion and uncertainty, especially for young children who are still developing their own worldviews. The child may struggle to understand which approach is most effective in navigating life's challenges.

Furthermore, the thinker's efforts to provide guidance and stability may be constantly undermined by the complainer's negativity. The thinker's message of hope, resilience, and accountability is drowned out by the complainer's constant barrage of complaints and external blame. In such an environment, it can be difficult for family members to find common ground or work together effectively. The tension between the two figures can lead to emotional strain, eroding the trust and communication that are essential for a healthy family dynamic.

In families where the complainer is dominant, the thinker may begin to feel isolated and frustrated. They may feel as though their efforts to maintain peace and offer solutions are futile in the face of constant negativity. Over time, the thinker may withdraw emotionally, leading to further disconnection within the family. The complainer, on the other hand, may feel unsupported and misunderstood, which can lead to more complaints and further entrenchment in their negative mindset.

Ultimately, the presence of both the thinker and the complainer within a family creates a delicate balance that requires constant effort and understanding. The thinker must be patient with the complainer, while the complainer must be willing to acknowledge the thinker's perspective. For the family to thrive, both figures must find a way to collaborate and create an environment where both growth and stability are prioritized.

In any family, the impact of the thinker and the complainer cannot be overstated. The thinker brings stability, growth, and solutions, while the complainer brings negativity, blame, and stagnation. When both forces are present, they create an intricate dynamic that requires constant effort to maintain balance. Families can thrive when they embrace the positive qualities of both figures, using the thinker's problem-solving abilities and the complainer's voice as an opportunity for improvement. But when one dominates, the family can quickly become mired in negativity and dysfunction. Understanding the roles of the thinker and the complainer within the family is crucial for fostering healthy communication, personal growth, and long-term success.

Which mindset do you see more of in your own life or household, the Complainer or the Thinker? How has that mindset shaped your decisions and relationships?

Chapter 2
The Mindset

When we look at how families evolve, what values they stand on, and which beliefs guide them through life's challenges, we often see two paths emerge: one of stagnation and complaint, and one of growth and thoughtful calculation. These paths are not accidental, nor are they tied exclusively to social background, luck, or innate intelligence. Rather, they stem from a foundational mindset, a mode of thinking that influences every choice, action, and reaction. Let's deepen our examination of the "complainer" and the "thinker," two diametrically opposed ways of approaching life. The choices made by each, the priorities they hold, and the values they nurture ripple outward to shape not only their personal destinies but also the family units that gather around them.

In Chapter 1, we explored how a complainer's perpetual negativity can infect an entire household and how a thinker's resilience and vision provide stability and growth. Now, it's time to probe deeper into what drives each mindset at the core. Why does one person remain fixated on survival and external validation, while another invests in a strategic, principled, and often self-reflective pursuit of success? Our discussion will move beyond surface-level analysis to examine the motivations, fears, and aspirations behind each.

The hope is that, by the end of this chapter, you'll not only recognize these mindsets in others but also discern elements of both within yourself. Only by cultivating self-awareness can we determine which mindset we've adopted and how that choice shapes our family's future. Whether you're currently stuck in a cycle of complaint or well on your way to becoming a thinker, these insights can guide you toward a more intentional, value-driven existence.

PART 1: The Complainer

Life places us on various routes. Some people begin their adult years determined to fulfill what they consider the 'basics' of success: getting a decent job, buying a house, having a family, maybe saving a little money along the way. At first glance, these goals seem practical, even admirable. After all, these are the standard yardsticks many of us use to measure our achievements in the modern world, particularly in a place like America, where the dream of owning property and providing for one's family holds a powerful allure.

However, for the complainer, **time spent striving for these basic goals** often morphs into a kind of hamster wheel. The initial motivation is seldom rooted in genuine passion or a sense of higher purpose. Instead, it's about meeting external expectations and doing what's 'normal' performing life's tasks so that society grants its nod of approval. The complainer typically exerts minimal effort just to reach a certain plateau of comfort or recognition, and once that plateau is reached, they seek validation from anyone willing to offer it.

Time Spent Striving for Basic Goals

It's not uncommon to encounter individuals who define their life's mission as checking boxes:

- **Obtain a steady job:** The complainer sees this as purely transactional, a means to receive a paycheck. There is little drive for excellence or advancement, so long as the paycheck arrives on schedule.
- **Buy a house (or rent a nicer apartment):** Achieving this might be fueled by the notion that property ownership or living in a better neighborhood is a sign of success. The house itself becomes a symbol, a tangible token of having "arrived."
- **Start a family:** It may be seen as the next natural step, rather than a conscious choice made from love, commitment, and the desire to nurture future generations.

At first glance, these goals appear worthy; who wouldn't want to secure a decent livelihood and have a safe place to call home? Yet the complainer's approach to these goals is often skewed. For him, each goal is a **destination** rather than part of an ongoing journey. He invests just enough time and energy to secure that job, purchase that home, or begin that family, and then effectively stalls out. Once he's checked the box, he feels he's done what society demands.

What remains unexamined is **why** he's done it and how these goals could serve a deeper personal mission or a broader family vision. There's no sense of real ownership or responsibility that stretches beyond the immediate transaction. Bills are paid (often begrudgingly), the house is maintained (minimally), and the family might receive the bare minimum in emotional and financial support. But once these basics are in place, the complainer sees himself as having "arrived," thus absolving himself of further, deeper efforts.

A Man Without True Vision

Here's where the real issue surfaces: **once his plateau is reached, the complainer seeks recognition from outside the very structure he has built.** Without a meaningful vision guiding him, he becomes restless, disillusioned, and uncertain of what to do next.

Take, for example, a man named Kyle. Kyle worked hard in his twenties to pay off debts, purchase a modest home, and secure a regular office job. By thirty, he's ticking boxes left and right: stable paycheck, mortgage, health insurance, maybe even a family. But inside, Kyle feels unfulfilled. The routine is suffocating. Rather than looking inward to ask deeper questions like "What do I truly value?" or "How can I make a meaningful contribution to my family or community?" he starts seeking excitement, acknowledgement, or a sense of being 'important' from other places.

He might over-invest in hobbies, chasing sports cars he can't afford, or turning to activities that provide a fleeting dopamine hit. He may start spending more time with friends or acquaintances who admire him for superficial reasons, perhaps he's the friend who can throw a party at his own house or the one who splurges on dinners and drinks in search of someone, anyone, to say, "'Wow, look at him!'"

At first, Kyle's wife and children may not notice. They see him as the responsible breadwinner who's always bragging about the house he purchased. But over time, the cracks begin to show. Kyle's real dissatisfaction, ironically, stems from the fact that his entire sense of identity was built around **reaching that plateau**, the job, the house, the outward display of 'success.'"Once that was done, he lost his driver, any deeper vision that might carry him forward.

The result? Kyle starts complaining about everything: how expensive groceries have become, how tough his job is, how he's 'underappreciated' by his family. He becomes irritated when his kids need extracurricular funds. He becomes resentful when the water heater breaks down. In short, he is lost, though he might not realize it consciously. All he knows is that he's unfulfilled and angry that the world hasn't given him a standing ovation for hitting the conventional milestones he was told to achieve.

How This Has Become the Norm for American Men

There's a wider cultural context here. While men across the globe face their own cultural and societal pressures, **the American narrative** often extols the virtues of independence, the ability to "pull yourself up by your bootstraps," and the external trappings of success. A house in the suburbs, a car or two in the garage, a reliable job, and a steady paycheck, these are taken as universal markers of having "made it."

In many ways, these standards were forged in the post-World War II era, where economic booms allowed many to own homes, support a family on a single income, and enjoy a certain brand of stability. Over time, the American Dream was mythologized into this neat checklist. For those who manage to meet these criteria, society offers a round of applause but not a deeper meaning.

For the complainer, this superficial notion of success can become a trap. Once he reaches a semblance of these milestones, there is little guidance on the next step. The culture rarely encourages him to ask how he can grow personally or spiritually, how he can invest in his children's emotional well-being, or how he might contribute to the community in a way that fulfills him beyond writing a mortgage check.

Consequently, many American men find themselves in Kyle's position: they've done the "right things," and yet they're unhappy, disconnected from their families, and mentally unprepared for life's broader responsibilities. Instead of exploring deeper questions like how to become a better husband, father, or community leader, they sink into a pattern of grumbling about how life turned out "unfair," forgetting that they themselves never established a guiding vision beyond those basic benchmarks.

The Consequences of This Approach

The fallout from a complainer's worldview can be severe:

- **Family Tension and Resentment:** When the man of the house exudes constant dissatisfaction, the entire home vibrates with that negativity. Children learn that "Dad is always upset about something," and spouses walk on eggshells, trying not to provoke him. This erodes trust and open communication.

- **Financial Instability Despite Appearances:** Even if the complainer has reached a moderate level of financial stability, his lack of vision can lead to poor long-term planning. He might squander extra income on quick fixes, much like Sam in Chapter 1, who did short-term repairs without thinking of the consequences. Over time, these choices can eat away at savings, lead to credit card debt, and jeopardize the family's future.

- **Emotional and Mental Exhaustion:** The mental toll on the complainer (and everyone around him) is immense. Constant frustration and the need for external recognition become a black hole of energy. He invests more time complaining than resolving problems or nurturing relationships.

- **Stalled Personal Growth:** Because the complainer's sense of self is tied to meeting externally defined goals, he rarely invests in personal development once those goals are met. He doesn't read, learn new skills, or pursue meaningful hobbies. His soul remains stagnant, unchallenged, and unfulfilled.

- **A Lost Legacy:** For those with children, the risk goes beyond the present. When children absorb this pattern, they, too, become adults who define success in the narrowest terms, then lament the absence of deeper satisfaction once the boxes are checked. This destructive pattern can echo down the generations.

The Need to Change the Mindset

In a society that largely pushes men to meet a superficial standard of success, **recognizing the problem** is half the battle. Many complainers never realize that their dissatisfaction stems from the absence of a genuine, internally driven vision, one that goes beyond finances and property ownership.

To break free, a complainer must reorient his entire approach to life. **He must shift his mindset to clarify his values** and learn to nurture the kind of personal growth that benefits not only himself but also his entire family. Instead of seeking external accolades for hitting a socially approved checkpoint, he can begin to ask:

- *What do I truly believe in?*
- *How can I use my position and resources to invest in my family's emotional and psychological well-being?*
- *What kind of father, husband, or brother do I want to be?*

Yet this is where the bigger challenge emerges, **confronting the selfishness** that most men (and, honestly, many women) experience. Selfishness here refers not just to wanting things for oneself, but to the narrower inability to see life as an interconnected tapestry. The complainer sees only his own burdens and not how those burdens could be shared or turned into opportunities for collective growth.

For instance, a complainer might gripe that his children's extracurricular activities cost too much. However, a shift in mindset would allow him to see that these very activities offer a chance to bond with his kids, support their talents, and guide them toward confidence and discipline. Instead of framing it as a financial drain, it could be seen as an investment in his family's legacy. The difference is subtle yet monumental; it pivots from "They're costing me" to "We're building something together."

In essence, the complainer must rewire his internal narrative. He must begin to see beyond his immediate frustrations and short-term goals, stepping into a broader perspective where each decision, each action, becomes part of a meaningful journey for both himself and those who depend on him. Only through this transformation can he shed the shackles of complaint and fully embrace life's deeper opportunities.

PART 2: The Thinker

If the complainer is defined by external validation and short-term thinking, **the thinker** stands in stark contrast:

calculated, introspective, and guided by principle rather than mere appearances. The thinker recognizes that life is rife with hardship and uncertainty, yet responds by adopting a mindset that is both **flexible** and **purposeful**.

We've seen glimpses of the thinker's characteristics in Chapter 1, someone like James, who not only endures challenges but learns from them, shaping his future endeavors with each lesson. Now, in this second chapter, we delve into how the thinker's underlying mindset evolves, especially under pressure, and why it's a fundamental key to building a sustainable family structure that thrives over time.

The Calculated Mindset Through the Process

The hallmark of the thinker's approach is **calculation**, not in a cold or manipulative sense, but in a deliberate, strategic manner. Where the complainer reacts to events often with frustration or blame, the thinker **plans**, **prepares**, and **prioritizes**.

Imagine a man named Victor, who dreams of starting a tech company. Like many entrepreneurs, he faces financial obstacles, fierce competition, and a host of personal sacrifices. However, unlike the complainer, Victor doesn't rush into the market out of a desire to boast or to earn quick admiration. He invests the time to study consumer needs, research his target industry, and plan his finances meticulously. Each decision whether about product development, hiring, or funding, is measured against his broader vision.

Yet the thinker's calculated nature isn't solely about success in business or finances. It's equally relevant in his personal life. When confronted with relationship challenges, say, an argument with a spouse or a misunderstanding with a teenager, the thinker avoids knee-jerk reactions. He attempts to see patterns, identify the root cause, and address it systematically.

- Is the argument with his spouse really about unpaid bills, or is it about deeper issues like feeling unappreciated or stressed?
- Is his teenager acting out because of a desire for freedom, or are they struggling with anxiety or peer pressure at school?

In each case, the thinker tries to unpack the situation rather than react blindly. This approach sets the tone for more constructive resolutions, forging trust and understanding within the family.

How the Mindset Is Influenced Through Pain

A crucial distinction between the thinker and the complainer is how each **processes pain**. For the complainer, pain or hardship is an occasion to blame external factors, such as the economy, the spouse, or the bosses. For the thinker, pain is a signal that something within his system or process needs to adapt.

The thinker's orientation toward pain is often based on **principles established through personal reflection** and prior experiences. Rather than allowing pain to defeat him, he uses it as a catalyst for change and adaptation. This is reminiscent of James in Chapter 1, who faced logistical, financial, and emotional hurdles in building his business, yet refused to let these hardships derail him. Instead, he refined his strategy, sought better resources, learned new skills, and eventually transformed his initial struggles into stepping stones for success.

Let's consider an example in a family context: Anthony is a father of two who just lost his job due to corporate downsizing. Initially, the loss is devastating, sparking fear about mortgage payments and the cost of raising his children. Yet Anthony approaches the crisis methodically.

- **Immediate Step:** He files for unemployment benefits and cuts non-essential spending to stabilize the family's finances.
- **Action Plan:** He updates his resume, reaches out to former colleagues, and invests time in online courses that can enhance his skill set.
- **Family Meeting:** He sits down with his spouse and children, explaining the situation honestly but with a focus on how they can work together, adjusting family activities, supporting each other's emotional well-being, and brainstorming ways to save money.

In this way, Anthony's mindset harnesses pain as a prompt for thoughtful action. He remains transparent, calm, and proactive, which reassures his family that while times are tough, they have a strategy in place.

The Foundation That Allows Him to Restore and Restructure

The thinker's guiding light is **a firm foundation**, a set of core values and principles that he can return to when life becomes uncertain. This foundation often includes:

- **Integrity:** A commitment to honesty and ethical behavior, even when cutting corners might be easier.
- **Responsibility:** Owning up to one's mistakes, accepting accountability for outcomes, and making amends where necessary.
- **Resilience:** Recognizing that setbacks are inevitable but not insurmountable.
- **Vision:** Having a clear picture of what success looks like not just financially but in terms of family well-being, community impact, and personal growth.

When adversity strikes, the thinker re-centers on these values. If he's faced with a decision that challenges his integrity, like padding expense reports to get some extra cash, his moral anchor prevents him from betraying his core principle. If he makes a mistake that threatens his family's financial stability, he doesn't bury his head in the sand; he accepts responsibility and puts in the necessary work to correct it.

This return to foundational principles isn't a one-time event; it's a recurring process. In the same way an architect checks a building's structural integrity after an earthquake, the thinker frequently inspects the integrity of his personal and professional life. Has he drifted from the guiding vision he set for himself and his family? Are the decisions he's making still aligned with his ethics?

This internal audit allows him to **restore and restructure** his mindset whenever necessary. When he identifies cracks in his thinking or notes that some of his habits no longer serve his vision, he corrects course. This ongoing cycle of reflection and recalibration prevents stagnation and ensures growth remains intentional.

Staying Focused on the Process

We've discussed how a complainer often fixates on external validation, applause for reaching a certain milestone, or ownership of a specific asset, leading to a sense of emptiness once that milestone is behind him. In stark contrast, **the thinker remains process-driven**.

Consider a marathon runner. If his only goal is to finish one race and then stop running forever, he might push hard, cross the finish line, and then complain about the soreness and injuries he got along the way. But a runner who is process-driven sees each race as part of a broader journey; he's continuously training, refining his technique, honing his nutrition, and exploring ways to maintain physical and mental health over the long haul.

Likewise, the thinker recognizes that achieving one objective, such as starting a successful business or buying a home, is just one phase. The real accomplishment lies in how well he can improve and iterate on his methods, keeping aligned with his overarching vision. Once the business is profitable, can he expand into new markets, explore charitable work, or mentor others? Once the home is purchased, can he make it an even warmer, more supportive environment for his family?

By **focusing on the process**, the thinker not only avoids complacency but also basks in the ongoing satisfaction that comes from continuous growth. He doesn't regard the journey as a grind for the sake of external praise. Instead, he finds intrinsic motivation in knowing that every day, every effort, is taking him closer to a more refined version of himself and a stronger, more cohesive family.

The Thinker's Vision Sets His Path for Success

Finally, we must address the core element that separates the thinker from the complainer: **vision**. It's not enough to merely avoid negativity or to strategize one's next move; the thinker needs a guiding light, a sense of **what he stands for** and **what he aims to achieve** in the grander scheme of life.

Vision for the thinker is not purely financial. It encompasses:

- **Family Harmony:** Fostering an environment where children feel heard and loved, and where spouses support each other's growth.

- **Community Impact:** Recognizing that personal success is intertwined with contributing to the broader social fabric.
- **Personal Evolution:** Continually developing skills, emotional intelligence, and moral character.
- **Legacy:** Building something that endures beyond one's lifetime, whether that's a business that provides jobs, a charitable initiative that benefits the less fortunate, or simply a family that carries forward strong values and integrity.

James from Chapter 1 exemplified this. His early hardships could have made him bitter, a perpetual complainer, or someone who chased only immediate profits. Instead, his core values, quality service, customer-centric focus, and a commitment to improving people's lives stayed with him. He sacrificed short-term comforts for the sake of long-term impact. Once he achieved a level of success, he didn't stop to bask in external admiration. He continued giving back to the community, mentoring others, and refining his vision.

When a thinker sees the world through this lens, **success** is not a destination but a continuum. Each achievement leads to new responsibilities and opportunities. Each failure becomes a lesson. And each sacrifice along the way, whether of time, finances, or personal comfort, feels justified because it advances a larger purpose.

Weighing the Two Mindsets in a Family Context

Now that we've dissected both the complainer and the thinker in granular detail, it's valuable to revisit how these two mindsets might clash or occasionally coexist within a single family. While Part 1 of this chapter highlighted the complainer's pitfalls, Part 2 sought to illuminate the thinker's strengths. The reality is that families are seldom black and white: rarely is there one person who is **only** a complainer or **only** a thinker. We carry bits of both, and under stress, we might oscillate from one mode to the other.

However, **dominant tendencies** do emerge, setting the tone of the household. In families dominated by complainers, negativity, blame, and short-sightedness often become the norm. Children and spouses learn to walk on eggshells, or they might even internalize that pattern, replicating it later in their own adult lives.

In contrast, a home guided by a thinker's mindset encourages open communication, long-term planning, and a balanced response to challenges. It doesn't mean that such a home is free from arguments or mistakes, far from it. However, it does imply a shared commitment to address problems at their root and to see them as stepping stones rather than insurmountable barriers.

Bridging the Gap: How a Complainer Can Transition Toward Thinking

A critical question arises: **Can the complainer evolve into a thinker?** The short answer is yes, but it requires conscious effort, humility, and a willingness to confront uncomfortable truths about oneself. Here are some steps that might guide such a transformation:

- **Self-Reflection:** Before any change can happen, the complainer must become aware of his patterns. This can involve journaling, seeking feedback from loved ones, or even attending therapy or counseling to identify the root causes of his dissatisfaction and blame-shifting.

- **Setting New Goals:** Instead of the standard checklist (job, house, car), delve into *why* these goals matter and what deeper aspirations might exist. Goals that tie into personal growth, learning a new skill, nurturing a child's talent, or improving relationship communication are inherently more sustaining.

- **Accepting Responsibility:** A complainer's default is to blame external factors. One of the most powerful acts of self-growth is taking ownership of mistakes and failures. Saying "I made an error, and here's how I'll fix it" is transformative, turning complaints into actionable insight.

- **Building Principles:** Identify key values, integrity, kindness, perseverance, and consciously integrate them into decision-making processes. Over time, these values become the foundation that the complainer-turned-thinker can rely on.

- **Sustaining the Shift:** Change is rarely linear. Old habits die hard. The emerging thinker must continually revisit his newfound principles, especially under stress, to ensure that negativity doesn't creep back in.

These steps, while straightforward, demand courage. They require an individual to face not just external challenges but also the more intimidating internal ones, fear, regret, guilt, and the vulnerability of acknowledging past mistakes. However, it is through this very confrontation that real growth and lasting transformation become possible.

Practical Applications: Transitioning the Family Dynamic

For a family currently mired in an atmosphere of complaint, negativity, or short-term thinking, **the shift** to a more solution-oriented, visionary mindset doesn't happen overnight. It's a collective effort. Here are some practical methods to facilitate this transition:

- **Family Meetings and Open Forums:** Schedule regular times to discuss both triumphs and challenges. The point is to create a safe space where each member can voice concerns, express gratitude, and propose ideas for improvement. This shared dialogue encourages accountability and solution-driven thinking.

- **Shared Goals and Vision Boards:** Encourage the entire family to create a 'vision board' together, perhaps on a corkboard in the living room or digitally on a shared platform. This board might include pictures and statements reflecting the family's collective dreams (e.g., family vacations, personal growth goals, charitable endeavors). By having a visual representation of shared ambitions, each family member is reminded that life is a journey, not a static series of tasks.

- **Celebrate Problem-Solving, Not Just Achievements:** When a child finds a clever way to study for an exam or a spouse devises a budgeting strategy to save money, celebrate these problem-solving efforts. This reinforces the process-oriented mindset, showing that how you arrive at success is just as important as success itself.

- **Model the Behavior:** If you're the one reading this book and striving to be more of a thinker, your actions will speak volumes. Children learn through observation, and spouses or extended family members often adapt to more constructive approaches when they see them in action. Each time you handle conflict with composure and foresight, you're setting a standard.

- **Encourage Self-Care and Education:** A crucial component of the thinker's mindset is ongoing learning, whether it's reading books on personal growth, attending workshops, or engaging in physical activities that promote health and clarity. Bringing the entire family into these practices can foster collective resilience.

The Larger Cultural and Societal Implications

Up to this point, we've primarily discussed family structures. However, the shift from complainer to thinker extends its reach into broader society. Communities and workplaces, too, benefit when more individuals adopt a visionary, problem-solving orientation. Conversely, they suffer from the stagnation and blame game that complainers bring.

Consider how local communities might flourish if more families made an intentional effort to live by the thinker's principles:

- **Community Projects:** Instead of complaining about potholes or a lack of green spaces, the thinker-minded community organizes clean-up days, fundraisers, or petitions for improving local infrastructure.

- **Economic Growth:** Entrepreneurs and professionals who apply a thinker's approach to their careers build sustainable businesses or excel in their professions, in turn creating job opportunities and mentoring future generations.

- **Social Cohesion:** Complaints about social divides, housing costs, or educational disparities are valid, but they only become catalysts for improvement when approached with the thinker's drive to plan, innovate, and collaborate.

All these improvements start at the micro level, within the family. Every child who grows up learning how to tackle problems with insight, compassion, and resilience carries those lessons into adulthood. Every parent who transforms from being a perpetual complainer into a thoughtful leader sends ripples of positive influence well beyond their immediate household.

Balancing Realism with Idealism

One potential misunderstanding might be to see the thinker's path as purely idealistic, assuming that if one just tries hard enough, or remains positive and strategic, everything will automatically work out. The reality is that **life remains unpredictable**. Economic downturns, health issues, unexpected tragedies, or simply being in the wrong place at the wrong time can derail even the most carefully laid plans.

Yet the thinker is not someone who denies reality. Rather, he acknowledges risk, adversity, and the limits of control. He remains **prepared** precisely because he respects life's unpredictability. Where the complainer sees chaos as proof that everything is rigged against him, the thinker sees chaos as an inevitable element that must be factored into one's strategy.

Thus, the thinker's mindset rests at the intersection of **realism** and **idealism,** believing in the potential to shape one's destiny while acknowledging that the world is chaotic and obstacles are real. This balancing act underlines why a strong internal foundation is essential. Without it, the storms of life can knock a person off course into cynicism or despair.

Throughout this chapter, we've dissected the internal workings of the complainer and the thinker, exploring how each views the world, sets goals, responds to obstacles, and influences the family unit. We see how easy it is for a person, especially within the American cultural framework, to become trapped in a cycle of complaint once basic goals are met. We also see the transformative power a visionary mindset can wield, not only in personal and professional success but also in cultivating a thriving family environment.

Change begins at the level of mindset. Whether you see more of the complainer or the thinker in your household, remember that mindsets aren't static. They're shaped by daily choices, habits, and patterns of thought. If there's a dominant complainer energy in your family, you can gradually shift it by asking different questions, celebrating problem-solving over blaming, and setting goals that resonate with deeper values rather than superficial benchmarks.

1. **Are there areas in your life where you catch yourself or others stopping at the bare minimum, then seeking applause?** Recognizing these patterns is the first step to breaking them.
2. **What would a deeply rooted vision look like for you?** Try to articulate it beyond finances, achievements, or superficial markers of success.
3. **When adversity strikes, do you find yourself complaining first or moving into solution mode?** Track this for a week. Awareness often precedes improvement.
4. **Are you willing to sacrifice short-term comfort to uphold your principles and follow your vision?** This question separates those who are only half

committed from those who are truly ready to embrace change.

5. **How can you reinforce a thinker's mindset in your family today?** Consider small, practical actions like an honest talk about a lingering issue, a family brainstorming session, or setting a new shared goal.

The transformation from complainer to thinker on both an individual and familial level is not about achieving perfection. It's about fostering an environment where every challenge becomes a lesson, every success becomes a platform for greater contribution, and every family member feels valued and empowered to grow. In this sense, building a strong family structure is more than a project; it is an ongoing practice of learning, adapting, and loving with intention.

Just as Chapter 1 urged us to reflect on our own families and personal experiences, Chapter 2 offers a deeper dive into the *why* behind these behaviors. We've journeyed through the mindset that stagnates once basic goals are met and the mindset that evolves into a strategic, principle-driven force for positive change. Which mindset best represents you or those around you? And more importantly, how will you use this understanding to shape a brighter future for yourself and your family?

Remember: **A family thrives when it is guided by vision and purpose, not by complacency and complaint.**

Chapter 3
Approach to Problem Solving

They say life is a series of problems to be solved, a constant stream of challenges that require our attention and response. How we approach these problems, how we frame them in our minds, and how we work toward solutions define not just our personal success but the atmosphere we create in our homes and businesses. The way we confront uncertainty shapes our relationships, our growth, and ultimately our legacy. This chapter explores two fundamentally different approaches to problem-solving that exist within families and how these approaches ripple outward to affect everyone connected to them.

Problem-solving is not just about finding answers; it's about the mindset we bring to the table when faced with difficulties. It's about whether we see problems as insurmountable obstacles or as opportunities for growth. The approach we take when confronted with challenges reveals our character, our values, and our potential for future success. More importantly, it establishes patterns that others around us, especially our children, may follow for generations to come.

In this chapter, we will continue our exploration of two distinct mindsets: the complainer and the thinker. We will examine how each approaches problem-solving and the ripple effects these approaches have on family dynamics. By understanding these contrasting methods, we can better recognize our own tendencies and make conscious choices about how we want to tackle life's inevitable challenges.

The Complainer

Uncertainty as the Enemy

For the complainer, uncertainty is not just uncomfortable; it is terrifying. When faced with a problem that doesn't have an immediate or obvious solution, the complainer experiences a sense of dread that permeates every aspect of their being. This feeling isn't simply a momentary hesitation or a fleeting worry; it's a deep-seated fear that manifests as physical discomfort. Their heart races, their palms sweat, and their mind begins to spin with worst-case scenarios. The unknown becomes not just a challenge but an enemy that must be defeated or avoided at all costs.

Take the example of Robert, a small business owner with a complainer mindset. When faced with a sudden drop in revenue, Robert doesn't see this as a temporary setback or an opportunity to reassess his business strategy. Instead, he experiences a crushing sense of uncertainty that paralyzes him. The questions pile up in his mind: What if the business fails completely? What will people think of me? How will I support my family? These questions aren't productive inquiries aimed at finding solutions; they're expressions of fear that trap Robert in a cycle of anxiety and inaction.

The complainer's relationship with uncertainty is one of avoidance. Rather than leaning into the discomfort and working through it, they attempt to escape it. This might manifest as procrastination, denial, or even aggressive attempts to control everything and everyone around them. Robert might put off looking at his financial statements, avoid meetings with his accountant, or snap at employees who bring him problems without immediate solutions. All of these behaviors stem from the same root cause: an inability to tolerate the discomfort of not knowing.

This aversion to uncertainty doesn't just affect the complainer's professional life; it seeps into their personal relationships as well. When faced with uncertainty in their marriage, in their parenting, or in their friendships, complainers often respond with the same fear-based reactions. They might withdraw emotionally, lash out at loved ones, or attempt to control family members' behaviors to create a false sense of certainty. The result is a family environment where honest communication is stifled, where problems are buried rather than addressed, and where growth is stunted by fear.

The irony is that by trying to avoid uncertainty, the complainer actually creates more of it. Their refusal to confront problems head-on means that issues are left unresolved, growing larger and more complex over time. Robert's business problems don't disappear because he ignores them; they compound, creating even more uncertainty in the future. His employees, sensing his avoidance, begin to lose confidence in his leadership, contributing to the very decline he fears. His family, witnessing his distress but never seeing him work through it productively, learns that problems are to be feared rather than faced. The uncertainty that the complainer so desperately tries to escape becomes a constant companion, growing stronger with each avoided challenge.

In many ways, the complainer's fear of uncertainty is a fear of their own inadequacy. Deep down, they doubt their ability to handle whatever might come their way. This self-doubt becomes a self-fulfilling prophecy: because they don't believe they can solve problems, they don't develop the skills needed to do so, which reinforces their belief that problems are insurmountable. It's a cycle that becomes increasingly difficult to break with each passing day.

The Emotional Response: Anger, Anxiety, and Confusion

When confronted with a problem, the complainer rarely responds with calm rationality. Instead, they are flooded with a cascade of emotions that overwhelm their ability to think clearly and act decisively. The three primary emotional responses, anger, anxiety, and confusion, create a toxic cocktail that clouds judgment and hinders effective problem-solving.

Anger is often the first and most visible response. The complainer feels a sense of injustice, a belief that they shouldn't have to deal with this particular problem or that others are to blame for their difficulties. This anger manifests in various ways: They might lash out at family members, criticize employees, or rage against external circumstances.

For example, when Robert's business faces financial difficulties, his immediate response might be to blame the economy, his competitors, or his staff for not working hard enough. This anger serves a purpose for the complainer; it temporarily alleviates their sense of helplessness by directing their energy outward rather than inward.

But beneath the anger lies a deeper emotion: **anxiety**. While anger is explosive and visible, anxiety is corrosive and often hidden. The complainer worries constantly about what might happen, imagining worst-case scenarios and dwelling on potential failures. Robert lies awake at night, his mind racing with thoughts of bankruptcy, public humiliation, and family disappointment. This anxiety paralyzes him, making it difficult to take even small steps toward solving his problems. He becomes trapped in a state of hypervigilance, constantly on alert for new threats but unable to address the ones already facing him.

The third emotional response, **confusion**, is perhaps the most debilitating. When faced with complex problems, the complainer often feels overwhelmed by the sheer number of variables and potential solutions. They struggle to organize their thoughts, to prioritize tasks, or to develop a coherent plan of action. Robert might sit at his desk, surrounded by financial statements and business plans, unable to determine where to begin or what actions to take. This confusion leads to procrastination and avoidance, as the complainer decides that if they can't solve the whole problem immediately, they won't attempt to solve any part of it.

These three emotional responses, anger, anxiety, and confusion, feed into each other, creating a cycle that's difficult to break. Anger fuels anxiety as the complainer worries about the consequences of their outbursts. Anxiety increases confusion as stress hormones flood the brain, inhibiting clear thinking. And confusion leads back to anger as the complainer becomes frustrated with their own inability to find solutions. This emotional cycle becomes a prison, trapping the complainer in an unproductive loop of negative feelings that prevent effective action.

The impact of these emotional responses extends beyond the complainers themselves. Family members, employees, and friends often become collateral damage, absorbing the complainer's negative emotions and adapting their own behaviors in response. Children may learn to hide problems rather than risk triggering a parent's anger. Spouses might take on more than their fair share of responsibilities to avoid causing anxiety. Employees might stop bringing up important issues, knowing that their boss will respond with confusion rather than leadership. In this way, the complainer's emotional responses create ripple effects throughout their social and professional circles, hampering collective problem-solving and creating an atmosphere of tension and unease.

Breaking free from this emotional cycle requires awareness and intentional effort. The complainer must learn to recognize their emotional responses as they occur, to pause before reacting, and to channel their feelings in more productive directions. This isn't about suppressing emotions, anger, anxiety, and confusion, which are natural human responses to challenge, but about preventing these emotions from dictating behavior and clouding judgment. It's about developing emotional intelligence alongside problem-solving skills, understanding that how we feel about a problem is often just as important as how we think about it.

The Self-Doubt Within: A Mind in Conflict

At the core of the complainer's ineffective approach to problem-solving lies a profound self-doubt that corrodes their confidence and undermines their efforts. This isn't just occasional uncertainty or healthy humility; it's a persistent, nagging belief that they are not capable of overcoming the challenges before them. This self-doubt manifests as an internal dialogue filled with negative predictions, harsh self-criticism, and limiting beliefs about one's own abilities.

The complainer's mind is often a battlefield where confidence and doubt wage a constant war. Even when they try to approach a problem constructively, a voice in their head questions every decision, predicts failure, and reminds them of past mistakes. Robert, for instance, might briefly consider a new marketing strategy for his business, only to immediately think: "This will never work. Remember the last campaign that failed? You're not cut out for this. Other business owners would know what to do, but you're just faking it."

This inner critic is relentless, offering no quarter and accepting no excuses. It magnifies small mistakes into catastrophic failures and dismisses successes as mere luck or coincidence. When the complainer does manage to solve a problem, they rarely give themselves credit. Instead, they attribute the positive outcome to external factors or downplay its significance. This pattern reinforces their self-doubt, as their mental scorecard only keeps track of failures while discounting wins.

The self-doubt within the complainer's mind creates a particular kind of cognitive dissonance. On one hand, they desire success, stability, and solutions to their problems. On the other hand, they don't truly believe they're capable of achieving these things. This internal conflict leads to half-hearted efforts, inconsistent action, and a tendency to give up at the first sign of difficulty. Why persist, after all, if failure seems inevitable?

This self-doubt extends beyond the complainer's assessment of their skills and abilities; it infects their sense of worthiness and value as a person. They question not just whether they can solve problems but whether they deserve success at all. This deeper level of self-doubt can be traced back to early experiences, family dynamics, or cultural messages that have been internalized over time. Perhaps Robert grew up with highly critical parents who emphasized his failures rather than his successes. Maybe he internalized societal messages about what success should look like or compared himself unfavorably to peers who seemed to have it all figured out.

The complainer's self-doubt doesn't exist in isolation; it affects how they interpret the world around them. They tend to take neutral comments as criticism, see potential opportunities as risks, and interpret others' success as evidence of their own inadequacy. When a friend offers advice on business strategy, Robert might hear it as a judgment of his incompetence rather than a gesture of support. When a competitor succeeds, he sees it as proof that he doesn't have what it takes, rather than as evidence that success is possible in his industry.

This distorted interpretation of reality creates a self-reinforcing cycle: self-doubt leads to negative interpretations of events, which in turn reinforce self-doubt. Breaking this cycle requires more than just positive thinking or hollow affirmations. It requires a fundamental shift in how the complainer relates to themselves and their capabilities. It calls for self-compassion rather than self-criticism, for realistic assessment rather than catastrophic thinking, and for a willingness to see failure as feedback rather than as a final verdict on one's worth or ability.

The journey from self-doubt to self-confidence is not a straight line. It involves setbacks, resistance, and moments of regression. The complainer who has spent years or decades questioning their own abilities won't transform overnight. However, with conscious effort, with small successes that build upon each other, and perhaps with the support of mentors, therapists, or coaches, change is possible. The inner critic can be tamed, the inner dialogue rewritten, and the self-doubt gradually replaced with a more balanced and accurate assessment of one's strengths, weaknesses, and potential for growth.

The Consequences: A Life and Family in Confusion

The complainer's approach to problem-solving characterized by fear of uncertainty, overwhelming emotional responses, and crippling self-doubt inevitably leads to consequences that affect every aspect of their life. These consequences aren't limited to the individual; they ripple outward, impacting family members, colleagues, and even future generations. The price of ineffective problem-solving is high, paid not just in missed opportunities and unresolved issues but in strained relationships and emotional well-being.

One of the most immediate consequences is a life filled with unaddressed problems. Because the complainer avoids, denies, or mishandles challenges, issues that could have been resolved with prompt attention are allowed to grow and multiply. Robert's initial cash flow problem, for instance, might evolve into serious debt, damaged supplier relationships, and staff turnover if left unaddressed. What began as a manageable issue becomes a crisis that threatens the very survival of his business. This pattern repeats across all areas of life: health concerns go unchecked until they become serious conditions; relationship tensions fester until they erupt in conflict; financial issues compound until they reach crisis levels.

The complainer's home becomes a reflection of their internal state: chaotic, tense, and reactive rather than proactive. Family members learn to tiptoe around issues, knowing that bringing up problems will trigger negative reactions rather than constructive solutions. Children growing up in this environment receive powerful messages about how to handle life's challenges. They learn that problems are sources of distress rather than opportunities for growth, that emotions like anger and anxiety should drive decision-making, and that avoiding issues is preferable to confronting them directly. These lessons become ingrained, shaping how the next generation will approach their own challenges.

The complainer's spouse often bears a disproportionate burden in the relationship. They may find themselves handling not only their own responsibilities but also picking up the slack for problems the complainer avoids. This imbalance creates resentment and exhaustion, straining the marriage and diminishing intimacy. The spouse may feel more like a caretaker or parent than an equal partner, constantly managing the complainer's emotions and cleaning up messes that could have been prevented with more effective problem-solving.

Professionally, the consequences are equally severe. The complainer develops a reputation for unreliability, emotional volatility, and ineffectiveness. Colleagues learn not to depend on them for crucial tasks, limiting their career advancement and opportunities for growth. Employees working under a complainer often experience low morale, high stress, and a lack of clear direction. The business itself suffers from inconsistent decision-making, missed opportunities, and reactive rather than strategic management. In Robert's case, what could have been a thriving enterprise instead becomes a source of constant stress and disappointment, perpetually on the brink of failure despite his hard work and good intentions.

Perhaps the most profound consequence is the impact on the complainer's mental and emotional well-being. Living in a state of chronic stress takes a toll on physical health, leading to issues like high blood pressure, compromised immune function, and sleep disturbances. Emotionally, the complainer experiences higher rates of anxiety, depression, and burnout. Their self-esteem erodes with each avoided challenge and unresolved problem, creating a negative feedback loop that becomes increasingly difficult to escape. The joy, satisfaction, and sense of accomplishment that come from effectively solving problems remain elusive, replaced by a persistent sense of victimhood and helplessness.

The complainer's approach to problem-solving affects not just the present but the future as well. Financial issues left unresolved limit options for retirement, education, and quality of life. Relationship patterns become entrenched, making it harder to establish healthy connections later in life. Business problems compound, narrowing the path to long-term success and security. The complainer finds themselves constantly putting out fires rather than building for the future, trapped in a reactive cycle that prevents true progress and growth.

Breaking free from these consequences requires more than just a change in problem-solving tactics; it demands a fundamental shift in mindset. The complainer must recognize the high cost of their current approach and commit to a different path, one that embraces uncertainty, manages emotions effectively, builds self-confidence, and addresses problems proactively. This transformation isn't easy, but the alternative, a life and family in perpetual disarray, provides powerful motivation for change.

The Thinker

Complex Challenges, Different Perspectives

The thinker, like the complainer, faces the same complex world filled with uncertainty, obstacles, and challenges. They experience the same market fluctuations, relationship difficulties, health concerns, and unexpected setbacks. The problems themselves are not different; what differs dramatically is how the thinker perceives and responds to these challenges. Where the complainer sees threats, the thinker sees puzzles to be solved. Where the complainer feels overwhelmed, the thinker feels engaged. This fundamental difference in perspective shapes everything that follows.

Consider Elizabeth, a business owner with a thinker's mindset. Like Robert, she faces fluctuations in revenue, staffing challenges, and competitive pressures. But when her business encounters a significant downturn, her first reaction isn't panic or blame. Instead, she experiences what psychologists call "productive curiosity," a desire to understand what's happening, why it's happening, and what can be done about it. The uncertainty doesn't disappear for Elizabeth, but it doesn't paralyze her either. She recognizes it as an inherent part of business and life, something to be worked with rather than feared.

This doesn't mean the thinker is immune to negative emotions. Elizabeth feels anxiety when her business struggles, experiences frustration when solutions aren't immediately apparent, and worries about the implications for her family and employees. The difference lies in how she relates to these emotions. Rather than being overwhelmed by them or allowing them to dictate her actions, she acknowledges them as natural responses and then creates space for more productive thinking. She might take a walk to clear her head, talk through her concerns with a trusted advisor, or journal about her feelings before turning her attention to practical solutions.

The thinker understands that complex problems rarely have simple causes or solutions. When faced with declining sales, Elizabeth doesn't immediately blame the economy, her marketing team, or bad luck. Instead, she adopts a systems thinking approach, recognizing that multiple factors are likely at play and that they interact in complex ways. She gathers data, analyzes trends, seeks input from various stakeholders, and considers both internal and external factors that might be contributing to the issue. This comprehensive approach allows her to develop more effective, holistic solutions than would be possible with a simplistic diagnosis.

Whereas the complainer often frames problems in absolute, catastrophic terms," My business is failing,' "My marriage is over," "My health is ruined," the thinker uses more nuanced, accurate language that creates space for solution-finding. Elizabeth might think, "Sales have declined by 15% over the past quarter, which is concerning but not unprecedented. We've navigated similar challenges before and learned valuable lessons that can help us now." This precise framing doesn't minimize the seriousness of the situation but does make it more approachable and actionable.

The thinker also differs from the complainer in their time orientation. Where the complainer is often trapped in the past (ruminating on previous failures or assigning blame) or catastrophizing about the future, the thinker maintains a balanced temporal perspective. Elizabeth acknowledges the past for the lessons it offers and plans for the future to create direction and purpose, but remains primarily focused on the present and on the actions that can be taken today to address current challenges and build toward desired outcomes. This present-focused orientation prevents the paralysis that comes from dwelling on unchangeable past events or becoming overwhelmed by hypothetical future scenarios.

Perhaps most importantly, the thinker approaches problems with a fundamental belief in their ability to improve situations, even if they can't always solve them completely. This sense of agency, what psychologists call an 'internal locus of control,' allows the thinker to take action even in the face of uncertainty. Elizabeth believes that her decisions and actions matter and that she can influence outcomes even when she can't control all variables. This belief sustains her motivation and resilience when facing complex challenges that might take time and multiple attempts to resolve.

The thinker's approach to complexity isn't about having all the answers or never making mistakes. It's about maintaining a perspective that facilitates problem-solving rather than problem-avoidance. It's about seeing challenges as an inevitable and potentially valuable part of life rather than as unfair burdens or insurmountable obstacles. This perspective doesn't make problems disappear, but it does transform how they're experienced and addressed, laying the groundwork for more effective solutions and greater resilience in the face of life's inevitable complexities.

Creating a World of Values Through Concepts

One of the thinker's most powerful tools is their ability to create conceptual frameworks that bring order to chaos and meaning to challenges. Where the complainer sees only problems, the thinker sees patterns. They develop mental models that help them understand the underlying structures of the challenges they face, allowing them to approach problems with greater clarity and purpose. This conceptual thinking isn't abstract intellectualism; it's a practical approach to making sense of a complex world and defining a path forward.

The thinker builds their conceptual framework around core values and principles that guide decision-making and provide stability amid uncertainty. Elizabeth, for instance, might identify integrity, excellence, innovation, and community as the foundational values of her business. These aren't just words on a mission statement; they're deeply held beliefs that inform how she approaches every aspect of her work. When faced with difficult decisions, she returns to these values for guidance: "Which option best reflects our commitment to integrity? How can we maintain excellence while adapting to changing circumstances? Where might innovation help us overcome this obstacle? How will this decision impact our community?"

These value-based concepts serve as anchors, providing stability and direction even when specific circumstances change. They allow the thinker to maintain consistency without rigidity and to adapt tactics while staying true to underlying principles. When Elizabeth's business faces a financial downturn, her values help her distinguish between essential cuts that streamline operations and harmful cuts that would compromise quality or ethics. Her decision-making remains coherent and values-aligned even under pressure, which builds trust with employees, customers, and partners.

The thinker also develops concepts that help them understand and navigate recurring patterns in their personal and professional lives. They recognize that while each problem has unique elements, many challenges share common structures or dynamics. Elizabeth might notice that certain types of client complaints tend to arise from similar misalignments in expectations. Rather than treating each complaint as a separate, unrelated incident, she develops a conceptual framework for understanding and addressing the underlying pattern. This pattern recognition allows for more efficient and effective problem-solving, as solutions can address root causes rather than just symptoms.

Another way the thinker creates order through concepts is by developing mental models of how systems work. Whether it's understanding market dynamics, family relationships, or personal health, the thinker builds internal maps that represent how different elements interact and influence each other. Elizabeth might develop a mental model of her business ecosystem, recognizing how changes in one area (like marketing strategy) affect others (like customer service demands or production schedules). This systems thinking allows her to anticipate ripple effects, identify leverage points for change, and avoid solutions that might create new problems elsewhere.

The thinker's conceptual frameworks also include temporal models, ways of understanding how past, present, and future connect. They recognize patterns over time, understand developmental stages, and appreciate how current actions create future possibilities or constraints. Elizabeth sees her business not as a static entity but as an evolving organization with distinct phases of growth, each with its own challenges and opportunities. This temporal perspective allows her to place current difficulties in a broader context: "This cash flow issue is typical of our growth stage and signals that we need to adjust our financial systems to accommodate our new size."

Perhaps most importantly, the thinker develops concepts around their own role and agency in problem-solving. They have clear ideas about what they can and cannot control, where their responsibilities begin and end, and how their actions influence outcomes. These concepts of personal agency are neither grandiose (believing they control everything) nor defeatist (believing they control nothing). Instead, they reflect a realistic assessment of influence and responsibility. Elizabeth understands that while she can't control the economy or competitors' actions, she can control her company's preparation, response, and adaptation. This concept of bounded agency keeps her focused on productive action rather than wasting energy on factors beyond her influence.

The thinker's world of values-based concepts isn't built overnight. It develops through experience, reflection, study, and conversation with others. It evolves as the thinker encounters new challenges, gains new insights, and refines their understanding. But over time, this conceptual framework becomes an invaluable asset, a mental architecture that brings clarity to confusion, purpose to action, and meaning to difficulty. It transforms problems from chaotic threats into comprehensible challenges that can be approached with wisdom and skill.

Understanding Wants vs. Needs: The Foundation of Effective Solutions

A critical distinction in the thinker's approach to problem-solving is their ability to differentiate between wants and needs, both their own and those of others. This distinction might seem simple on the surface, but it requires significant self-awareness, emotional intelligence, and honest assessment. The thinker recognizes that wants are desires, preferences, and wishes for things we would like to have but can live without. Needs, on the other hand, are essential requirements for well-being, growth, and fulfillment that cannot be compromised without significant negative consequences.

Elizabeth demonstrates this distinction in how she approaches business challenges. When facing financial constraints, she carefully separates the nice-to-haves from the must-haves. She might want a larger office space, the latest technology, or an expanded team, but she recognizes that the business needs financial stability, reliable core services, and a focused strategy. This clarity allows her to make difficult decisions with confidence, cutting expenses that serve wants while protecting investments that address fundamental needs.

The thinker applies this same distinction to personal life. They understand that while they might want constant approval, perfect comfort, or immediate gratification, what they actually need is meaningful connection, purposeful work, and continuous growth. This understanding helps them avoid the traps of materialism, people-pleasing, or short-term thinking that often derail effective problem-solving. When family tensions arise, for instance, Elizabeth recognizes that while she might want agreement or avoidance of difficult conversations, the family needs honest communication, mutual respect, and collaborative problem-solving.

This understanding extends to how the thinker perceives others as well. Where the complainer might see only demands or disappointments in their interactions with family members, employees, or customers, the thinker sees expressions of underlying needs, sometimes awkwardly or indirectly communicated, but legitimate nonetheless. When an employee repeatedly misses deadlines, Elizabeth looks beyond the surface behavior to understand what need might be unmet: Is there a need for clearer instructions? Additional training? A more manageable workload? By addressing the underlying need rather than just reacting to the surface want (an extension or exception), she creates more sustainable solutions.

The thinker's ability to distinguish between wants and needs also helps them prioritize effectively when facing multiple challenges. Not all problems are created equal, and resources (time, energy, money, attention) are always limited. By identifying which issues threaten genuine needs and which affect only preferences or conveniences, the thinker can allocate resources more strategically. Elizabeth might delay addressing office complaints about the brand of coffee in the break room (a want) to focus on resolving a critical supply chain disruption that threatens the business's ability to serve customers (a need).

This distinction becomes particularly important in family dynamics, where different members may have competing wants but shared needs. The thinker recognizes that while family members might want different things, one spouse wants to save for the future while the other wants to enjoy experiences now, one child wants more independence while another wants more structure, the family as a whole needs financial security, emotional connection, and mutual respect. By focusing conversations on these shared needs rather than conflicting wants, the thinker helps the family find common ground and develop solutions that address fundamental requirements while accommodating individual preferences where possible.

The thinker also understands that needs exist in a hierarchy, with some being more fundamental than others.

Drawing on concepts like Maslow's hierarchy, they recognize that physiological and safety needs generally must be addressed before higher-level needs like belonging, esteem, and self-actualization. This understanding helps them avoid the trap of working on higher-level problems while foundational issues remain unresolved. Elizabeth ensures that her business maintains financial stability and operational safety before investing in projects related to brand prestige or market expansion. In her family life, she makes sure basic needs for security and connection are met before addressing issues related to personal achievement or self-expression.

Perhaps most importantly, the thinker recognizes their own responsibility in meeting their needs rather than expecting others to fulfill them. Where the complainer often places the burden of their happiness or success on external factors, other people, circumstances, or luck, the thinker takes ownership of identifying and addressing their own needs. They develop self-sufficiency without becoming isolated, and they develop interdependence without becoming dependent. This balanced approach to needs creates a foundation for resilience and effectiveness in all areas of life.

The Thinker's Vision: From Possibility to Provision

One of the most distinctive characteristics of the thinker is their ability to transform vision into reality to bridge the gap between what could be and what is. This isn't mere daydreaming or wishful thinking; it's a disciplined process of imagining better possibilities and then methodically working to bring them into existence. The thinker's vision extends beyond immediate problem-solving to encompass longer-term aspirations and broader impact, creating a sense of purpose and direction that sustains them through difficulties.

Elizabeth's approach to her business illustrates this capacity. When she founded her company, she didn't just see it as a way to make a living; she envisioned it as a vehicle for creating value, providing meaningful work, and serving her community. This vision wasn't vague or unrealistic; it included specific goals, values, and approaches that differentiated her business from competitors. Her vision provided a clear direction for daily decisions and a compelling narrative that attracted like-minded employees, partners, and customers.

The thinker's vision isn't static; it evolves as circumstances change and new information emerges. When facing challenges, Elizabeth doesn't abandon her vision but refines it, adapting specific elements while maintaining core principles. If market conditions shift or customer needs change, she adjusts her strategies and tactics accordingly, but the underlying purpose, the "Why" behind her business, remains consistent. This balance of flexibility and consistency allows her to navigate difficulties without losing sight of her larger goals.

What distinguishes the thinker's vision from mere fantasy is their commitment to turning vision into provision, to creating tangible results that benefit themselves and others. Elizabeth doesn't just dream about success; she develops detailed plans, allocates resources effectively, builds necessary systems, and executes consistently. Her vision provides direction, but her action creates results. When obstacles arise, she doesn't retreat into wishful thinking but instead gets creative about finding alternate paths to her goals.

The thinker's capacity for vision extends to their personal life as well. They envision the kind of family relationships they want to foster, the environment they want to create in their home, and the values they want to instill in their children. This family vision guides their parenting decisions, relationship priorities, and household management. When faced with family challenges, whether it's behavioral issues with children, communication problems with a spouse, or external pressures on the family unit, the thinker returns to this vision for guidance and inspiration.

One key aspect of the thinker's visionary capacity is their ability to see potential in others. Where the complainer often focuses on others' shortcomings and limitations, the thinker recognizes untapped capabilities and growth opportunities. Elizabeth sees her employees not just as they are but as they could become with proper support, training, and challenge. This perspective transforms how she manages her team; rather than merely assigning tasks and monitoring performance, she invests in development and creates opportunities for growth. This approach not only benefits the employees but also strengthens the organization by building capability and commitment.

The thinker also demonstrates visionary thinking in how they approach problems. Rather than seeing difficulties as mere obstacles to be removed, they often recognize them as opportunities for innovation and improvement. When Elizabeth's business faces a customer complaint or operational breakdown, she doesn't just aim to restore the status quo; she looks for ways to emerge stronger than before. The problem becomes a catalyst for examining systems, challenging assumptions, and developing better approaches. This transformative mindset turns challenges into stepping stones toward a better future rather than mere setbacks to be overcome.

Central to the thinker's visionary capacity is their ability to maintain hope and optimism without denying reality. They don't ignore problems or pretend difficulties don't exist; they acknowledge challenges honestly but refuse to be defined or limited by them. Elizabeth doesn't minimize the seriousness of a cash flow crisis or pretend that a key client's departure isn't concerning. But alongside this realism, she maintains the conviction that solutions exist, that adaptation is possible, and that growth can emerge from difficulty. This balanced perspective, neither naive optimism nor pessimistic defeatism, enables perseverance through tough times.

The thinker's vision provides more than just practical direction; it offers meaning and purpose that sustain motivation during challenging periods. When immediate rewards are scarce and problems abound, the connection to a larger purpose prevents burnout and despair. Elizabeth's commitment to her business vision helps her persist through difficult quarters or market downturns. Her family vision sustains her through the inevitable challenges of raising children and maintaining a healthy marriage. This sense of purpose transforms obligation into a calling and effort into meaningful work.

Education and Awareness: Preparing for Complexity

The thinker's approach to problem-solving is inseparable from their commitment to continuous learning and heightened awareness. They recognize that effective solutions require relevant knowledge, accurate information, and a clear understanding of context. Rather than relying solely on intuition, habit, or conventional wisdom, the thinker actively educates themselves about the challenges they face and the systems within which they operate. This educational mindset becomes a powerful advantage when navigating life's inevitable complexities.

Elizabeth embodies this approach in how she develops her business acumen. She doesn't assume that her initial training or past experience fully equips her for current challenges. Instead, she continuously updates her knowledge through reading industry publications, attending relevant conferences, participating in executive education programs, and engaging with mentors and peers. She stays informed about market trends, technological developments, regulatory changes, and evolving best practices. This ongoing education isn't just academic; it's practical knowledge that directly enhances her decision-making and problem-solving capabilities.

The thinker's educational commitment extends beyond formal learning to include a broader awareness of their environment and the factors that influence it. Elizabeth pays attention to economic indicators, cultural shifts, demographic changes, and emerging technologies that might affect her business. She maintains relationships with diverse stakeholders, customers, suppliers, industry colleagues, and community members who provide different perspectives and insights. This environmental scanning allows her to anticipate challenges rather than merely reacting to them, to prepare for emerging trends rather than being surprised by them.

A crucial aspect of the thinker's educational approach is their willingness to seek expertise beyond their own. They recognize the limitations of their knowledge and experience and aren't threatened by others who know more about specific areas. When facing legal challenges, Elizabeth consults qualified attorneys rather than relying on her limited understanding of the law. When addressing technical issues, she engages experts rather than assuming she can figure it out herself. This willingness to learn from others reflects not insecurity but confidence; the thinker is secure enough to acknowledge what they don't know and wise enough to seek guidance from those who do.

The thinker's commitment to education is matched by their dedication to self-awareness. They understand that effective problem-solving requires not just external knowledge but internal insight and understanding of their own biases, triggers, strengths, and blind spots. Elizabeth regularly reflects on her decision-making processes, examining how her personality, past experiences, and preferences influence her judgments. She seeks feedback from trusted advisors who can help her identify patterns she might miss on her own. This self-awareness allows her to compensate for personal tendencies that might interfere with optimal problem-solving, such as overconfidence in certain areas or avoidance of particular types of challenges.

The thinker's educational mindset is characterized by curiosity rather than certainty. Where the complainer often assumes they already know why problems occur and who's to blame, the thinker approaches difficulties with genuine questions and a desire to understand. When her business experiences an unexpected setback, Elizabeth doesn't jump to conclusions but instead asks probing questions: What factors contributed to this situation? What information might I be missing? What assumptions am I making that should be examined? This curiosity leads to deeper understanding and more effective solutions than would be possible with a rigid, certainty-based approach.

A particularly valuable aspect of the thinker's educational approach is their ability to learn from failure and setbacks. Rather than seeing mistakes as evidence of incompetence or bad luck, they view them as valuable feedback and opportunities for growth. When a new initiative doesn't produce the expected results, Elizabeth conducts a thorough after-action review, examining what worked, what didn't, and why. She encourages her team to share insights without fear of blame, creating a learning culture that improves collective problem-solving capacity over time. This approach transforms failures from mere disappointments into stepping stones toward future success.

The thinker's commitment to education and awareness extends to their family life as well. They recognize that effective parenting, strong marriages, and healthy family dynamics require knowledge, skills, and understanding that don't come automatically. Elizabeth reads books on child development to better understand her children's needs at different stages. She and her spouse attend marriage enrichment workshops to strengthen their communication skills. The family discusses current events and cultural issues at dinner, developing critical thinking skills and awareness of the world beyond their immediate experience. This educational emphasis prepares family members to navigate complex situations with wisdom and discernment.

Perhaps most importantly, the thinker's educational mindset creates resilience in the face of unexpected challenges. By continuously learning and developing awareness, they build a reservoir of knowledge, skills, and perspectives that can be drawn upon when facing novel problems. When unprecedented situations arise, whether a global pandemic, a disruptive technology, or a family crisis without precedent in their experience, the thinker isn't paralyzed by the unfamiliarity. Their habit of learning and awareness-building has prepared them to adapt, to transfer knowledge from one domain to another, and to approach even unprecedented challenges with confidence and competence.

This educational approach represents a fundamental difference between the thinker and the complainer. Where the complainer often relies on the same limited knowledge and perspectives year after year, growing increasingly out of touch with changing realities, the thinker continuously updates their understanding and expands their awareness. This difference becomes more pronounced over time, as the gap between reality and the complainer's outdated perception widens, while the thinker maintains relevance and effectiveness through ongoing learning and awareness.

The thinker's commitment to education and awareness isn't just about accumulating information; it's about developing wisdom, the ability to apply knowledge appropriately in specific contexts. Elizabeth doesn't just know business theories; she understands how to adapt them to her particular industry, company size, market position, and team composition. She doesn't just memorize parenting techniques; she discerns which approaches will work with each child's unique temperament and needs. This contextual intelligence, developed through continuous learning and heightened awareness, allows the thinker to navigate complexity with a sophistication that the complainer, trapped in simplistic or outdated thinking, cannot match.

How These Approaches Shape Family and Business

The contrast between the complainer's and the thinker's approaches to problem-solving extends far beyond individual outcomes. These distinct mindsets create ripple effects that influence family dynamics, business performance, and community impact. Understanding these broader implications helps us appreciate why problem-solving approaches matter not just for personal success but for collective well-being.

In the family context, the complainer's approach creates an atmosphere of tension, reactivity, and avoidance. Children learn that problems are to be feared rather than faced, that emotional outbursts are an acceptable response to challenges, and that blaming others is preferable to taking responsibility. These lessons become ingrained, often carried forward into adulthood and passed down to the next generation. The complainer's family often experiences higher levels of conflict, less effective communication, and fewer opportunities for genuine connection. Problems that could be resolved through collaborative effort instead become sources of ongoing strife and division.

The thinker's family, by contrast, develops a culture of resilience, cooperation, and growth. Children learn by example that challenges can be approached with curiosity rather than fear, that emotions can be acknowledged without becoming overwhelming, and that taking responsibility leads to greater agency and effectiveness. Family members develop problem-solving skills through guided practice, tackling age-appropriate challenges with parental support that gradually gives way to greater independence. The thinker's family isn't free from problems, no family is, but they develop a collective capacity to address difficulties in ways that strengthen rather than weaken their bonds.

In the business context, the differences are equally pronounced. The complainer's business typically operates in crisis mode, lurching from one problem to the next without developing sustainable systems or strategic direction. Employees learn to hide problems rather than address them promptly, knowing that bringing bad news will trigger blame rather than constructive action. Innovation stalls as people become risk-averse, fearing the consequences of failure in a culture where mistakes are punished rather than learned from. Customer relationships suffer as service issues are denied, minimized, or addressed superficially rather than resolved at their root cause.

Conversely, the thinker's business develops a problem-solving culture that becomes a competitive advantage. Employees are empowered to identify issues early and contribute to solutions, knowing their input is valued and that addressing problems promptly prevents larger complications. Innovation flourishes in an environment where calculated risks are encouraged and failures are seen as valuable learning opportunities. Customer relationships strengthen as service issues are addressed thoroughly and systematically, often resulting in greater loyalty than existed before the problem arose. The business develops resilience that allows it to weather industry downturns, competitive challenges, and unexpected disruptions that might cripple less adaptable organizations.

These contrasting approaches also influence community impact. The complainer's business tends to have a transactional relationship with its community, taking what it needs while giving back minimally and reluctantly. Community problems are seen as someone else's responsibility, even when the business contributes to them or has the capacity to help address them. The complainer's family similarly tends to isolate itself from community involvement, viewing community challenges as threats to avoid rather than opportunities to contribute.

The thinker's business and family, on the other hand, often become positive forces in their communities. They recognize the interconnection between their success and community well-being, understanding that thriving communities create environments where businesses and families can flourish. The thinker applies the same problem-solving mindset to community challenges that they bring to personal and business issues: seeking to understand root causes, collaborating with others who bring different perspectives and resources, and taking appropriate responsibility rather than waiting for others to act. This engagement creates social capital that benefits not just the thinker and their immediate circle but the broader community as well.

Perhaps most significantly, these contrasting approaches to problem-solving shape the legacy that extends beyond immediate outcomes to influence future generations. The complainer's approach tends to create a diminishing legacy, as unresolved problems compound over time and dysfunctional patterns are perpetuated. Children carry forward limiting beliefs and ineffective strategies, businesses fail to adapt to changing conditions, and opportunities for positive impact are missed. The complainer's influence typically peaks early and then declines as their reactive approach proves increasingly inadequate for evolving challenges.

The thinker's approach, by contrast, creates an expanding legacy, as effective problem-solving creates platforms for further growth and development. Children internalize empowering beliefs and practical skills that serve them throughout life, businesses build capabilities that allow them to evolve and thrive long-term, and contributions to community well-being create lasting positive change. The thinker's influence often grows over time as the compounding benefits of their approach to challenges become increasingly evident.

This legacy dimension underscores why understanding and adopting effective problem-solving approaches matter so deeply. It's not just about resolving today's challenges more effectively, though that's certainly important. It's about creating patterns that will shape outcomes for years and potentially generations to come. It's about establishing cultures in families, businesses, and communities that nurture growth, resilience, and positive contribution rather than perpetuating dysfunction, fragility, and isolation.

The good news is that problem-solving approaches can be learned and improved. The complainer is not permanently fixed in their mindset; with awareness, motivation, and practice, they can develop more effective ways of addressing challenges. Thinkers aren't born with perfect problem-solving skills; they develop them through experience, education, and intentional effort. By understanding these contrasting approaches and their implications, we gain insight into our own tendencies and opportunities for growth. We can make conscious choices about how we want to approach life's inevitable problems and what kind of legacy we want to create through our response to challenges.

Which approach characterizes your response to challenges? What impact is your problem-solving style having on your family, your work, and your community?

And most importantly, what steps might you take to develop a more effective approach that will serve not just your immediate needs but your long-term legacy?

Chapter 4
Family Value System

Values are the foundation upon which we build our lives. They guide our choices, define our priorities, and shape how we interact with the world around us. When it comes to families, these values become even more important. They create the atmosphere in which children grow, marriages develop, and legacies form. Some families have clear, consistent values that provide stability and direction. Others operate with shifting, unclear values that create confusion and insecurity.

This chapter explores how our two familiar characters, the complainer and the thinker, approach values within their families. We'll see how their different mindsets create entirely different environments for their loved ones. More importantly, we'll see how these value systems impact not just daily life but the family's long-term development and success.

The Complainer

Searching for Solid Ground

Tom sits at his kitchen table, bills spread out before him, his face tight with worry. His wife Emily quietly makes dinner, careful not to disturb him when he's in "one of those moods." Their children, sensing the tension, retreat to their rooms. This scene plays out regularly in their home, not because of a genuine financial crisis, but because of Tom's approach to life's challenges.

As a complainer, Tom doesn't have a clear, consistent set of values that guide his decisions and responses. Instead, he reacts to each situation based on his emotions in the moment, creating an unpredictable environment for his family. One day, he might insist that family time is most important, canceling overtime work to attend his daughter's soccer game. The next week, he might miss the championship match for that same overtime, explaining that "providing for the family has to come first." This inconsistency isn't intentional deception; Tom genuinely believes what he's saying in each moment. But without a stable value system, his priorities shift with his moods and circumstances.

This lack of clear values creates significant challenges for Tom's family. His children never quite know which dad they'll encounter, the one who prioritizes their activities or the one who's too stressed about work to engage. His wife can't reliably predict which expenses will be considered essential and which will trigger a lecture about budgeting. Family plans are tentative at best, subject to cancellation when Tom's focus shifts. Over time, this inconsistency erodes trust and security within the family.

Tom's approach to values extends beyond scheduling and finances to fundamental questions of character and behavior. He tells his children that honesty matters, yet they've heard him call in "sick" to work when he simply wanted a day off. He emphasizes the importance of healthy habits but reaches for fast food and beer when stressed. He values education in theory but rarely makes time to help with homework or attend school events. These contradictions don't make Tom a bad person; they simply reflect his lack of a coherent value system that can guide consistent behavior across different situations.

The complainer's value vacuum doesn't develop overnight. It usually forms gradually through a series of compromises and reactions to life's pressures. Tom didn't set out to create confusion; he simply never took the time to identify and commit to core values that could provide stability amid life's inevitable changes. Without this foundation, he finds himself constantly adjusting to whatever seems most urgent or comfortable in the moment, creating the impression that his values change with the wind.

When Support Systems Become Life Changers

Despite the challenges created by the complainer's inconsistent values, there is hope for positive change. Often, this transformation begins when the complainer connects with supportive individuals who demonstrate a more stable approach to life. For Tom, this lifeline came through an unexpected source, his brother-in-law Mark, who had built a successful business and family life based on clear, consistent values.

At first, Tom resisted Mark's influence, viewing his brother-in-law's advice as judgment or criticism. "You don't understand my situation," Tom would say, listing all the unique challenges and pressures he faced. Mark listened patiently, neither arguing nor backing down from his perspective. Over time, through consistent examples rather than lectures, Mark began to show Tom an alternative way of approaching life's challenges.

When Tom complained about his boss's unreasonable demands, Mark asked questions about Tom's long-term career goals and how his current position aligned with those goals. When Tom vented about financial pressures, Mark shared how his family had developed a budget based on their values rather than reacting to each bill as it arrived. Most importantly, Mark demonstrated through his own family life the stability and joy that come from having clear, consistent values that guide decisions and priorities.

Gradually, Tom began to see how his reactive approach to life was creating unnecessary stress and conflict. He noticed how Mark's family seemed to navigate similar challenges with less drama and more confidence. Tom started to wonder if the problem wasn't his circumstances but his approach to them. This realization marked the beginning of a significant shift in Tom's mindset.

Support systems often function this way for complainers, not by rescuing them from difficulties, but by showing them a different way to interpret and respond to those difficulties. The right mentor, friend, or family member can help the complainer see beyond immediate reactions to identify the values that should guide their choices. They offer not just emotional support but a new perspective that challenges the complainer's assumption that they are merely victims of circumstance.

For Tom, Mark's influence gradually expanded to include other positive voices. He joined a men's group at a local community center, where he met others who were intentionally building their lives around clear values. He started reading books recommended by these new friends, discovering frameworks for identifying and living by core principles. These expanded connections reinforced the lessons he was learning from Mark, creating a network of support that encouraged his developing growth mindset.

This support system became truly transformative when Tom began to apply what he was learning. With encouragement from Mark and his new friends, Tom sat down with Emily to identify their most important family values. The conversation was awkward at first; they had never explicitly discussed such matters, but eventually, they agreed on five core values: integrity, family connection, growth, service, and financial stewardship. This simple exercise gave them a common language and framework for making decisions, reducing the reactivity that had characterized their family life.

The impact of this shift rippled throughout the family. When their teenage son wanted to quit the basketball team mid-season because it was "too hard," Tom and Emily could point to their family value of commitment and growth through challenges. When an opportunity for promotion required potentially moving to another city, they evaluated the option based on how it would affect their value of family connection rather than just the financial benefit. Having explicit values didn't eliminate difficult choices, but it provided a stable foundation for making those choices thoughtfully rather than reactively.

The Light Beyond Familiar Territory

Though Tom has begun to recognize the benefits of having clear values, he still struggles with fully embracing this new approach. His heart is in the right place; he genuinely wants the best for his family and himself, but stepping out of familiar patterns causes him significant stress. Like many complainers who begin to see a better way, Tom longs for the light beyond his comfortable territory but finds the journey challenging.

This tension manifests in various ways. Tom might enthusiastically commit to new family values on Sunday, but revert to old patterns by Wednesday when work pressures mount. He attends parenting workshops with Emily but finds himself falling back on the harsh disciplinary tactics he experienced as a child when his kids misbehave. He agrees with the concept of financial planning based on values, but still makes impulsive purchases when feeling stressed or insecure. This inconsistency isn't evidence of insincerity but reflects the difficult reality of changing deeply ingrained habits of thought and behavior.

The transition from complainer to thinker involves more than intellectual agreement with new concepts; it requires rewiring neural pathways established over decades. Tom finds himself caught between knowing and doing, between understanding better approaches and implementing them consistently. This gap creates internal conflict that sometimes manifests as defensiveness, especially when Emily or the children point out contradictions between his stated values and actual behaviors.

What Tom is experiencing is a common phenomenon in personal growth: the discomfort that comes with expanding beyond familiar limitations. The complainer's mindset, for all its drawbacks, offers a kind of comfort in its familiarity. There's security in believing that external factors are to blame for one's circumstances and that consistent values are impossible in an unpredictable world. Abandoning these beliefs requires not just adopting new ideas but developing new identities and new ways of seeing oneself and one's place in the world.

This transition period can be particularly challenging for relationships. Emily, encouraged by Tom's initial enthusiasm for change, might become disappointed or frustrated when he falls back into old patterns. The children, having experienced the instability of shifting values for years, might be skeptical of their father's transformation, waiting to see if it will last before fully trusting the new family atmosphere. These reactions, though understandable, can make Tom feel unsupported in his growth efforts, tempting him to retreat to familiar complainer territory where at least the expectations are clear.

Despite these challenges, glimmers of light continue to draw Tom forward. He experiences moments of clarity when making decisions based on values rather than reactions, which feel natural and right. He notices the positive response from his family when he maintains consistency between his words and actions. He observes how conflicts resolve more quickly and constructively when everyone refers to shared family values. These moments of success, though interspersed with setbacks, provide motivation to continue the difficult work of transformation.

Indulging in Low-Impact Comforts

As Tom navigates the challenging journey from reactive to value-based living, he sometimes seeks comfort in activities and purchases that provide temporary relief but little lasting impact. This tendency, common among complainers, beginning to recognize the limitations of their mindset, represents an attempt to find a middle ground between old patterns and new aspirations. Tom isn't ready to fully commit to the discipline required by clear values, but isn't satisfied with his previous approach to life.

This compromise often manifests as indulgence in what might be called "low-impact comfort" activities or purchases that provide momentary pleasure without requiring significant change or commitment. Tom might buy the latest smartphone, believing the technology will somehow make him more organized and productive, without addressing the underlying habits that create chaos in his life. He might sign up for a gym membership but attend sporadically, allowing him to feel virtuous about "prioritizing health" without actually developing consistent exercise habits. He might browse self-help books but apply the concepts selectively, taking only the parts that feel comfortable and ignoring more challenging insights.

These indulgences serve a psychological purpose for the complainer in transition. They create an illusion of progress without demanding the deep, sometimes painful work of genuine transformation. When Tom buys exercise equipment for the home, he can temporarily quiet the voice that urges him toward better health habits. When he organizes his workspace but doesn't address his tendency to procrastinate on difficult tasks, he can feel accomplished without confronting deeper issues of discipline and focus. These half-measures provide just enough satisfaction to reduce the urgency of complete change.

The pattern becomes particularly evident in how Tom approaches family time. He might plan elaborate weekend activities, trips to amusement parks, expensive dinners out, or costly sporting events that create memorable experiences but don't address the daily disconnection that characterizes his relationship with his children. These special occasions allow him to feel like a good father without changing the everyday habits that would truly strengthen family bonds. Emily notices this pattern but hesitates to point it out, not wanting to discourage Tom's attempts, however imperfect, to prioritize family.

This approach extends to Tom's work life as well. Rather than addressing fundamental issues with his career path or work habits, he focuses on surface changes, reorganizing his office, trying new productivity apps, or complaining about different aspects of his job. These activities create movement without progress, giving the impression of addressing problems without actually solving them. Colleagues and supervisors notice the inconsistency, further reinforcing Tom's belief that his workplace doesn't appreciate his efforts.

The complainer's tendency to indulge in low-impact comforts reflects a deeper struggle with delayed gratification and long-term thinking. Value-based living requires the ability to forego immediate pleasures for greater future benefits and to withstand temporary discomfort for lasting improvement. Tom understands this concept intellectually but finds the emotional reality challenging. When stress mounts or results don't come quickly, the temptation to fall back on familiar indulgences becomes powerful.

This pattern of indulgence without impact creates a particular kind of frustration. Tom spends money and energy on activities and purchases that promise transformation but deliver only temporary relief. Over time, he accumulates possessions and experiences that were supposed to change his life but instead clutter his home and schedule. The gap between expectation and reality reinforces his complainer's tendency to blame external factors rather than examining his own choices and commitments.

Breaking this cycle requires honest self-assessment and greater alignment between values and actions. For Tom to move beyond low-impact indulgences, he needs to clarify what truly matters to him and his family, then make choices that consistently reflect those priorities. This doesn't mean eliminating all pleasures or pursuing an austere lifestyle, but rather ensuring that resources, time, money, energy, and attention are allocated in ways that create lasting value rather than merely temporary comfort.

The journey from indulgence to impact isn't easy or straightforward. Tom will likely continue to vacillate between value-based decisions and comfort-seeking behaviors as he works to establish new patterns. What matters isn't perfection but direction, gradually moving toward greater consistency between stated values and daily choices. With continued support from Emily, Mark, and other positive influences, Tom can learn to find deeper satisfaction in living according to clear principles rather than chasing the next indulgence.

The Thinker

Building on Bedrock

In contrast to Tom's shifting priorities and inconsistent principles, Jason has built his life and family around clearly defined values that provide stability amid life's inevitable changes. As a thinker, Jason doesn't just react to circumstances as they arise; he interprets and responds to them through the lens of core principles that remain constant regardless of external conditions. This approach creates a foundation of bedrock rather than sand, a solid platform upon which he can construct a meaningful life and nurture a thriving family.

Jason's value system didn't develop overnight or without effort. Early in his marriage to Sarah, they recognized the importance of identifying and articulating the principles that would guide their life together. Through thoughtful conversation, reading, and observation of families they admired, they gradually clarified five core values: integrity, growth, service, relationship, and stewardship. These weren't just nice-sounding words but deeply held convictions about what matters most in life, convictions they revisit regularly and apply consistently to decisions large and small.

What makes Jason's approach particularly effective is how he translates abstract values into concrete behaviors and decisions. Integrity isn't just a concept he praises; it's demonstrated in how he honors commitments, speaks truthfully even when uncomfortable, and takes responsibility for mistakes rather than blaming others. Growth isn't merely an inspirational poster on his wall; it's reflected in his regular reading habits, his willingness to receive feedback, and his encouragement of family members to embrace challenges rather than avoid them. Each value finds expression in daily choices that reinforce and demonstrate what the family truly believes.

This consistency between stated values and lived experience creates a powerful learning environment for Jason and Sarah's children. Unlike Tom's kids, who must navigate the confusion of shifting priorities and contradictory messages, Jason's children receive clear, consistent guidance about what matters and why. When their son considers quitting a difficult project, Jason doesn't simply tell him to persevere; he explains how persistence connects to the family's value of growth through challenges. When their daughter faces a friendship dilemma, Sarah helps her think through options in light of their values of integrity and relationship. These conversations do more than solve immediate problems; they equip the children with decision-making frameworks they can apply throughout life.

The thinker's value system also creates stability during difficult times. When Jason's company went through downsizing and his position was eliminated, the family certainly felt the financial and emotional impact of this setback. However, their response wasn't determined by fear or immediate comfort but by their core values. They made budget adjustments based on their principle of stewardship, preserved family rituals that supported their value of relationships, and approached the job search as an opportunity for growth rather than merely a necessary evil. These value-based responses didn't eliminate the challenge but provided direction and meaning amid uncertainty.

Jason's clear values extend beyond his immediate family to shape his engagement with the broader community. His commitment to service leads him to volunteer regularly and include his children in these activities, teaching them that contributing to others' well-being is an essential part of a fulfilling life. His value of relationship influences how he maintains connections with extended family, invests in friendships, and builds networks within his professional field. His emphasis on growth shapes how he approaches civic engagement, seeking to understand complex issues rather than adopting simplistic positions. Through these various expressions, Jason's values create ripple effects that extend far beyond his own household.

The thinker's approach to values doesn't mean rigid adherence to rules or traditions for their own sake. Jason and Sarah regularly reassess how their core principles should be applied in changing circumstances and as their children develop. Their value of integrity remains constant, but how they help their teenage daughter understand and live this value differs from the approach they took when she was younger. Their commitment to growth continues, but the specific challenges they encourage their son to tackle evolve as his capabilities expand. This combination of stable principles and flexible applications allows their value system to remain relevant and effective through different life stages and circumstances.

Building and Maintaining Reality

For the thinker, values aren't just abstract concepts or occasional considerations; they form the blueprint for constructing and maintaining a cohesive reality for themselves and their family. Jason doesn't simply hope for the best or react to whatever circumstances arise; he actively builds the life he envisions, using his values as guiding principles for decisions both major and minor. This proactive approach creates a sense of agency and purpose that contrasts sharply with the complainer's feeling of being perpetually at the mercy of external forces.

Jason's construction of reality begins with vision, a clear picture of what he wants his life and family to embody. This vision isn't about specific achievements or possessions but about qualities and experiences: a home characterized by warmth and authenticity, work that contributes meaningfully to others, relationships marked by depth and mutual growth, and a legacy of positive impact. His values provide both the foundation and the framework for this vision, ensuring that what he builds will have integrity and lasting significance.

The daily work of constructing this reality involves countless small decisions that align with these values. When Jason considers job opportunities, he evaluates them not just by salary and benefits but by how they fit with his values of service, growth, and family connection. When he and Sarah make parenting decisions, they consider not just immediate behavioral outcomes but the long-term character development of their children. When they allocate family resources, time, money, energy, and attention, they prioritize experiences and investments that reflect and reinforce their core principles.

Maintaining this reality requires ongoing attention and adjustment. Jason and Sarah hold regular family meetings where they discuss how well their actions align with their stated values and where adjustments might be needed. They create family traditions that reinforce key principles, like service projects during holiday seasons or celebration rituals that honor growth and achievement. They establish boundaries that protect their priorities, sometimes saying no to activities or opportunities that, while attractive in some ways, would undermine their core values if pursued.

The thinker's approach to building and maintaining reality includes preparing for inevitable challenges and setbacks. Jason doesn't naively assume that having clear values will prevent difficulties; instead, he develops contingency plans and financial buffers that provide stability when unexpected situations arise. He cultivates relationships and skills that create resilience before they're urgently needed. This preparedness reflects the thinker's understanding that maintaining a value-aligned reality isn't about avoiding problems but about responding to them in ways that preserve core principles even under pressure.

Central to this maintenance work is the thinker's commitment to consistency between words and actions. Jason recognizes that values declared but not demonstrated quickly lose credibility, especially with children who naturally watch what parents do more than what they say. When he makes a mistake that contradicts family values, losing his temper during a stressful moment, for instance, he acknowledges the lapse, makes appropriate amends, and recommits to the principle, modeling both accountability and growth. This integrity between statement and behavior establishes trust that strengthens the family's shared reality.

The reality Jason and Sarah build isn't isolated from the larger world but intentionally connected to it in value-aligned ways. They create opportunities for their children to engage with diverse perspectives and experiences while providing the guidance needed to interpret these encounters through their family's value lens. They discuss current events and cultural trends at the dinner table, helping their children develop critical thinking skills rooted in core principles. This engagement with the broader world prepares their children to maintain their own value-aligned reality even when they eventually leave home.

Navigating Obstacles with Skill and Purpose

Life presents challenges to everyone, regardless of mindset or value system. What distinguishes the thinker is not an absence of obstacles but a skillful approach to navigating them that maintains alignment with core values. Jason faces the same kinds of difficulties Tom encounters: work pressures, relational tensions, financial setbacks, and parenting challenges, but his response to these situations reflects a fundamentally different perspective and skill set.

When confronted with problems, Jason's first instinct isn't complaint or blame but curiosity and assessment. Rather than immediately reacting emotionally, he takes time to understand the situation fully: What exactly is happening? What factors contributed to this challenge? What elements can he influence, and what must he accept? This thoughtful analysis doesn't mean endless deliberation; Jason recognizes when quick action is needed, but it does prevent the knee-jerk responses that often make situations worse rather than better.

Once he understands the challenge, Jason frames it within the context of his values. A potential job loss isn't just a financial threat but an opportunity to demonstrate his commitment to growth and integrity. A conflict with his teenage son isn't merely a battle of wills but a chance to deepen their relationship through honest communication. A health scare becomes not just a source of worry but an occasion to reassess priorities and practice stewardship of physical well-being. This value-based framing transforms obstacles from mere problems to be solved into meaningful parts of a larger life narrative.

The thinker's approach to obstacles includes drawing on accumulated wisdom and skills developed through intentional practice. Jason has invested time in learning effective communication techniques that help him navigate conflicts constructively. He's developed financial disciplines that provide options when unexpected expenses arise. He's cultivated emotional intelligence that allows him to recognize and manage his reactions during stressful situations. These capabilities aren't innate but acquired through deliberate effort and consistent application, another expression of the thinker's commitment to growth and preparation.

Jason also recognizes the value of community in overcoming obstacles. Unlike the complainer, who often isolates during difficulties out of shame or pride, the thinker builds and maintains relationships that provide support, perspective, and practical help when challenges arise. Jason and Sarah have cultivated friendships with couples in different life stages who can offer wisdom from their experiences. They participate in community groups that share their values and provide mutual assistance during difficult times. They maintain strong family connections that create safety nets for various types of needs.

The thinker's navigation of obstacles is characterized by flexibility within principled boundaries. Jason doesn't rigidly adhere to specific methods or plans when circumstances change, but maintains a commitment to underlying values that guide adaptation. When financial pressures required scaling back on certain expenses, he and Sarah found creative ways to honor their value of family connection without spending money, instituting game nights, exploring free community events, and discovering natural areas for outdoor adventures. The specific activities changed, but the core principle remained intact.

Perhaps most importantly, Jason approaches obstacles with confidence rooted in previous experiences of growth through challenge. Unlike Tom, whose self-doubt undermines his problem-solving abilities, Jason has accumulated a track record of successfully navigating difficulties while maintaining his values. This history doesn't create arrogance but does foster realistic optimism about his capacity to handle whatever comes his way. When he tells his children, "We'll figure this out," it's not empty reassurance but a statement grounded in the lived experience of obstacles transformed into opportunities.

The Path to Success

While the complainer's direction often shifts with circumstances and emotions, the thinker maintains a consistent course guided by clearly defined values and goals. Jason's path to success isn't without adjustments; he responds to new information and changing conditions, but the underlying direction remains steady, creating momentum that carries him and his family through inevitable challenges and toward meaningful achievements.

This consistency begins with clarity about what constitutes "success" in the first place. For Jason, success isn't defined primarily by external markers like income level, job title, or possessions but by alignment between values and lifestyle. A successful day isn't necessarily one where everything goes according to plan, but one where responses to whatever happens reflect core principles. A successful career isn't measured just by advancement or recognition but by contribution and growth. A successful family life isn't indicated by perfection but by authentic connection, shared purpose, and mutual support.

With this definition of success established, Jason can evaluate opportunities and make decisions based on whether they support or detract from his true goals. When offered a promotion that would significantly increase his income but require travel that would undermine family relationships, he declined, recognizing that the apparent advancement would actually move him further from success as he defined it. When considering housing options, he and Sarah chose a modest home in a community aligned with their values rather than stretching for a more impressive property that would create financial stress and limit their ability to give generously.

The thinker's unwavering path doesn't mean slavish adherence to specific plans but rather a consistent orientation toward guiding stars that remain fixed even when routes must change. When Jason's initial career path hit unexpected obstacles, he didn't abandon his professional goals but found alternative ways to express his values through work. When their first approach to a parenting challenge proved ineffective, he and Sarah adjusted their methods while maintaining their commitment to raising children who embodied the family's core values. This combination of flexible tactics and stable strategy allows the thinker to maintain progress even when facing detours and delays.

Jason's commitment to his chosen path extends through seasons of apparent stagnation when visible progress slows or temporarily stops. Unlike the complainer, who often abandons goals when immediate results aren't evident, the thinker understands that meaningful achievements frequently require periods of foundation-building, obstacle-clearing, or capacity development that don't show immediate external results. During a year when career advancement seemed stalled, Jason focused on developing skills and relationships that later proved crucial for unexpected opportunities. When their son went through a difficult phase that tested their parenting approach, Jason and Sarah maintained consistent boundaries and expectations that eventually bore fruit in renewed connection and growth.

The unwavering quality of the thinker's path creates particular benefits for children, who thrive on consistency and clear expectations. Jason and Sarah's kids don't have to guess what matters to their parents or wonder if today's priorities will be abandoned tomorrow. This stability doesn't mean rigidity; their parents respond to each child's unique needs and adapt approaches as they mature, but it does provide a reliable framework within which growth can occur safely. The children develop confidence that comes from understanding boundaries and values that remain constant even as specific applications evolve with age and circumstance.

Self-Awareness in Service of Values

A distinctive quality of the thinker's approach to values is the cultivation of self-awareness that supports rather than undermines principled living. Jason recognizes his own tendencies, both strengths and weaknesses, and develops strategies that help him maintain alignment between values and actions despite human limitations. This honest self-assessment creates both humility and efficacy, allowing him to work with rather than against his own nature in pursuit of what matters most.

Jason acknowledges that, at times, his commitment to achievement and excellence can slide into unhealthy perfectionism that creates unnecessary stress for himself and his family. Rather than denying this tendency or allowing it to operate unchecked, he has developed specific practices that help him maintain balance: regular conversations with Sarah, who provides perspective when his standards become excessive, intentional celebration of "good enough" outcomes in appropriate situations, and meditation practices that help him distinguish between helpful and harmful forms of ambition. This self-awareness doesn't eliminate his perfectionist tendencies but does prevent them from undermining his deeper values of relationship and well-being.

The thinker's self-awareness extends to the recognition of seasons and rhythms in their capacity and needs. Jason understands that his energy, focus, and emotional reserves fluctuate based on various factors, such as work demands, family situations, physical health, and natural temperament. Rather than maintaining rigid expectations regardless of circumstances, he adjusts self-expectations appropriately while maintaining core commitments. During particularly demanding work periods, he might simplify family activities while preserving essential connection times. When sensing emotional depletion, he might schedule additional renewal practices that restore his ability to engage authentically with loved ones. These adjustments aren't compromises of values but recognition of what's needed to sustain them long-term.

This awareness also includes honest recognition of how selfishness can manifest in seemingly value-aligned choices. Jason notes his tendency to sometimes use work achievements, even those that align with his value of contribution, as an escape from the emotional demands of family life. He observes how his commitment to growth can occasionally become self-focused rather than oriented toward service. Rather than denying these tendencies or harshly judging himself for them, he brings them into conscious awareness where they can be addressed constructively. This honesty with himself creates the possibility of adjustment and improvement rather than unconscious rationalization.

The thinker's self-awareness includes recognition of their own limitations and needs for support. Jason doesn't pretend to have all the answers or abilities required for the life he envisions. He identifies areas where he needs help, whether with practical skills, emotional intelligence, specialized knowledge, or simply additional perspectives, and actively seeks resources to address these gaps. Unlike the complainer, whose insecurity leads to defensiveness about limitations, the thinker's security allows honest acknowledgment of areas needing development or assistance. This openness to learning and support greatly enhances the capacity for consistent value-aligned living.

One of the most important aspects of the thinker's self-awareness is recognition of their impact on others, particularly family members. Jason regularly reflects on how his words and actions affect Sarah and their children, noticing patterns that either support or undermine the family atmosphere they want to create. When he observes that his communication style during stress creates distance rather than connection, he doesn't blame others' sensitivity but takes responsibility for developing more effective approaches. When he notices positive ripple effects from certain behaviors, he intentionally incorporates these into regular practice. This attention to impact rather than just intention helps align behavior with values across various relationships and contexts.

The self-awareness Jason cultivates doesn't lead to self-absorption but actually enhances his availability to others. By understanding his own patterns, triggers, and tendencies, he can respond more thoughtfully and less reactively to family needs and interpersonal dynamics. His awareness of personal limitations creates genuine humility that facilitates mutual learning and growth. His recognition of how selfishness can manifest in subtle ways allows him to make choices that truly serve others rather than merely appear generous while meeting his own needs. In these ways, self-knowledge becomes a powerful tool in service of the values he holds most dear.

The contrasting approaches to values demonstrated by Tom and Jason create dramatically different trajectories not just for their own lives but for generations that follow. Each man is building a legacy, whether intentionally or not, through the value system he establishes and demonstrates to his children and community. Understanding these different paths can help us examine our own approach to values and make conscious choices about the legacy we wish to leave.

Despite genuine love for his family and moments of clarity about what truly matters, Tom creates a legacy characterized by inconsistency and reaction to circumstances. His children learn that values are flexible conveniences rather than foundational principles, that what's important changes based on external pressures rather than internal convictions. They absorb the message that immediate comfort takes precedence over long-term fulfillment, that appearances matter more than substance, and that circumstances rather than choices determine outcomes. Unless Tom completes his transition from complainer to thinker, these lessons will likely shape his children's approach to decisions, relationships, and challenges throughout their lives.

Jason, through thoughtful development and consistent demonstration of clear values, establishes a legacy of principle-centered living that will influence his family for generations. His children internalize not just specific values but the meta-lesson that having clear, consistent principles provides direction and meaning amid life's inevitable changes and challenges. They develop decision-making frameworks that will serve them in situations their parents never anticipated. They witness and absorb approaches to obstacles that demonstrate agency rather than victimhood. They experience firsthand the benefits of aligning actions with deepest convictions, creating motivation to continue these patterns in their own adult lives.

These different legacies extend beyond immediate family to impact communities and even societies. Tom's reactive, inconsistent approach to values contributes to fraying social fabric, as his fluctuating commitments make him an unreliable community member, and his children learn citizenship patterns characterized by convenience rather than conviction. Jason's stable, principle-centered approach strengthens social connections, as his reliable contributions build community trust, and his children learn patterns of engagement that prioritize collective well-being alongside personal fulfillment.

The good news embedded in this chapter is that value systems can be developed and refined at any point in life. Tom's journey, though incomplete, demonstrates that even those with complainer tendencies can begin to recognize the importance of clear, consistent values and take steps toward more principle-centered living. Change isn't instantaneous; neural pathways and family dynamics established over the years take time to redirect, but the movement toward greater clarity and consistency is possible with awareness, support, and persistent effort.

The first step in this journey is an honest assessment of our current approach to values. Do our actions consistently reflect our stated principles, or do we find ourselves making frequent exceptions and justifications? Do our children see alignment between what we say matters and how we allocate time, money, and attention? Do we have explicit, articulated values that guide decisions, or do we react to each situation based on immediate feelings and circumstances? These questions, answered truthfully, can reveal whether we're building on bedrock or shifting sand.

For those who recognize complainer tendencies in their approach to values, the path forward begins with clarity about what truly matters most. This isn't about adopting someone else's value list but about identifying and articulating principles that reflect the deepest convictions about what constitutes a meaningful life. With these core values established, the next step is examining decisions and behaviors in light of these principles, noticing areas of alignment and disconnection. Where gaps exist, strategies can be developed to bring actions into greater consistency with stated values, creating integrity that builds trust and stability for the entire family.

Whether we currently resemble Tom or Jason in our approach to values, we all face the same fundamental question: What legacy of values do we want to leave for those who follow us? The answer to this question, revealed more through our daily choices than our occasional declarations, will shape not just our own life satisfaction but the lives of generations to come. By developing and consistently demonstrating clear, meaningful values, we provide those we love with the most valuable inheritance possible: a foundation of principles upon which they can build lives of purpose, integrity, and fulfillment.

Chapter 5
Accountability

Part 1: The Complainer

The moment of mistake arrives with a familiar weight, heavy, uncomfortable, threatening. For the Complainer, this moment is not an opportunity for growth, but a potential catastrophe to be avoided at all costs. Mark sits in his small home office, surrounded by mounting bills and overdue notices, the physical manifestation of his financial chaos. A credit card statement shows multiple overdraft fees, late payment penalties, and interest charges that have ballooned beyond recognition. Yet, instead of examining the root causes, Mark's mind immediately begins its well-worn narrative of external blame.

"The bank's fee structure is predatory," he mutters, shuffling papers with increasing agitation. "These interest rates are impossible for anyone to manage." The statement is partially true, but it skillfully sidesteps the more critical questions: Why did the overdrafts occur? What financial decisions led to this moment? These are inquiries Mark refuses to entertain.

The psychology of avoidance is a complex terrain, and Mark has become an expert navigator of its most treacherous paths. His home reflects this internal landscape: papers are scattered haphazardly, bills are stuffed into drawers, and financial documents are hidden behind outdated magazines.

Each hidden statement is a small monument to his resistance, a physical representation of the mental barriers he's constructed.

His wife, Sarah, has witnessed this pattern for years, watching as Mark's financial decisions become increasingly erratic. Early in their marriage, she had hopes of collaborative financial planning. Those hopes have gradually eroded, replaced by a survival strategy of careful observation and minimal intervention. She's learned that direct confrontation only intensifies Mark's defensive mechanisms.

Financial literacy is more than understanding numbers; it's about understanding oneself. For the Complainer, this represents a terrain too treacherous to navigate. Mark's financial illiteracy isn't merely about a lack of knowledge—it's a deliberate resistance to learning. When Sarah suggests they attend a financial planning workshop, he dismisses the idea. "Those are just scams designed to sell you something," he declares, effectively constructing another wall between himself and potential growth.

The Roots of Resistance

The origins of Mark's approach can be traced back to his childhood. Growing up in a household where financial stress was a constant companion, he learned early that money was a source of conflict and anxiety. His father, a factory worker prone to sudden job losses, would respond to financial challenges with a mixture of rage and resignation. Mark internalized this response, developing a survival mechanism that prioritized emotional protection over financial health.

"Money talks were always fights in our house," Mark once admitted to Sarah during a rare moment of vulnerability early in their relationship. "Dad would get the bills, mom would cry, and we kids would disappear into our rooms." These formative experiences created a template that Mark would unconsciously follow throughout his adult life—avoidance as a form of self-preservation.

This early programming manifests in Mark's adult life as an almost allergic reaction to financial planning. When Sarah attempts to discuss their retirement strategy, his body language shifts immediately. His shoulders tense, his breathing becomes shallow, and his responses become clipped and defensive. These aren't conscious choices, but visceral reactions to perceived threat—the emotional equivalent of touching a hot stove.

The sad irony is that Mark's avoidance creates precisely the financial instability he fears. By refusing to engage with financial reality, he ensures that crises will continue to emerge, seemingly from nowhere. A surprise car repair becomes a financial emergency rather than an anticipated expense. A routine medical procedure transforms into a budget catastrophe. Each incident reinforces his belief in a hostile, unpredictable financial world.

This resistance manifests in a complex psychological dance. Each financial misstep becomes an opportunity not for reflection, but for an elaborate narrative of victimhood.

Missed payments aren't the result of poor budgeting or impulse spending, but elaborate conspiracies involving employers, banks, or economic systems. The credit card statement isn't a record of his choices, but evidence of an unfair world.

The Contagion of Blame

The impact of this approach extends far beyond personal finances. Mark's children observe this pattern of evasion, learning that accountability is something to be feared rather than embraced. When his teenage son comes home with a poor grade, Mark's first response isn't to discuss study strategies or understand the underlying challenges. Instead, he immediately questions the teacher's fairness, the grading system, and the school's methodology.

"These standardized tests are meaningless," Mark will say, effectively teaching his son that responsibility is a burden to be deflected, not a skill to be developed. The lesson is subtle but profound. His children are absorbing a worldview where personal agency is replaced by a narrative of perpetual victimhood.

His daughter's approach to competitive swimming reveals the generational impact of this mindset. When she fails to qualify for a championship meet, her immediate response mirrors her father's pattern—blaming the timing equipment, the coaching decisions, and the pressure of the moment. The possibility that additional training or technique refinement might improve future performances remains unexplored.

Mark's workplace reflects the same pattern. Promotions seem to slip away; opportunities become missed connections. Yet, he never considers his own role in these professional setbacks. Each rejected proposal, each overlooked project, becomes another piece of evidence in his ongoing narrative of external persecution.

His colleagues have learned to navigate around Mark's defensive mechanisms. Team meetings become carefully choreographed dances, with colleagues anticipating and deflecting potential moments of personal accountability. It's an exhausting performance, maintained not out of malice, but out of a collective understanding of Mark's psychological fragility.

"Mark has some great ideas," his supervisor once confided to a colleague, "but working with him requires constant reassurance that any feedback isn't personal criticism." This accommodation creates a temporary peace but ultimately limits Mark's professional growth. Without honest feedback, without genuine accountability, his skills stagnate. The same presentation mistakes, the same strategic oversights, appear repeatedly in his work, invisible to him but increasingly apparent to others.

The Feedback Loop of Financial Avoidance

The most insidious aspect of the Complainer's approach to accountability is its self-reinforcing nature. By consistently avoiding genuine reflection, Mark ensures he'll never develop the skills necessary to improve. Each blamed external factor becomes another brick in a wall of learned helplessness. Financial challenges aren't problems to be solved, but permanent conditions to be endured.

This cycle creates a peculiar relationship with financial information. Mark simultaneously seeks and avoids financial data. He'll obsessively check account balances but resist creating a comprehensive budget. He'll research investment opportunities without ever implementing a concrete plan. This contradictory approach creates the illusion of financial engagement without the substance.

The psychological mechanism at work is a form of self-protection. By maintaining a state of partial knowledge, Mark preserves his ability to blame external forces. Complete information would require complete responsibility—a prospect too threatening to contemplate. This selective engagement with financial reality allows him to maintain the comforting narrative that his challenges are imposed rather than created.

This isn't to suggest Mark doesn't suffer. He experiences genuine stress and real anxiety about his financial situation. But this suffering becomes another tool of evasion—a performance of victimhood that paradoxically prevents actual change. His complaints are not calls for improvement, but elaborate defenses against personal responsibility.

Sleep often eludes him. Nights become extended sessions of worry and recrimination, but notably absent from these midnight reflections is any genuine self-examination. The mental loop remains consistent: external forces have created these problems, circumstances have conspired against him, and the system is rigged. By morning, exhaustion has replaced anxiety, but the underlying patterns remain unchanged.

The Relational Cost

Sarah watches this pattern with a mixture of frustration and resignation. She's tried multiple approaches, gentle guidance, direct confrontation, and collaborative planning—but Mark's resistance remains impenetrable. Their conversations about money inevitably devolve into arguments where he becomes defensive, transforming financial dialogue into emotional warfare.

The financial strain isn't just about numbers. It's about trust, about the fundamental contract of partnership. Each deflected responsibility creates a small fracture in their relationship. Their intimacy becomes transactional, defined more by shared expenses and household management than by genuine emotional connection.

"Sometimes I feel like I'm raising three children instead of two," Sarah confides to her sister during a rare moment alone. The statement isn't meant as criticism, but as an expression of profound weariness. The constant vigilance required to navigate Mark's defensive patterns has created an emotional exhaustion that permeates their relationship.

Their children absorb these tensions with the uncanny perception typical of young people. They learn to modulate their requests based on the household's financial barometer. They develop an intuitive understanding of when to approach their father about expenses and when to redirect requests to their mother. This adaptation might seem benign, even clever, but it represents a profound lesson in emotional manipulation rather than financial literacy.

Mark's relationship with credit is particularly revealing. Where others might see credit as a tool for financial flexibility, he experiences it as a form of persecution. Each credit card feels like a potential trap, and each loan is a conspiracy designed to undermine his financial stability. He fails to understand that credit, properly managed, can be a pathway to financial opportunity.

This misunderstanding stems from a deeper psychological mechanism. Credit requires a level of forward-thinking and the capacity to plan and strategize, which directly conflicts with the Complainer's reactive approach to life. Planning requires acknowledging potential future challenges, a skill Mark has systematically avoided developing.

The credit system, with its emphasis on payment history and responsibility, becomes a mirror reflecting truths Mark refuses to acknowledge. His credit score—a numerical representation of financial accountability—remains perpetually depressed, not due to major financial catastrophes, but through a series of small evasions and deflections that compound over time.

The Family Legacy

The tragedy isn't just the financial instability, but the relational damage. Trust erodes with each deflected responsibility. Their children learn that transparency is dangerous, that admitting mistakes invites criticism rather than support. The family system becomes a complex network of unspoken tensions, with financial stress acting as a constant, low-grade fever.

Family gatherings become performances of normalcy, carefully choreographed to avoid triggering Mark's defensive patterns. Holiday gift-giving becomes a minefield of potential conflict, with Sarah carefully managing expectations and expenses to prevent inevitable post-holiday financial drama. Vacations, if they occur at all, are shadowed by Mark's constant commentary on costs and value, his enjoyment perpetually compromised by financial anxiety.

The children learn to manage their father's emotions rather than express their own needs. His daughter becomes adept at framing requests in ways that minimize his defensive response. His son develops an unsettling financial secretiveness, hiding small purchases and saving gift money in hidden locations throughout the house. These aren't acts of typical teenage rebellion, but adaptive strategies developed in response to an emotionally unsafe financial environment.

Mark's approach to accountability represents more than individual failure—it's a broader psychological mechanism of protection. By never fully acknowledging his role in creating his circumstances, he maintains a fragile sense of self-worth. Admitting mistakes would require dismantling carefully constructed narratives of external persecution.

Yet, beneath the complaints and deflections, there's a vulnerability. Mark isn't inherently malicious. He's trapped in a psychological mechanism designed to protect him from perceived shame, from the terrifying prospect of genuine self-examination. His complaints are a defense mechanism, a way of maintaining an illusion of control in a world that feels overwhelmingly complex.

In his quiet moments, rare though they may be, Mark sometimes glimpses the reality of his situation. These flashes of insight arrive unexpectedly—while watching his son's baseball game, during a rare peaceful moment with Sarah, in the predawn stillness before the household awakens. In these moments, he feels the weight of his patterns and senses the damage his approach has created. But these insights remain fragile, easily displaced by the more familiar narrative of external blame when the next challenge arrives.

The path toward genuine accountability remains available, but the first step requires the courage to acknowledge a simple truth: the common denominator in all these financial challenges is himself. Until this recognition occurs, the pattern will continue, creating ripples of consequence that extend far beyond bank accounts and credit scores, shaping the emotional landscape of his family for generations to come.

Part 2: The Thinker

In stark contrast stands Elena, a woman who approaches accountability with the precision of an architect designing a complex structure. Where the Complainer sees mistakes as threats, Elena views them as valuable blueprints for personal development.

Her office, a meticulously organized space, reflects her approach to life. Bookshelves lined with financial texts, carefully maintained spreadsheets, and color-coded folders documenting every significant financial decision. This isn't mere organization; it's a philosophy, a way of understanding the world through systematic reflection and continuous improvement.

Embracing the Moment of Truth

The moment Elena discovers a financial misstep, her response is immediate and methodical. When she realizes she's missed a credit card payment, she doesn't launch into a narrative of external blame. Instead, she opens a spreadsheet, analyzes the incident, and develops a system to prevent future occurrences.

"I need to understand what happened here," she tells her husband, David, her tone curious rather than defensive. "Was this a systematic failure or a one-time oversight?" This question isn't rhetorical—it's the beginning of a genuine investigation. Elena understands that accountability begins with an accurate assessment.

Her approach is rooted in a deep understanding of personal psychology. Elena recognizes that accountability isn't about perfection, but about honest engagement with one's choices. Each financial decision is carefully considered, not as an isolated event, but as part of a broader life strategy.

This clarity allows Elena to separate her self-worth from her mistakes. A financial misstep doesn't indicate personal failure, but an opportunity for systemic improvement. This nuanced understanding creates an emotional safety that allows for honest self-evaluation without crushing self-judgment.

The Foundations of Financial Literacy

Growing up, Elena witnessed a different approach to financial management. Her parents, both educators, treated financial literacy as a critical life skill. Family discussions around the dinner table often involved nuanced conversations about budgeting, investment, and financial planning. These weren't lectures, but collaborative explorations of economic principles.

"My father would explain compound interest using my allowance as an example," Elena recalls with a smile. "He'd show me how saving even small amounts could grow significantly over time." These early lessons weren't just about numbers, but about relationships, with money, time, and future goals.

For Elena, financial literacy isn't an abstract concept but a dynamic living practice. She approaches money with the same intellectual rigor she applies to her professional work as a research scientist. Each financial decision is a hypothesis to be tested, and each mistake is an opportunity for recalibration.

Her professional background as a research scientist profoundly influences her approach to personal finance. In her laboratory, mistakes aren't failures but essential data points in the journey of understanding. She applies this same principle to her financial life, viewing each unexpected expense or missed opportunity as valuable information.

This approach creates a remarkable stability, not just in her accounts, but in her emotional relationship with money. Financial challenges still occur—unexpected medical expenses, market fluctuations, career transitions—but these events are processed as variables to be incorporated rather than disasters to be avoided.

Teaching Through Example

When her daughter encounters an academic challenge, Elena's approach is transformative. "Let's break down what happened," she'll say, sitting beside her child. "What worked in your study approach? What didn't? How can we adjust?" This isn't an interrogation, but a collaborative exploration of growth.

One particularly illuminating incident occurred when her son received a disappointing grade on a science project. Rather than immediately contacting the teacher or questioning the grading criteria, Elena helped him analyze the project itself. "Let's look at the areas where you excelled and the areas that need improvement," she suggested. Together, they identified specific weaknesses and developed strategies for future assignments.

The benefits of such an approach extend far beyond immediate problem-solving. Elena's children learn that mistakes are not shameful incidents to be hidden, but valuable data points in the ongoing experiment of personal development. They witness vulnerability as a strength, not a weakness.

This approach creates a particular kind of resilience—not the rigid stubbornness of denial, but the flexible strength of adaptation. Her children face challenges with a confidence born not from false praise, but from experienced competence. They've developed the metacognition to analyze their performance and adjust accordingly—a skill that will serve them throughout their lives.

The Partnership of Accountability

Her husband, David, appreciates this approach, having seen how it transforms potential conflicts into opportunities for mutual understanding. When financial challenges arise, they become collaborative problem-solving sessions rather than battlegrounds of blame and defensiveness.

"Before I met Elena," David reflects, "I saw budgeting as a form of restriction. Now I understand it's actually about freedom—the freedom to make informed choices rather than reactive decisions." This shift in perspective has transformed not just their financial landscape but the emotional texture of their relationship.

Their family finances are a testament to this approach. Regular family meetings discuss not just expenses, but financial goals, investment strategies, and personal growth. Their children are active participants, learning financial principles not through lectures, but through genuine engagement.

A recent family discussion about vacation planning demonstrates this philosophy in action. Rather than simply announcing a destination or budget, Elena and David presented options with associated costs, asking their children to help analyze the value of different experiences. This wasn't just about the vacation itself, but about developing critical thinking skills within a financial context.

The Architecture of Financial Responsibility

Accountability, in Elena's worldview, is fundamentally about agency. By consistently taking responsibility, she maintains control over her narrative. Each acknowledged mistake becomes a stepping stone, not a stumbling block. Her credit score reflects this approach—consistently strong, built through deliberate, thoughtful financial choices.

Her understanding of credit is particularly sophisticated. Where others might see credit as a simple tool for purchasing, Elena recognizes it as a complex system with both opportunities and limitations. She uses credit strategically—leveraging rewards programs, maintaining optimal utilization ratios, and strategically timing applications to maximize benefits while minimizing credit inquiries.

This nuanced approach extends beyond personal finance to broader economic understanding. Elena recognizes that individual financial decisions exist within larger economic systems. She stays informed about policy changes, market trends, and emerging financial technologies. This knowledge isn't academic—it directly informs her decision-making, allowing her to adapt strategies as conditions change.

The contrast with the Complainer's approach couldn't be more profound. Where Mark sees a credit card statement as a document of persecution, Elena sees it as a communication, a set of information to be understood and integrated. Her financial literacy isn't just about knowing numbers, but about understanding the complex human systems that create those numbers.

Imperfection as Information

This doesn't mean Elena is perfect. She makes mistakes and experiences setbacks. But her fundamental orientation towards these moments is one of curiosity rather than defensiveness. “Interesting,” she’ll say, examining an unexpected expense. “What can I learn from this?”

A particularly challenging period occurred during an economic downturn that impacted her research funding. The laboratory budget was cut significantly, creating both professional and personal financial strain. Rather than becoming mired in resentment or anxiety, Elena approached the situation with her characteristic analytical mindset.

“We need to reassess our priorities, both at work and at home,” she told David during this period. Together, they created temporary spending reductions, identified potential alternative income sources, and developed contingency plans for various scenarios. The situation remained challenging, but their response transformed a potential crisis into a manageable challenge.

Her professional network reflects this approach. As a research scientist, Elena is known not just for her technical skills but for her capacity to transform challenges into opportunities. Colleagues seek her out not just for her expertise, but for her unique approach to problem-solving.

The Legacy of Financial Empowerment

The financial education she provides her children goes beyond practical skills. It’s a comprehensive approach to understanding personal agency, risk management, and continuous learning. Her teenage children already demonstrate a level of financial sophistication rare among their peers.

"Mom taught us to think about money as a tool, not a goal," her daughter explains to a friend struggling with financial decisions. This simple distinction represents a profound shift in orientation—money becomes a means of creating value rather than a source of anxiety or an end in itself.

Her children are absorbing more than financial strategies—they're learning a fundamental life philosophy. Responsibility isn't a burden, but a form of empowerment. Mistakes aren't endpoints, but beginnings of more sophisticated understanding.

This education creates a particular kind of confidence. Unlike the brittle certainty that comes from denial, this is the grounded confidence of genuine competence. Her children approach financial decisions with neither fear nor recklessness, but with thoughtful consideration of consequences and opportunities.

Strategic Credit Management

Elena's approach to credit is particularly illuminating. Where others might see credit as a potential trap, she views it as a strategic tool. She understands credit not as a method of immediate gratification, but as a long-term financial instrument that, when used wisely, can create opportunities for growth and stability.

This doesn't mean she approaches credit recklessly. Each credit decision is carefully analyzed, considering not just immediate needs but long-term financial health. She teaches her children that credit is a responsibility, not a right—a nuanced lesson that goes far beyond simple financial instruction.

Her family's emergency fund demonstrates this approach in action. Unlike Mark, who experiences unexpected expenses as devastating surprises, Elena anticipates these events. "It's not a question of if emergencies will happen, but when," she explains to her children. The emergency fund isn't just financial protection—it's a concrete demonstration of foresight and responsibility.

The broader implications of this approach extend beyond finance. Her children learn that responsible planning creates freedom rather than restriction. The emergency fund allows for confident decision-making during challenging times—a stark contrast to the panic-driven choices that financial instability often creates.

The Architecture of a Meaningful Life

In the grand landscape of human development, Elena represents a different approach to personal growth. Accountability becomes not a performance of virtuousness, but a genuine, ongoing practice of self-improvement.

This approach creates a particular quality of presence. Elena engages fully with each moment, whether challenging or joyful, because she's not burdened by unacknowledged mistakes or unresolved tensions. The energy that other people expend on defense and denial becomes available for genuine engagement with life.

The difference between the Complainer and the Thinker isn't about perfection. It's about orientation. One sees the world as a series of things happening to them; the other sees themselves as active participant, constantly learning, constantly growing.

As the financial landscape becomes increasingly complex, this approach isn't just beneficial—it's essential. In a world of changing economic realities, the ability to take genuine, honest accountability becomes a critical survival skill.

Elena's life is a testament to this approach. Not a life without challenges, but a life characterized by resilience, continuous learning, and a profound understanding that personal growth is an ongoing journey, not a destination.

The architecture of responsibility she's created serves as a blueprint for others, not to be replicated exactly, but to inspire similar structures built on the foundation of genuine accountability. In a world increasingly characterized by deflection and blame, her approach offers a refreshing alternative—a life built on the steady ground of responsibility rather than the shifting sands of evasion.

Chapter 6
Differences of Repetitive Choices

Life unfolds not through single, dramatic decisions, but through patterns of choices repeated day after day, year after year. These repetitive choices in how we respond to challenges, manage our resources, and interact with loved ones eventually crystallize into the architecture of our existence. What appears as fate or circumstance to the casual observer is often the culmination of thousands of small decisions, each reinforcing a particular direction or mindset. The repetitive choice becomes not just what we do, but who we are.

In our continuing exploration of the complainer and the thinker, we now turn to this critical dimension of human experience. How do these contrasting mindsets approach the repetitive choices that shape their days and, ultimately, their lives? What happens when patterns become so ingrained that they're no longer recognized as choices at all? And how does awareness or the lack thereof transform the landscape of possibility?

Part 1: The Complainer

The Crisis of an Undiscovered Self

Greg stands at the kitchen counter, mechanically preparing his morning coffee with the same distracted movements he's used for years. The ritual is so familiar that his hands operate independently of his conscious mind, which is already occupied with rehearsing grievances about the upcoming workday. The coffee will be too bitter, as it often is, but he'll drink it anyway, adding extra sugar to mask the taste rather than adjusting his brewing method. This small pattern of accepting frustration rather than addressing its cause echoes throughout his life in ways he has never paused to consider.

For the complainer, the most profound crisis isn't external circumstance but the fundamental disconnection from the self. Greg doesn't know himself in the way that matters for meaningful growth or change. He has never developed the habit of genuine self-reflection, of examining the patterns that shape his experiences and the choices that reinforce those patterns. This absence of self-discovery isn't merely a philosophical concern; it's a practical limitation that confines him to reactive rather than intentional living.

"I'm just not a morning person," Greg will say when explaining his perpetual tardiness to work, as though this were an immutable characteristic rather than a pattern that could be examined and potentially changed. "That's just how the world works," he'll declare when describing the office politics he finds so frustrating, never considering how his own behaviors might contribute to or perpetuate these dynamics. These statements aren't merely observations; they're declarations of identity that simultaneously explain and excuse the repetitive choices that shape his reality.

This crisis of an undiscovered self didn't emerge suddenly. It developed gradually through life influences that subtly shaped Greg's perceptions and responses. His father, a man who viewed life as something that happened to him rather than something he actively shaped, modeled a particular way of moving through the world. His early workplace experiences, where initiative was often punished rather than rewarded, reinforced the safety of passive complaint over active problem-solving. His social circle, composed largely of others who share his worldview, continually validates his perspective through mutual commiseration.

These influences haven't merely affected Greg; they've become so deeply integrated into his perception that he no longer recognizes where they end and his authentic self begins. His complaints about his boss, his marriage, and his financial situation all feel like objective assessments of external reality rather than expressions of a particular mindset he's adopted. The narratives he's absorbed have become the lens through which he views all experience, invisible precisely because they're the mechanism of seeing itself.

This lack of self-awareness creates a peculiar kind of stagnation. Without recognizing the patterns that shape his experience, Greg remains locked in repetitive choices that produce predictable results. Each day begins with the same hurried morning routine, continues with the same workplace frustrations, and ends with the same evening escapism through television or social media. These aren't conscious choices made with awareness of alternatives, but automatic responses to stimuli, reactions rather than decisions.

"That's just who I am," Greg will say when his wife suggests a different approach to handling their teenage son's academic struggles. This statement reveals the fundamental limitation of the complainer's self-concept. Identity becomes not a dynamic, evolving expression of growth and choice, but a fixed set of characteristics that justify continued patterns regardless of their effectiveness. This rigid self-definition becomes both prison and shield, confining growth while protecting from the vulnerability of genuine change.

The tragedy isn't that Greg makes poor choices, but that he doesn't recognize them as choices at all. His sense of agency, the awareness that he is actively creating his experience through decisions, has been replaced by a narrative of circumstances happening to him. This narrative isn't merely an interpretation of reality; it has become his reality, the water in which he swims without recognizing it as water.

The Made-Up Lifestyle

What Greg experiences as "just life" is, in fact, a made-up lifestyle, a construct built from accumulated habits, absorbed influences, and unexamined assumptions. This lifestyle wasn't consciously designed or deliberately chosen, but emerged from a thousand small surrenders to the path of least resistance. Yet, having never paused to examine its foundations, Greg experiences this constructed reality as the inevitable and unchangeable nature of existence itself.

This made-up lifestyle manifests in concrete ways across all dimensions of Greg's life. His morning routine, rushed, chaotic, and anxiety-producing, isn't the only possible way to begin a day, but he approaches it as though it were an immutable law of nature rather than a series of choices that could be reconfigured. His financial habits, including impulsive spending followed by anxiety about bills, aren't inevitable consequences of his income level, but patterns he's never seriously examined or attempted to modify. His communication style with his wife and children, reactive, defensive, and often dismissive, isn't the only way to engage with loved ones, but it's the only way he knows because he's never invested in developing alternatives.

The irony is that Greg believes himself to be highly observant and analytical about the world around him. He readily identifies flaws in systems, mistakes in others' thinking, and injustices in social structures. Yet this outward-focused analysis never turns inward to examine his own patterns with the same critical eye. He can articulate in exhaustive detail why his workplace culture is dysfunctional, but remains blind to how his own behavior contributes to that dysfunction. He can identify precisely why the education system is failing his son, but cannot see how his own modeling of avoidance and excuse-making influences his child's approach to academic challenges.

This one-way analysis creates a peculiar blind spot where personal responsibility should be. Greg experiences himself as a helpless observer of life's disappointments rather than an active participant in creating his reality. "What can you do?" becomes his reflexive response to difficulties, a rhetorical question that assumes its own answer: nothing. This perceived helplessness isn't just a perspective; it's a self-fulfilling prophecy that ensures continued patterns of reaction rather than proactive change.

The complainer's made-up lifestyle becomes increasingly rigid over time, calcifying into habits so ingrained they feel like destiny. Each repetition of a pattern, whether it's how Greg responds to criticism at work, manages household finances, or handles disagreements with his wife, deepens the neural pathways associated with that behavior, making it increasingly automatic and resistant to change. What began as a tendency becomes a habit, then a defining characteristic, and finally an identity that seems immutable.

"This is just how things are for people like me," Greg might say when comparing his financial struggles to those of more affluent acquaintances. This statement reveals the ultimate limitation of the complainer's perspective: the inability to imagine that different choices could lead to different outcomes. The made-up lifestyle has become so convincing, so all-encompassing, that alternatives seem not just difficult but impossible, not just unfamiliar but unnatural.

The Trap of Repetitive Choices

This unexamined, unconsciously constructed lifestyle leads inevitably to repetitive choices and decisions made not from conscious intention but from ingrained habit and unquestioned assumptions. Greg doesn't decide to procrastinate on important projects; he simply follows the familiar pattern of avoidance that has characterized his approach to challenges for decades. He doesn't choose to react defensively to his wife's suggestions; he automatically employs the protective mechanisms he's used since childhood without considering their impact or effectiveness.

These repetitive choices create a closed loop of experience. Certain behaviors produce predictable results, which then reinforce the very worldview that generated those behaviors in the first place. When Greg procrastinates on work projects and then must rush to meet deadlines, the resulting stress and subpar performance confirm his belief that work is inherently overwhelming and unrewarding. When he reacts defensively to his wife's suggestions and she withdraws in frustration, this reinforces his perception that relationships are naturally contentious and unsatisfying. Each cycle deepens the grooves of his existing patterns, making deviation increasingly difficult.

The most insidious aspect of this trap isn't just that it produces continued difficulties, but that it severely limits Greg's experience of life itself. Like a person who orders the same dish at every restaurant, never experiencing the full range of culinary possibilities, the complainer becomes trapped in a narrow band of experience defined by familiar patterns and predictable outcomes. The rich variety of potential responses, the creative possibilities that emerge from trying new approaches, and the growth that comes from stepping beyond comfortable habits all remain unexplored territories.

This limitation becomes particularly evident in Greg's relationships. His interactions with his wife have fallen into such predictable patterns that both parties can anticipate exactly how conversations will unfold before they begin. His relationships with colleagues follow the same scripts day after day, year after year. Even his parenting approach remains static, unchanged by evolving research on child development or the changing needs of his growing children. These relationships don't evolve or deepen over time but simply repeat familiar dynamics in slightly different contexts.

The repetitive choices extend beyond specific behaviors to encompass thought patterns and emotional responses as well. Greg's mental habit of immediately identifying what's wrong in any situation has become so automatic that he's incapable of experiencing an event without simultaneously critiquing it. His emotional response of frustration when faced with obstacles has become so ingrained that it arrives instantaneously, before he's had time to consciously assess the situation. These internal patterns, though less visible than external behaviors, are equally restrictive, creating a prison of perception that defines what's possible.

Living in the Moment, But Not in Awareness

By this point in his life, Greg has achieved what many would consider success: a stable job, home ownership, and a family. Yet beneath these outward markers of achievement lies a profound limitation: his focus and viewpoint lack the expansiveness needed to truly push through life's challenges toward meaningful growth. Instead, he exists in a peculiar state of living in the moment, but without the awareness that would make those moments truly rich or significant.

This state differs profoundly from the mindful presence often celebrated in spiritual traditions. Greg isn't fully experiencing the present moment with open awareness; he's reacting to it through the limited lens of his habitual patterns. When he sits at the dinner table with his family, he isn't truly present with them, appreciating their unique qualities, listening deeply to their experiences, and connecting authentically. Instead, he's mentally rehearsing workplace grievances, scrolling through his phone, or half-listening while formulating his own next statement. This isn't presence but absence disguised as participation.

The complainer's version of "living in the moment" lacks both backward reflection and forward vision. Greg rarely examines past experiences to extract meaningful lessons that might inform better choices. Difficult situations are processed not as valuable data for growth but as further evidence of life's inherent unfairness. Similarly, his vision of the future remains limited to vague hopes unconnected to concrete plans or consistent actions. He might wish for better finances or improved relationships, but these desires never crystallize into the sustained effort required for actual transformation.

This combination of unreflective past and unplanned future creates a peculiar kind of present, one that feels simultaneously overwhelming and empty. Greg experiences the immediate pressures of daily responsibilities, workplace demands, and family needs with intense stress, yet without the sense of meaning or purpose that comes from connecting these challenges to a larger life narrative. Each day becomes simply another round of familiar frustrations to be endured rather than a meaningful chapter in an evolving story of growth and contribution.

The limitation of the complainer's momentary focus becomes particularly evident in how Greg handles success. When things go well, a project is completed, a bill is paid off, and a pleasant family dinner is held, he experiences temporary relief rather than genuine satisfaction. Without a larger context of purpose or growth, achievements become merely brief respites from struggle rather than meaningful milestones in an intentional journey. The question "What's next?" rarely arises because success is seen as an endpoint rather than a stepping stone toward further development.

This narrow temporal focus creates a strange paradox: Greg feels perpetually behind while simultaneously lacking a clear destination. The immediate demands of each day create a sense of constantly playing catch-up, yet without a compelling vision of what all the effort is building toward.

Work becomes simply the means to pay bills rather than an expression of value or contribution. Parenting becomes a series of problems to manage rather than the cultivation of human potential. Marriage becomes a domestic arrangement rather than a journey of mutual growth and deepening intimacy.

The complainer's life thus unfolds as a series of disconnected moments rather than an integrated journey. Like a traveler so focused on immediate obstacles that he never consults his map or remembers his destination, Greg moves through life reacting to whatever appears directly before him, without the context that would give those reactions meaning or direction. This approach creates the illusion of engaged living while missing the deeper possibilities of human experience, the capacity to learn from the past, envision the future, and find meaning in the connection between the two.

The tragedy isn't that Greg fails to achieve conventional success, but that the success he does achieve feels hollow and insufficient. Without the awareness that comes from self-discovery and intentional choice, even accomplishments become simply new settings for familiar patterns of complaint and frustration. The house purchased after years of saving becomes not a source of security and pride but a new focus for grievances about maintenance costs and property taxes. The promotion at work becomes not a recognition of value and contribution but a new source of stress and unreasonable expectations.

Perhaps the most poignant aspect of the complainer's predicament is that transformation remains possible at any moment. Greg is not irrevocably condemned to his limiting patterns; the potential for greater awareness, more conscious choice, and expanded experience exists in every interaction and every decision. Yet without recognizing that broader possibilities exist, he remains trapped in repetitive choices that create the same results while expecting different outcomes—a definition of insanity that manifests in the chronic dissatisfaction that characterizes his existence.

Part 2: The Thinker

The Strength of Small Successes

Bruce stands in his home office, contemplating the small plant on his desk. Six months ago, it was barely a seedling, vulnerable and uncertain. Today, through consistent care and attention, it has grown into a thriving presence that transforms the space around it. He smiles, recognizing in this simple organism a metaphor for his own approach to life, the power of small, consistent actions compounding over time to create meaningful change.

Unlike the complainer, who dismisses minor achievements in favor of focusing on what remains imperfect, the thinker finds profound value in small successes. Bruce doesn't just note these victories; he actively harvests their psychological and practical benefits, using them as fuel for the larger vision that guides his choices. This appreciation isn't mere positive thinking or naive optimism, but a strategic approach to maintaining momentum and building the resilience necessary for long-term achievement.

When Bruce completes a challenging work project, he doesn't immediately shift focus to the next demand without acknowledgment. Instead, he takes time to recognize what was accomplished, what was learned, and how this achievement connects to his broader professional goals. This reflection isn't self-congratulatory indulgence but practical psychology; he understands that consciously processing successes builds the confidence and motivation necessary for tackling the next challenge.

This approach extends beyond professional achievements to encompass the full spectrum of life's dimensions. When his daughter masters a difficult piano piece after weeks of practice, Bruce doesn't simply offer a cursory "good job" before moving on. He sits with her to discuss the process, appreciating not just the end result but the persistence and problem-solving that made it possible. When he and his wife successfully navigate a difficult conversation about family finances, he acknowledges this as an important strengthening of their partnership, not merely a task completed.

Bruce's valuing of small successes reflects a sophisticated understanding of how meaningful change actually occurs. He recognizes that transformative achievements rarely happen in dramatic, single moments but through consistent effort applied over time. The major professional recognition, the significant financial milestone, the deepened relationship, these outcomes that might appear sudden to outside observers are actually the culmination of hundreds of small choices and minor victories that created the conditions for a breakthrough.

This perspective creates a particular kind of patience that distinguishes the thinker from the complainer. Where Greg might abandon efforts that don't produce immediate, dramatic results, Bruce maintains consistent investment in processes he values, trusting that meaningful outcomes emerge through persistence rather than sporadic intensity. His exercise routine, his mentoring of junior colleagues, and his development of new professional skills all reflect this patient persistence, the trust that small actions compound into significant results over time.

The thinker's appreciation of small successes connects directly to the strength of vision that guides his choices. Each minor achievement serves not just as a momentary satisfaction but as confirmation that the larger direction is sound, that the values and principles informing his decisions are creating the life he intends to build. When Bruce sees positive results from the parenting approach he and his wife have thoughtfully developed, this doesn't just feel good in the moment; it strengthens his commitment to the family culture they're intentionally creating.

This connection between small successes and larger vision creates a positive feedback loop fundamentally different from the complainer's cycle of frustration and avoidance. Each achievement, however minor, provides evidence that intentional choice matters, that consistent effort produces results, and that the vision guiding these choices is viable. This evidence, in turn, strengthens commitment to continued aligned action, creating a self-reinforcing cycle of progress and motivation that builds momentum over time.

The Calculated Movement

The thinker's approach to repetitive choices is characterized by a quality of calculated movement, deliberate, thoughtful action guided by clear intention rather than habitual reaction or unexamined impulse. Bruce doesn't simply respond to life as it happens; he moves through it with purpose, evaluating choices not in isolation but in relation to the larger life he's intentionally creating.

This calculated movement begins with awareness, the recognition that even seemingly small, routine decisions carry significance when repeated over time. Bruce understands that his morning routine shapes not just the beginning of his day but, through repetition, the quality of his life. His choices about how to respond to workplace challenges create not just immediate outcomes but lasting patterns that define his professional identity. His approach to family conversations establishes not just a momentary connection but the enduring culture of his household.

With this awareness as a foundation, Bruce approaches repetitive choices with a particular kind of discernment. He regularly evaluates habitual patterns, asking not just whether they're comfortable or familiar, but whether they align with his values and contribute to his vision. When he notices that his evening habit of checking work emails has begun to erode family dinner conversations, he doesn't simply continue the pattern because it's established. He recognizes the misalignment with his values and intentionally designs a different approach that better serves his priority of meaningful family connection.

This willingness to reconsider established patterns distinguishes the thinker from the complainer. While Greg continues ineffective behaviors simply because they're familiar, Bruce approaches habitual patterns with both respect for their efficiency and willingness to modify them when necessary. His morning routine isn't changed on a whim, but neither is it maintained when it no longer serves its purpose. His financial habits are reviewed regularly rather than continuing unexamined indefinitely. His communication patterns with his wife and children evolve as he learns more effective approaches rather than calcifying into unchangeable traits.

The calculated nature of the thinker's movement doesn't mean rigid adherence to predetermined plans regardless of circumstances. Bruce remains responsive to changing conditions, unexpected opportunities, and new information. What distinguishes his adaptability from the complainer's reactivity is the thoughtful evaluation that precedes change. When Bruce adjusts his approach, it's not from frustration or impulsivity, but from careful consideration of how the adjustment aligns with underlying values and contributes to long-term vision.

This thoughtful, intentional approach creates a particular quality of consistency without rigidity. Bruce's choices demonstrate clear patterns that reflect his values, reliability in commitments, presence with family, excellence in work, and integrity in relationships, yet these patterns can accommodate the natural variability of life circumstances. A challenging work period might temporarily alter how family time is structured, but not whether it remains a priority. Financial setbacks might change specific spending decisions, but not the underlying commitment to responsible stewardship. This flexible consistency creates both stability and adaptability, a balanced approach to life's inevitable variations.

Avoiding Misaligned Repetition

The thinker's calculated approach to repetitive choices includes not just what to continue, but what to change or eliminate when patterns no longer serve their purpose. Bruce doesn't avoid all repetition; he recognizes the value of productive routines and consistent habits. What he actively avoids is misaligned repetition, continuing patterns that conflict with values or undermine long-term vision simply because they're established or familiar.

This discernment manifests in Bruce's careful evaluation of how he invests time. When he notices that his habit of accepting every meeting request at work has begun to fragment his days and prevent deeper focus on priority projects, he doesn't continue the pattern simply because it's expected. Instead, he develops a more selective approach to meetings that better aligns with his professional goals and values. This isn't about avoiding difficulty or responsibility, but about ensuring that repetitive choices support rather than undermine what matters most.

The same discernment applies to financial patterns. Bruce and his wife regularly review their spending habits, not just tracking amounts but evaluating whether expenditures reflect their actual priorities. When they notice that dining out has increased while family activities have decreased, they don't simply continue the pattern because it's convenient. They realign spending to better reflect their stated priority of meaningful family experiences. This ongoing evaluation prevents the gradual drift that often occurs when repetitive choices remain unexamined over time.

Perhaps most significantly, Bruce applies this discernment to thought and emotional patterns as well as external behaviors. When he catches himself falling into repetitive worry about scenarios he can't control, he doesn't continue the mental habit simply because it's familiar. He implements practices that redirect attention toward productive problem-solving or present engagement. When he notices a pattern of irritation arising during particular family interactions, he examines the triggers and assumptions involved rather than accepting this as an unchangeable aspect of relationship dynamics.

This avoidance of misaligned repetition requires particular courage when patterns are reinforced by social expectations or cultural norms. When Bruce's colleagues express surprise at his decision to decline a prestigious committee appointment that would have compromised family commitments, he doesn't abandon his carefully considered choice to conform to professional expectations. When extended family pressure pushes toward holiday traditions that create stress rather than connection, he and his wife don't simply continue patterns out of obligation. This willingness to evaluate and potentially modify socially reinforced patterns demonstrates the thinker's commitment to alignment over approval, to meaningful choice over social conformity.

The thinker's approach to avoiding misaligned repetition isn't about constant upheaval or rejection of all tradition. Bruce values stability and recognizes the psychological and practical benefits of well-established routines. What distinguishes his approach is the regular evaluation of whether specific patterns continue to serve their intended purpose, whether they remain aligned with current values and circumstances, and whether they contribute to or detract from the larger vision guiding his choices. This ongoing assessment prevents the calcification that transforms productive habits into limiting constraints over time.

The Alignment of Goals, Timelines, and Choices

A defining characteristic of the thinker's approach to repetitive choices is the consistent alignment between goals, timelines, and daily decisions. Bruce doesn't just have aspirations; he has a coherent system where long-term vision connects to medium-term objectives, which in turn inform immediate choices. This alignment creates a meaningful context for repetitive decisions, transforming them from isolated habits into consistent contributions toward intended outcomes.

Bruce's professional development exemplifies this alignment. His long-term vision of creating innovative solutions in his field connects to specific mid-range goals, completing specialized certifications, developing particular expertise, and establishing key professional relationships. These goals then inform daily choices about where to invest time, which skills to develop, and how to approach workplace challenges. This isn't rigid adherence to a predetermined plan, but dynamic alignment that creates coherence across different time horizons.

The same principle applies to family life. Bruce and his wife don't just hope for strong connections with their children; they establish clear intentions about the family culture they want to create, set specific objectives for different developmental stages, and make daily choices that consistently reinforce these priorities. The decision to maintain family dinner as a phone-free zone isn't an isolated rule but a specific application of their broader commitment to meaningful communication and presence with each other. The monthly family outings aren't random activities but intentional investments in shared experiences that build the connections they value.

This alignment extends to financial choices as well. Bruce doesn't make spending decisions in isolation, but in relation to clearly defined short, medium, and long-term financial goals. The decision to live below their means isn't deprivation but a strategic allocation of resources toward priorities like educational opportunities for their children, eventual financial independence, and the capacity for meaningful giving. Daily financial choices gain significance through connection to these larger intentions, transforming routine decisions into meaningful participation in a coherent life strategy.

What makes this alignment particularly powerful is how it transforms the experience of setbacks and challenges. When inevitable difficulties arise, a project fails, a financial setback occurs, or a family conflict emerges, Bruce doesn't experience these as evidence that effort is futile or that his approach is fundamentally flawed. Instead, he places these challenges within the context of his larger journey, seeing them as natural variations in the path toward meaningful goals rather than devastating failures that undermine the entire enterprise.

This perspective creates a particular kind of resilience that distinguishes the thinker from the complainer. Where Greg might abandon an exercise program after missing several sessions, seeing this as evidence of inevitable failure, Bruce recognizes such lapses as normal variations in a longer process. The missed sessions don't invalidate the overall approach or goal, but simply require recalibration and renewed commitment. This resilience applies across all life domains, allowing the thinker to maintain consistent direction despite the inevitable imperfections of actual implementation.

The alignment between goals, timelines, and choices also creates a particular quality of presence different from the complainer's momentary focus. Bruce is fully engaged with current activities, but this engagement occurs within the context of meaningful progression. When he helps his daughter with homework, he's not just completing a daily task but participating in her educational development. When he invests time in a challenging work project, he's not just meeting immediate deadlines but developing capabilities relevant to long-term professional goals. This connection between present action and future intention creates depth of meaning that the complainer's disconnected approach cannot access.

The Power of Realistic Expectations

Central to the thinker's approach to repetitive choices is a sophisticated understanding of how expectations shape experience and outcomes. Bruce doesn't subscribe to either naive optimism that ignores constraints or pessimistic fatalism that assumes failure. Instead, he cultivates realistic expectations—assessments of what's possible that account for both genuine limitations and authentic potential. This balanced perspective transforms how repetitive choices are experienced and sustained over time.

The power of realistic expectations becomes evident in how Bruce approaches new initiatives. When beginning a fitness program, he doesn't expect dramatic transformation within weeks, nor does he assume the effort will inevitably be abandoned. He anticipates gradual progress with natural variations, understanding that sustainable physical change occurs through consistent effort over extended periods. This realistic timeline prevents both the disappointment that comes from unrealized rapid results and the complacency that arises from underestimating what's possible through persistent effort.

This approach extends to professional development. Bruce recognizes that mastering new skills requires time, involves inevitable awkwardness during learning phases, and includes plateaus where progress seems temporarily stalled. Rather than becoming discouraged when these natural aspects of learning emerge, he anticipates them as expected parts of the development process. This realistic expectation prevents the premature abandonment that often occurs when development doesn't follow an idealized, smooth trajectory of constant improvement.

Parenting particularly highlights the value of realistic expectations. Bruce and his wife recognize that children's development includes natural phases of both connection and differentiation, cooperation and resistance, progress and regression. When their teenage son goes through a period of increased independence and decreased communication, they don't catastrophize this as relationship failure or evidence of parenting mistakes. They recognize it as a natural developmental phase that requires adjustment in approach rather than abandonment of core values or boundaries. This realistic perspective allows consistent parenting despite the inevitable variations in how that parenting is received and expressed at different stages.

Financial progress similarly benefits from realistic expectations. Bruce and his wife understand that building financial security occurs through consistent choices over extended periods, with natural variations in results based on market conditions, unexpected expenses, and changing circumstances. Their financial plan acknowledges these variations rather than assuming a perfect, linear progression. This realistic approach prevents the discouragement that often leads to abandoned financial disciplines when short-term results don't match idealized expectations.

The thinker's realistic expectations extend beyond outcomes to include the process itself. Bruce anticipates that maintaining any valuable practice, whether exercise, financial discipline, relationship investment, or professional development, will sometimes feel difficult, uninspiring, or even burdensome. Rather than interpreting these natural variations in motivation as evidence that the activity isn't "right" or sustainable, he recognizes them as normal aspects of any meaningful long-term commitment. This realistic expectation of variable motivation allows him to maintain valuable practices even during periods of reduced enthusiasm or increased challenge.

Perhaps most powerfully, Bruce's realistic expectations create a particular approach to completion and achievement. He understands that meaningful accomplishment occurs not through sporadic intensity but through sustained, consistent effort applied over time. Each small step, the workout completed despite fatigue, the difficult conversation initiated despite discomfort, the financial discipline maintained despite temptation, represents genuine progress toward intended outcomes. This recognition of incremental achievement sustains motivation through the extended middle phases of any significant undertaking, where visible results often lag behind invested effort.

Over the years of repetition, this approach to realistic expectations creates a profound difference between the thinker's experience and the complainer's frustration. While Greg remains caught in cycles of unrealistic hopes followed by inevitable disappointment, Bruce builds steady progress through consistent alignment between expectations and actions. The gap between aspiration and achievement gradually narrows, not through lowered standards but through the power of realistic assessment combined with persistent effort. This alignment creates the sustainable success that the complainer glimpses but never quite achieves, the natural fruit of choices made consistently over time in service of a clear and meaningful vision.

The contrasting approaches to repetitive choices revealed through Greg and Bruce's experiences highlight a fundamental truth about human development: we become what we repeatedly do. The complainer's unexamined patterns create a life characterized by reaction rather than intention, by frustration rather than fulfillment. The thinker's calculated choices create a life of meaningful progression, of values expressed through consistent action, of vision gradually manifested through persistent effort.

The good news embedded in this examination is that patterns can change, that greater awareness remains possible at any point in life's journey. Even deeply ingrained habits can be modified when brought into conscious awareness and addressed with intention and persistence. The complainer's repetitive choices aren't inevitable destiny but patterns that can be recognized, evaluated, and gradually transformed through the very power of repetition that created them, this time applied with awareness rather than automaticity.

The journey from complainer to thinker begins with a single, crucial step: the recognition that our current patterns reflect choices rather than unchangeable reality. This awareness, however uncomfortable initially, opens the door to genuine possibility, the opportunity to align our repetitive choices with our deepest values and most meaningful aspirations. Through this alignment, gradually developed and consistently maintained, we create not just different outcomes but different selves moving from the limitations of unconscious reaction to the possibilities of intentional creation.

Chapter 7
Consequences of Action

The weight of accumulated choices eventually becomes impossible to ignore. Where once there might have been flexibility, options, and the possibility of different directions, patterns solidify into reality with the persistence of water carving through the stone. What begins as a series of seemingly insignificant decisions, how to respond to a challenge, whether to take responsibility or deflect blame, and how to approach each day's demands, eventually crystallizes into the fundamental architecture of existence itself.

The consequences of our actions don't arrive as dramatic revelations or sudden reversals of fortune. Instead, they emerge gradually, like the slow formation of a riverbed, carved deeper with each passing season until what was once a gentle slope becomes an irreversible canyon. Some people find themselves standing at the bottom of such canyons, wondering how they arrived there, unable to see the countless small erosions that created their current reality. Others recognize the power of accumulated action and deliberately shape their landscape, understanding that today's choices are tomorrow's circumstances.

This chapter examines how the complainer and the thinker experience the long-term consequences of their contrasting approaches to life. We'll see how years of different patterns create entirely different realities, not just in external circumstances but in the very capacity to envision and create change. The tragic irony is that both individuals began with similar potential, similar resources, and similar opportunities. The divergence in their outcomes reflects not luck or circumstance but the compound interest of repeated choices played out across the decades of their lives.

Part 1: The Complainer

The Architecture of Limitation

Robert sits in his cramped apartment, surrounded by the physical manifestations of twenty years of reactive living. The furniture, secondhand and mismatched, tells the story of emergency purchases made when previous items broke down beyond repair. The walls, painted a dingy beige by a landlord who chose the cheapest option, reflect a man who has never quite managed to create the stability needed for home ownership. At fifty-two, Robert has achieved a kind of equilibrium, not the dynamic balance of purposeful living, but the static balance of a life that has settled into the grooves carved by decades of complaint and avoidance.

The pit Robert finds himself in wasn't dug in a day, nor was it created by any single catastrophic event. Instead, it represents the accumulated consequence of thousands of small choices, each seeming reasonable or necessary at the time but collectively creating a reality far removed from the life he once imagined possible. The credit cards maxed out to cover emergencies that better planning might have anticipated. The jobs left me frustrated rather than working through challenges. The relationships were abandoned when difficulties arose rather than addressed with patience and skill. Each decision seemed justified in isolation, but together, they formed a pattern of limitation that now defines his existence.

This isn't the poverty of someone who never had opportunities, but the constrained circumstances of someone who consistently chose short-term relief over long-term building. Robert has worked steadily throughout his adult life, sometimes holding jobs that paid reasonably well. Yet his financial situation remains perpetually precarious because his approach to money reflects his approach to everything else: reactive, defensive, and focused on immediate concerns rather than future consequences. When unexpected expenses arose, his response was to find ways to cover them rather than to examine why they consistently caught him unprepared. When windfalls occurred, tax refunds, bonuses, and gifts from relatives disappeared into immediate gratification rather than strategic investment in future stability.

The apartment itself reflects this pattern. The leaky faucet that Robert has lived with for six months, because calling the landlord feels like too much of a hassle. The broken cabinet door that he's rigged with duct tape rather than properly repaired. The outdated electronics function poorly but represent purchases he can't afford to replace. Each of these items tells the story of someone who has learned to accept degradation as normal and who has internalized the belief that better circumstances are beyond his control or capability.

What makes Robert's situation particularly tragic isn't the material limitations themselves but the psychological framework that makes escape seem impossible. He has developed such an ingrained pattern of seeing obstacles as insurmountable that opportunities for improvement become invisible. When his neighbor mentions a job opening at a company that might offer better prospects, Robert's immediate response focuses on why it probably wouldn't work out: the commute would be difficult, they probably want someone younger, and the interview process would be too stressful. This isn't a realistic assessment, but learned helplessness expresses itself as practical wisdom.

The architecture of limitation extends beyond physical circumstances to encompass relationships, possibilities, and dreams. Robert's social circle consists primarily of others who share his worldview, reinforcing the narrative that their shared struggles represent the inevitable lot of ordinary people rather than the predictable result of particular approaches to life's challenges. Their conversations revolve around complaints about employers, government, family members, and circumstances, creating an echo chamber that validates external blame while preventing the internal examination that might lead to change.

His relationship with his adult daughter exemplifies this dynamic. Sarah, now thirty, maintains contact with her father but has learned to keep their interactions superficial and brief. She loves him but has grown weary of conversations that inevitably become litanies of grievance about how unfairly life has treated him. She sees the same patterns that defined her childhood still playing out in his current circumstances: the same excuses, the same blame, the same refusal to consider how his own choices might have contributed to his difficulties. Her attempts to offer practical suggestions are met with explanations of why they won't work until she's learned to simply listen and offer generic sympathy rather than engage in problem-solving efforts that only generate defensiveness.

The Internal Prison

The most insidious aspect of Robert's situation isn't the external limitations but the internal blockages that make change seem impossible. Years of avoiding responsibility and deflecting blame have created a psychological prison more confining than any physical circumstance. His mind has become a closed system, filtering all information through the lens of victimhood and external causation. New ideas that might offer pathways to improvement are automatically rejected as impractical or irrelevant to his situation. Feedback that might illuminate self-defeating patterns is interpreted as criticism or misunderstanding of his unique challenges.

This internal blockage manifests in his relationship with learning and growth. Robert hasn't read a non-fiction book in years, hasn't taken a class or workshop, and hasn't sought mentorship or guidance from anyone who might offer different perspectives on his challenges. When others mention personal development resources, his response is immediate dismissal: "Those things are for people who don't understand real life." This rejection isn't just about specific resources but about the entire concept that individual change is possible or necessary. In Robert's worldview, problems are things that happen to people, not things that people help create through their choices and responses.

The psychological prison extends to his emotional landscape as well. Robert experiences a narrow range of feelings, primarily variants of frustration, resentment, and resignation. The broader spectrum of human emotion, genuine joy, contentment, excitement about possibilities, and satisfaction from meaningful work remains largely inaccessible because these states require the kind of agency and engagement that his defensive patterns have systematically eroded. When moments of potential happiness arise, they're quickly overshadowed by mental habits that focus on what's wrong, what's missing, or what will inevitably go bad.

Sleep provides little respite from this internal prison. Robert's nights are often restless, his mind cycling through familiar grievances and worries without ever arriving at actionable insights or peaceful resolutions. He wakes tired, not just from poor rest but from the mental exhaustion of carrying unresolved tensions that he lacks the tools to address constructively. This chronic stress manifests in physical symptoms, headaches, digestive issues, and general fatigue, which become additional sources of complaint rather than signals that lifestyle changes might be beneficial.

The internal blockages also prevent Robert from recognizing patterns in his own behavior. He genuinely doesn't see the connection between his defensive responses and others' eventual withdrawal from a relationship with him. He can't perceive how his focus on problems creates a problem-saturated reality that becomes self-perpetuating. He remains blind to the ways his expectations of disappointment actually contribute to disappointing outcomes. This lack of self-awareness isn't willful blindness but the natural result of years spent looking outward for sources of difficulty rather than inward for sources of agency.

Habits as Reality

By this stage of his life, Robert's patterns have become so deeply ingrained that they no longer feel like choices but like fundamental aspects of reality itself. His morning routine of checking his phone for news that inevitably irritates him, his workday pattern of finding fault with colleagues and systems, and his evening habit of numbing frustration through television or internet browsing behaviors have become as automatic as breathing. He doesn't choose to complain about his circumstances; complaining has become his default mode of processing experience.

This transformation of habits into perceived reality creates a peculiar form of imprisonment. Robert genuinely believes that his responses are the only reasonable reactions to his circumstances that anyone in his position would naturally feel and behave as he does. The possibility that different responses might create different outcomes doesn't register as realistic because his patterns have become so automatic that alternatives remain invisible. When his supervisor makes a request, Robert's immediate internal response is irritation at the unreasonableness of the demand. When his ex-wife mentions financial obligations, his instant reaction is defensiveness about his limited resources. When his daughter suggests ways he might improve his situation, his reflexive response is to explain why such suggestions don't apply to his unique circumstances.

These habitual patterns create their own momentum, making change increasingly difficult as time passes. Each repetition of a complaint or defensive response deepens the neural pathways associated with that behavior, making it more likely to occur automatically in the future. The complainer's patterns become self-reinforcing not through conscious choice but through the natural tendency of the brain to strengthen frequently used connections. What began as a tendency gradually becomes a compulsion, then an identity, and finally, a seemingly unchangeable aspect of reality.

The most tragic aspect of this process is how it transforms Robert's relationship with possibility itself. Dreams, aspirations, and visions of different outcomes gradually fade not through conscious abandonment but through simple neglect. When the mind is occupied with processing current difficulties and past grievances, little energy remains for imagining alternative futures. The creative capacity that once allowed Robert to envision different circumstances gradually atrophied from disuse, leaving him trapped not just in current limitations but in the inability to conceive of transcending them.

This contracted relationship with the possibility affects every area of Robert's life. Career advancement becomes unthinkable because he can only see the obstacles and unfairness in any workplace hierarchy. Financial improvement seems impossible because he focuses exclusively on current constraints rather than potential strategies for gradual enhancement. Relationship fulfillment appears unrealistic because he anticipates disappointment and prepares defensively for the inevitable conflict. These aren't accurate assessments of reality but the predictable perceptions of someone whose habits of thought have been shaped by years of defensive reaction rather than proactive engagement.

The Avoidance of Consequences

One of the most striking aspects of Robert's approach to life is his elaborate system for avoiding full awareness of how his choices create his circumstances. This avoidance isn't conscious deception but a sophisticated psychological mechanism that protects him from the discomfort of recognizing his own role in creating his limitations. When faced with evidence that his actions have contributed to negative outcomes, Robert's mind automatically shifts to external explanations that preserve his sense of victimhood while preventing the learning that might lead to change.

This avoidance manifests in his relationship with feedback from others. When his daughter gently suggests that his persistent negativity might be affecting their relationship, Robert doesn't hear this as valuable information about the impact of his behavior. Instead, he interprets it as evidence that she doesn't understand the legitimate challenges he faces or that she's being influenced by her mother's perspective. When former colleagues mention that his critical attitude created difficulties in team dynamics, he doesn't consider how his communication style might need adjustment. Instead, he concludes that they were part of the workplace politics that made his position untenable.

The financial realm provides particularly clear examples of consequence avoidance. When Robert's credit score declined due to late payments and missed obligations, he focused his attention on the unfairness of credit reporting systems rather than on the spending and payment patterns that created the negative marks. When collection agencies contact him about outstanding debts, he experiences these calls as harassment rather than as predictable results of borrowing money without reliable repayment plans. When his car insurance premiums increase after traffic violations, he complains about the insurance industry's greed rather than examining his driving habits.

This pattern of consequence avoidance extends to health outcomes as well. Robert's chronic stress, poor sleep, and physical complaints are experienced as things that happen to him rather than as natural results of lifestyle choices. He doesn't connect his persistent headaches to the mental habit of focusing on problems, his digestive issues to emotional stress patterns, or his fatigue to the lack of meaningful physical activity. Instead, these symptoms become additional sources of complaints about the unfairness of aging and the inadequacy of healthcare systems.

Perhaps most significantly, Robert avoids recognizing how his patterns affect others, particularly those who love him. When relationships become strained or distant, he attributes this to others' unrealistic expectations or inability to appreciate his genuine struggles. When his daughter limits their contact or his friends gradually become unavailable for social activities, he experiences this as further evidence of life's general unfairness rather than as a possible consequences of his own behavioral patterns. This avoidance protects him from painful self-examination but also prevents the relational learning that might improve his connections with others.

The sophistication of Robert's avoidance system lies in its ability to transform consequences into additional grievances. Each negative outcome becomes not a signal for behavior change but a confirmation that life is inherently difficult and unfair. This transformation serves the psychological function of maintaining his worldview while preventing the growth that might occur if consequences were experienced as information rather than persecution.

Survival Mode Mastery

After decades of reactive living, Robert has developed genuine expertise in what might be called survival mode, the ability to maintain basic stability in the face of persistent challenges without ever transcending those challenges. This isn't the dramatic survival of emergency situations but the grinding competence of someone who has learned to navigate chronic limitations with minimal expectations and maximum resilience to disappointment. In his own way, Robert has become masterful at managing a life that never quite works but never completely falls apart.

This survival expertise manifests in practical skills that shouldn't be underestimated. Robert knows how to stretch limited financial resources across competing demands, how to negotiate payment plans with creditors, how to find acceptable housing within tight budget constraints, and how to maintain employment despite frequent frustration with workplace dynamics. These are genuine capabilities, developed through necessity and refined through repetition. The tragedy isn't that these skills lack value but that they've become the ceiling rather than the floor of Robert's capabilities.

His survival mastery includes emotional strategies as well as practical ones. Robert has developed a remarkable tolerance for disappointment, frustration, and unmet needs. He can absorb criticism without complete devastation, continue functioning despite chronic stress, and maintain basic social relationships even when they provide limited satisfaction. This emotional resilience represents a genuine achievement, particularly given the challenging circumstances he's navigated throughout his adult life. Yet this same resilience can become a barrier to growth when it enables continued acceptance of limitations that might otherwise motivate change.

The social aspects of Robert's survival expertise are equally sophisticated. He has learned to maintain relationships within a narrow band of engagement that avoids triggering his defensive responses while preventing genuine intimacy. He can participate in casual conversations without revealing the depth of his dissatisfaction, attend family gatherings without creating major conflicts, and maintain workplace relationships that function adequately, if not enthusiastically. These social skills allow him to remain connected to the human community despite the limitations of his psychological framework.

Robert's survival mastery extends to his self-concept as well. He has developed ways of thinking about his situation that preserve dignity and self-respect despite external circumstances that might otherwise feel crushing. His narrative of being someone who faces unusual challenges with reasonable responses protects him from despair while preventing the kind of honest self-assessment that might reveal opportunities for change. This psychological survival mechanism serves important functions, but it also creates resistance to growth-oriented perspectives that might initially feel threatening to his carefully constructed sense of self.

The Comfort of Familiar Limitation

Perhaps the most profound consequence of Robert's long-term patterns is how they've created a kind of comfort in limitation that makes change seem not just difficult but undesirable. After years of developing expertise in managing constrained circumstances, Robert has achieved a form of stability that, while not satisfying, is predictable and familiar. He knows how to navigate his current reality, understands its rhythms and requirements, and has developed competence in managing its challenges. The prospect of different circumstances, even potentially better ones, introduces uncertainty that feels more threatening than the known difficulties of his current situation.

This comfort with limitation manifests in Robert's response to opportunities that might improve his circumstances. When his nephew offers to help him explore career opportunities in a growing industry, Robert's immediate focus is on the risks and uncertainties involved rather than the potential benefits. The effort required to learn new skills, the vulnerability of job interviews, and the possibility of failure in unfamiliar territory—these aspects of change feel more daunting than the predictable frustrations of his current position. The known difficulties have become manageable through familiarity, while unknown opportunities feel overwhelmingly uncertain.

The same dynamic appears in Robert's approach to relationships. While he frequently complains about loneliness and the superficiality of his social connections, he resists invitations to social activities that might lead to deeper relationships. New social situations require energy, vulnerability, and the risk of rejection or disappointment. The familiar isolation, though unsatisfying, doesn't demand the emotional investment that developing meaningful connections would require. In this way, Robert's complaints about his social life serve the psychological function of expressing dissatisfaction while avoiding the actions that might address that dissatisfaction.

Even Robert's physical environment reflects this comfort with limitations. His apartment, while far from ideal, represents a known quantity that doesn't require the energy, risk, or change that moving would involve. The inconveniences and inadequacies of his current housing are familiar inconveniences that he's learned to navigate. The prospect of searching for something better introduces variables—different neighborhoods, new landlords, moving expenses, adjustment periods—that feel more burdensome than the known problems of his current situation.

This pattern creates what psychologists recognize as learned helplessness, but Robert experiences it as practical wisdom. His focus on obstacles and potential problems isn't perceived as pessimism but as a realistic assessment based on extensive life experience. His resistance to change isn't recognized as fear but as prudent caution. His acceptance of limitation isn't acknowledged as resignation but as a mature recognition of life's inherent constraints. These reframings allow Robert to maintain dignity and self-respect while avoiding the vulnerability that genuine change would require.

The Story of Success

In the most poignant turn of his psychological journey, Robert has developed a narrative of his life that frames his current circumstances not as the result of limiting patterns but as evidence of his resilience and practical wisdom. This story of success isn't delusional but represents a genuine reframing that allows him to find meaning and dignity in circumstances that might otherwise feel crushing. According to this narrative, Robert is someone who has successfully navigated unusual challenges, maintained stability despite difficult circumstances, and avoided the mistakes that have derailed others in similar situations.

Within this framework, Robert's financial limitations become evidence of his refusal to compromise his integrity through the kind of career compromises that might have brought greater income but less personal authenticity. His relationship challenges become proof of his unwillingness to settle for superficial connections that require hiding his true thoughts and feelings. His modest living circumstances become demonstrations of his ability to find contentment without the material excess that drives others to unhappiness and debt.

This reframing extends to Robert's interaction with others who appear more successful in conventional terms. Rather than experiencing their achievements as evidence of possibilities he might have pursued, he sees them as examples of different priorities and values. Their financial success reflects their willingness to sacrifice personal time and family relationships for income. Their career advancement demonstrates their comfort with workplace politics and compromise. Their seemingly stable relationships are based on avoiding difficult conversations and maintaining superficial harmony.

In Robert's narrative, his complaints about life's unfairness become expressions of moral clarity rather than defensive reactions. His criticism of workplace dynamics reflects his commitment to fairness and integrity rather than his inability to navigate complex social systems. His frustration with financial pressures demonstrates his recognition of economic injustice rather than his lack of strategic planning. This reframing transforms what might be seen as limitations into expressions of values and principles.

The story of success that Robert has constructed isn't entirely without foundation. He has indeed demonstrated resilience in the face of challenges, maintained basic stability despite limited resources, and preserved personal authenticity in environments that might have encouraged compromise. These achievements deserve recognition and respect. The limitation of his narrative isn't that it's false but that it's incomplete, emphasizing the genuine strengths he's developed while overlooking the growth opportunities that his patterns have prevented him from recognizing or pursuing.

Part 2: The Thinker

The Daily Architecture of Excellence

Marcus begins each day at 5:30 AM with a routine that reflects not rigid obsession but thoughtful design. The extra hour before his family wakes allows for activities that ground him in purpose and prepare him for intentional engagement with the day ahead. Physical exercise, strategic reading, and reflective planning combine to create a foundation of energy, knowledge, and clarity that influences every subsequent interaction and decision. This isn't about perfection or controlling all variables but about establishing initial conditions that support the kind of day he wants to create.

His exercise routine exemplifies the thinker's approach to repetitive choices. Rather than sporadic, intense workouts that inevitably fail, Marcus has developed a sustainable program that accommodates the natural variations of energy, schedule, and motivation while maintaining consistent forward momentum. Some days include vigorous cardio sessions, others focus on strength training, and some consist of gentle stretching and mobility work. The specific activities vary based on circumstances, but the commitment to physical investment remains constant, creating compound benefits that extend far beyond physical fitness to encompass mental clarity, emotional resilience, and the confidence that comes from honoring commitments to oneself.

The reading component of Marcus's morning routine demonstrates how the thinker approaches intellectual development. Rather than random consumption of information, his reading follows a carefully considered strategy that supports his professional goals, personal growth, and contribution to his family and community. Biography and history provide perspectives on human achievement and challenges. Business and psychology texts offer frameworks for understanding systems and relationships. Philosophy and spirituality deepen his appreciation for meaning and purpose. This curated approach to learning creates a rich foundation of knowledge and wisdom that informs decision-making across all areas of life.

The planning aspect of Marcus's morning routine illustrates his approach to intentional living. This isn't a detailed schedule of every moment but a thoughtful consideration of priorities, values, and opportunities within the context of current circumstances and long-term goals. He reviews his calendar not just for logistical preparation but to identify where he can add the most value, create meaningful connections, or advance important projects. He considers his family's needs and schedules, looking for opportunities to provide support, encouragement, or simply present engagement. This planning process transforms a potentially reactive day into a proactive expression of values and priorities.

By the time his family wakes, Marcus has already invested significant energy in preparing himself to engage fully with the relationships and responsibilities that matter most. This preparation isn't about controlling outcomes but about bringing his best self to whatever the day requires. When his teenage daughter needs help with a challenging project, he's mentally and emotionally available rather than distracted by his own unmet needs. When his business partner calls with an urgent decision, he can respond from a centered place rather than reactive stress. When unexpected challenges arise, he has the psychological resources to address them creatively rather than defensively.

This daily architecture of excellence extends throughout Marcus's day in ways both visible and subtle. His approach to business meetings reflects the same intentionality as his morning routine. He prepares not just for the logistics of agenda items but for the human dynamics that will influence outcomes. He considers not just what needs to be accomplished but how to accomplish it in ways that strengthen relationships and build long-term value. His interactions with employees reflect his understanding that leadership is ultimately about developing others' capabilities rather than simply extracting performance.

The Format of Prestige

After fifteen years of consistent, values-based choices, Marcus has created what might be called a "format of prestige," not the empty status-seeking that characterizes so much contemporary ambition, but the genuine respect and influence that naturally emerges when competence is combined with character over extended periods. His business has grown not through aggressive self-promotion or corner-cutting but through the compound effect of excellence applied consistently across all dimensions of operation.

The diagrams and organizational structures that now characterize Marcus's company reflect his systematic approach to creating sustainable success. These aren't bureaucratic complexities imposed to control people, but thoughtful frameworks designed to support human flourishing while achieving meaningful objectives. The company's organizational chart doesn't just show reporting relationships but reflects careful consideration of how different personalities and skill sets can complement each other most effectively. The operational procedures don't simply ensure compliance but create conditions where employees can excel while maintaining the quality standards that define the company's reputation.

Marcus's approach to hiring demonstrates how the thinker's long-term perspective shapes immediate decisions. Rather than simply filling positions with the most immediately qualified candidates, he considers how potential employees align with the company's values and contribute to its evolving culture. He looks for character traits that predict long-term success: resilience in the face of challenges, willingness to take responsibility for mistakes, commitment to continuous learning, and genuine care for customer outcomes. This approach sometimes means passing on candidates with impressive credentials in favor of those who demonstrate the attitudes and values that support sustained excellence.

The company's training and development programs reflect Marcus's understanding that investing in people creates compound returns that extend far beyond immediate productivity. New employees don't just learn job functions but are introduced to the thinking frameworks and decision-making principles that guide the organization. Ongoing education isn't limited to technical skills but includes personal development, communication training, and leadership preparation. This comprehensive approach to human development creates a workforce that doesn't just perform tasks but thinks strategically and acts responsibly across all dimensions of their roles.

Customer relationships exemplify how the thinker's approach to consequences shapes business practices. Marcus's company doesn't just deliver products or services but creates experiences that reflect genuine care for client success. When problems arise, as they inevitably do in any complex enterprise, the company's response is guided by principles of accountability, creative problem-solving, and long-term relationship building rather than damage control or blame avoidance. This approach has created a client base characterized not just by satisfaction but by loyalty and advocacy that generates sustainable growth through referrals and repeat business.

The physical environment of Marcus's offices tells the story of his approach to creating conditions for excellence. The workspace is designed not for impressive appearances but for functionality, collaboration, and well-being. Natural light, ergonomic furniture, and thoughtfully organized common areas support both productivity and job satisfaction. Art and greenery create an atmosphere that nurtures creativity and reduces stress. Technology is implemented not because it's cutting-edge but because it genuinely improves efficiency or enhances the quality of work and customer service.

Dealing with Consequences Constructively

The thinker's approach to consequences differs fundamentally from the complainer's avoidance or blame-shifting. When Marcus faces negative outcomes, whether from his own mistakes or external circumstances beyond his control, his response is characterized by honest assessment, strategic learning, and constructive action; this doesn't mean he enjoys difficulties or remains unaffected by setbacks, but that he has developed the psychological and practical frameworks necessary to transform challenges into growth opportunities.

A recent example illustrates this approach in action. When a major client unexpectedly terminated their contract due to budget constraints, the immediate impact on Marcus's company was significantly reduced revenue, potential layoffs, and the psychological challenge of losing a relationship that had been central to the business for several years. Rather than falling into blame for the client's decision-making or worrying about factors beyond his control, Marcus's response was systematic and focused on elements within his influence.

The first step was an honest assessment of the situation, both the external factors that contributed to the loss and any internal elements that might have made the company vulnerable to such disruptions. This evaluation revealed that while the client's budget constraints were genuine and largely unpredictable, the company had become overly dependent on a single large contract—a strategic vulnerability that Marcus had recognized but not adequately addressed. Rather than seeing this insight as a source of self-criticism, he experienced it as valuable strategic information that could inform better future decisions.

The second step involved transparent communication with employees about the challenge and the company's response strategy. Rather than minimizing the difficulty or creating false optimism, Marcus shared both the reality of the situation and his confidence in the company's ability to navigate it successfully. This communication included acknowledging his own role in creating vulnerability through over-dependence on a single client, demonstrating the kind of accountability that builds rather than undermines leadership credibility. Employees responded not with panic or blame but with the kind of problem-solving energy that emerges when people trust their leader's honesty and competence.

The third step focused on the strategic response that would not only address the immediate challenge but also strengthen the company's long-term resilience. This included accelerated efforts to diversify the client base, the development of new service offerings that could create additional revenue streams, and temporary cost reductions that would maintain financial stability without compromising core capabilities or employee morale. Each element of the response was evaluated not just for immediate effectiveness but for its contribution to sustainable competitive advantage.

Marcus's approach to this setback demonstrates how the thinker transforms consequences into strategic intelligence. The loss of the major client became not just a problem to solve, but also information about industry trends, client needs, and company vulnerabilities that informed better future positioning. The temporary financial pressure became an opportunity to evaluate and streamline operations in ways that created greater efficiency and resilience. The challenge to employee morale became a chance to demonstrate and reinforce the company's values and commitment to its people.

The Path of Development

What distinguishes Marcus most clearly from Robert isn't the absence of difficulties but the presence of a development mindset that transforms challenges into stepping stones toward greater capability and contribution. Each obstacle becomes not just something to overcome but something to learn from, each success becomes not just something to enjoy but something to build upon, and each interaction becomes not just something to manage but something to optimize for mutual benefit and growth.

This development orientation manifests in Marcus's approach to skills and capabilities. Rather than seeing his current knowledge and abilities as fixed assets, he treats them as starting points for continued expansion. When industry changes require new technical knowledge, he doesn't resist the learning curve but embraces it as an opportunity to strengthen the company's competitive position. When leadership challenges require new interpersonal skills, he doesn't avoid the discomfort of growth but seeks out training, mentoring, and practice opportunities that develop greater effectiveness.

The same development mindset shapes Marcus's approach to relationships, both personal and professional.

His marriage isn't something he achieved and now maintains, but something he continues to develop and deepen. Regular conversations with his wife about their individual growth, shared goals, and evolving needs ensure that their relationship adapts and strengthens rather than stagnating or deteriorating over time. His parenting approach recognizes that effective guidance of children requires continuous learning about child development, communication techniques, and the changing cultural context in which his children are growing up.

Marcus's financial approach exemplifies development thinking applied to resources. Rather than seeing money as something to accumulate or spend, he views it as a tool for creating value, opportunities, and security that support his family's flourishing and his ability to contribute meaningfully to his community. Investment decisions are evaluated not just for potential returns but for alignment with values and contribution to long-term goals. Spending choices reflect consideration of how purchases support or detract from the life he and his family are intentionally creating.

Professional relationships within Marcus's company demonstrate how development orientation creates compound benefits over time. Rather than simply managing employees to achieve current objectives, Marcus invests in their growth and development with the understanding that their increasing capabilities benefit not just them individually but the entire organization. This approach has created a culture where people genuinely enjoy their work, take pride in their contributions, and refer talented friends to join the team. The result is a self-reinforcing cycle where excellence attracts excellence, and a development mindset spreads throughout the organization.

Strategic Vision and Tactical Flexibility

The consequence of Marcus's consistent, values-based approach to decision-making is the development of what might be called strategic vision combined with tactical flexibility. He has clarity about long-term direction and core principles while maintaining the adaptability necessary to navigate changing circumstances and unexpected opportunities. This combination allows him to make decisions quickly and confidently because they're guided by established frameworks rather than requiring complete analysis from scratch each time.

Marcus's strategic vision encompasses multiple dimensions of life and operates across different time horizons. Professionally, he has clear intentions about the kind of company he wants to build, the type of clients he wants to serve, and the impact he wants to create in his industry and community. Personally, he has articulated goals for his marriage, his role as a father, his contribution to his extended family, and his involvement in community organizations. Financially, he has established objectives for security, growth, and generosity that guide both earning and spending decisions. This comprehensive vision provides context for daily choices and prevents the kind of scattered effort that produces mediocre results across all areas.

The tactical flexibility component of Marcus's approach allows him to adapt methods while maintaining strategic direction. When economic conditions shift, he adjusts business strategies without abandoning core values or long-term goals. When family circumstances change, he modifies approaches to parenting or marriage while preserving the fundamental commitments that define those relationships. When new opportunities arise, he evaluates them based on established criteria rather than being distracted by every attractive possibility that emerges.

This combination of strategic vision and tactical flexibility has created what Marcus experiences as a sense of flow in his life. Decisions feel natural rather than forced, opportunities align with capabilities and values rather than creating internal conflict, and daily activities contribute to meaningful progress rather than simply filling time. This doesn't mean life is easy or without challenges, but that challenges are met from a centered place with clear priorities and proven capabilities.

The contrast with Robert's experience couldn't be more pronounced. Where Robert feels perpetually behind and reactive, Marcus feels engaged and proactive. Where Robert experiences life as a series of problems that happen to him, Marcus experiences life as a series of opportunities to express values and develop capabilities. Where Robert's patterns have created a narrowing spiral of limitation,

Marcus's patterns have created an expanding spiral of possibility and contribution.

Perhaps most significantly, Marcus has developed confidence in his ability to handle whatever circumstances might arise. This isn't naive optimism or denial of life's genuine uncertainties, but a realistic assessment based on his track record of successfully navigating challenges through consistent application of sound principles. When new difficulties emerge, he doesn't panic or become overwhelmed because he has accumulated evidence that a thoughtful response guided by clear values typically produces acceptable outcomes even in difficult situations.

This confidence extends to his family's security and well-being. Marcus's children are growing up with the psychological foundation that comes from witnessing competent, caring leadership in action. They're learning that challenges are normal parts of life that can be addressed effectively through preparation, clear thinking, and persistent effort. They're absorbing models of how to treat others, how to approach work, how to handle money, and how to navigate relationships that will serve them throughout their lives, regardless of the specific circumstances they encounter.

The consequences of Marcus's actions have created not just external success but internal integration, the alignment between values and behavior that produces genuine satisfaction and sustainable motivation. His work feels meaningful because it expresses his commitment to excellence and service. His family relationships feel fulfilling because they reflect his priorities and receive his genuine investment. His financial situation feels secure because it's built on consistent habits aligned with long-term goals rather than short-term reactions to immediate pressures.

Looking forward, Marcus can see the trajectory that his patterns are creating. The foundation he's built will continue to support growth and contribution regardless of external changes. The capabilities he's developed will adapt to new challenges and opportunities as they arise. The relationships he's cultivated will provide both personal satisfaction and practical support throughout his life. The principles he's established will guide decisions in situations he hasn't yet encountered but will inevitably face as life continues to unfold.

The ultimate consequence of the thinker's approach is the creation of a life that feels authentic, meaningful, and sustainable—not perfect or without difficulty, but characterized by the deep satisfaction that comes from knowing that daily choices reflect the deepest values and contribute to outcomes that matter. This isn't luck or privilege but the natural result of patterns maintained consistently over time, the compound interest of conscious choice applied across the decades of human life.

In examining these two approaches to life's consequences, we see not just different outcomes but different relationships with the fundamental questions of human existence: What matters most? How should we respond to difficulty? What kind of legacy do we want to create? The complainer and the thinker have answered these questions through their choices, and their circumstances reflect those answers with the precision of mathematical equations played out over time. The good news is that these patterns remain changeable for anyone willing to examine them honestly and invest in the patient work of transformation that creates different consequences through different choices.

The Mathematics of Accumulated Choice

The stark contrast between Robert and Marcus illustrates a fundamental truth about human experience: life operates according to a kind of mathematics where small choices compound over time to create dramatically different outcomes. This isn't the dramatic mathematics of lottery tickets or sudden windfalls but the patient mathematics of compound interest applied to every dimension of human existence. Each choice carries forward into the next choice, creating momentum that either supports or undermines the life we claim to want.

Robert's financial situation exemplifies this mathematical reality. His pattern of addressing immediate pressures without considering long-term consequences has created what economists call a "poverty trap"—a self-reinforcing cycle where short-term survival strategies prevent the accumulation of resources necessary for long-term stability.

When his car needs repairs, the emergency prevents him from building savings. When savings are absent, the next emergency becomes a crisis requiring expensive solutions like high-interest loans or credit card debt. Each emergency response makes the next emergency more likely and more costly, creating a mathematical progression toward increasing limitations.

Marcus's approach demonstrates the opposite mathematical trajectory. His early investments in emergency funds, skill development, and relationship building created resources that made challenges more manageable. When his major client canceled their contract, he had financial reserves that prevented panic decisions, professional relationships that opened new opportunities, and a reputation that attracted replacement business. Each strategic choice created conditions that made subsequent strategic choices more possible and more effective, generating a mathematical progression toward increasing capability and opportunity.

The mathematics extends beyond financial outcomes to encompass health, relationships, and personal development. Robert's pattern of avoiding difficult conversations has created relationship dynamics where problems compound rather than resolve. His habit of managing stress through distraction rather than addressing its sources has created physical and emotional patterns that generate more stress. His tendency to blame external factors has prevented the learning that might break negative cycles, ensuring their continuation with mathematical precision.

Marcus's contrasting patterns demonstrate how positive choices create their own momentum. His commitment to honest communication has built relationships characterized by trust and mutual support. His approach to stress through exercise, reflection, and problem-solving has created resilience that prevents problems from overwhelming him. His habit of learning from difficulties has developed capabilities that make future difficulties more manageable, creating an upward mathematical spiral of competence and confidence.

The Inheritance of Patterns

Perhaps the most profound consequence of these contrasting approaches lies in what each man passes on to the next generation. Robert and Marcus aren't just creating their own futures; they're establishing patterns that their children will inherit, either as assets or liabilities that shape possibilities for decades to come.

Robert's daughter Sarah has learned to navigate the world with the assumption that circumstances are fundamentally outside personal control, that relationships are sources of disappointment, and that financial security is something that happens to other people. These lessons weren't taught through lectures but absorbed through years of witnessing her father's responses to life's challenges. When Sarah faces her own difficulties, she automatically applies the problem-solving approaches she observed growing up: blaming external factors, avoiding uncomfortable conversations, and accepting limitations as normal. These inherited patterns make her success more difficult, not because she lacks ability or opportunity, but because she lacks the internal frameworks necessary to recognize and capitalize on possibilities.

The financial impact of inherited patterns is particularly clear in Sarah's life. Having never witnessed effective financial planning or strategic resource management, she approaches money with the same reactive patterns her father modeled. She lives paycheck to paycheck, not because her income is necessarily inadequate, but because she lacks the knowledge and habits necessary for building financial stability. When emergencies arise, she experiences them as evidence of life's unfairness rather than as predictable events requiring advance preparation. Her father's financial patterns have become her patterns, perpetuating limitations across generations.

Marcus's children are inheriting a dramatically different set of assets. They're growing up with the assumption that challenges can be addressed through thoughtful planning and persistent effort, that relationships can be sources of mutual growth and support, and that financial security is created through consistent, wise choices over time. These assumptions weren't taught through formal instruction but absorbed through daily observation of how their father approaches life's demands. When Marcus's son faces academic challenges, he doesn't immediately blame teachers or circumstances but considers how he might modify his study strategies or seek additional help. When his daughter encounters social difficulties, she applies communication skills and conflict resolution approaches she's witnessed at home.

The inheritance extends beyond specific skills to encompass fundamental orientations toward life itself. Marcus's children are developing what psychologists call "internal locus of control"—the belief that their choices significantly influence their outcomes. This orientation creates resilience in the face of setbacks, motivation to develop capabilities, and confidence that effort directed toward meaningful goals will eventually produce results. Robert's daughter has inherited the opposite orientation, "external locus of control," which creates vulnerability to depression, reduced motivation for personal development, and acceptance of outcomes as predetermined rather than influenced by choice.

The Ripple Effects of Leadership

The consequences of these contrasting approaches extend beyond immediate family to influence the broader communities where Robert and Marcus live and work. Each man's patterns create ripple effects that either strengthen or weaken the social fabric around them, demonstrating how individual choices contribute to collective outcomes.

Robert's workplace experience illustrates how the complainer's patterns affect others. His focus on problems rather than solutions creates an atmosphere where colleagues become defensive rather than collaborative. His tendency to blame external factors discourages the kind of honest evaluation that might improve systems or processes. His resistance to feedback prevents the learning that might benefit not just him but his entire team. Over time, these patterns contribute to workplace cultures characterized by mediocrity, defensiveness, and resignation rather than excellence, innovation, and growth.

The community impact of Robert's approach is more subtle but equally significant. His withdrawal from civic engagement, his focus on personal grievances rather than collective solutions, and his modeling of limitation rather than possibility all contribute to community environments where problems seem insurmountable and individual agency appears minimal. When community organizations need volunteers, Robert's response focuses on why such efforts won't work rather than how he might contribute. When neighborhood issues arise, his participation emphasizes obstacles rather than opportunities. These responses, multiplied across many individuals with similar patterns, create communities characterized by resignation rather than resilience.

Marcus's influence operates through different mechanisms toward different outcomes. His workplace leadership creates environments where people feel valued, challenged, and supported in their growth. His approach to problems as opportunities for innovation encourages creative thinking and collaborative problem-solving. His modeling of accountability and continuous learning establishes cultural norms that elevate everyone's performance. Employees in Marcus's company don't just complete their jobs; they develop capabilities, take initiative, and contribute to an organizational culture that attracts and retains excellent people.

The community impact of Marcus's approach is equally positive. His involvement in civic organizations focuses on practical solutions rather than philosophical complaints. His financial success creates opportunities for charitable giving that support community initiatives. His modeling of principled leadership inspires others to take greater responsibility for collective outcomes. When community challenges arise, Marcus's response emphasizes what can be done rather than why it can't be done, contributing to community cultures characterized by possibility and proactive engagement.

The Long View of Consequence

As Robert and Marcus enter their fifties, the long-term consequences of their contrasting approaches become increasingly apparent not just in their current circumstances but in the trajectories they're creating for their remaining years. The patterns established over decades don't just influence present outcomes; they determine the range of possibilities available for the future.

Robert's trajectory points toward increasing limitations and decreasing options. His health challenges, created by years of stress and poor self-care, will likely require more attention and resources as he ages. His financial situation, characterized by minimal savings and accumulated debt, offers little cushion for the healthcare costs and reduced earning capacity that often accompany later life. His relationship patterns, defined by emotional distance and mutual frustration, provide limited social support for navigating age-related challenges. His professional skills, underdeveloped due to years of minimal investment in growth, will become increasingly obsolete in changing economic conditions.

Perhaps most significantly, Robert's psychological patterns create resistance to the adaptations that successful aging requires. His habit of blaming external factors will make it difficult to accept the physical changes and shifting social roles that accompany later life. His pattern of avoiding difficult conversations will prevent the kind of family discussions necessary for effective elder care planning. His tendency to focus on problems rather than possibilities will make it challenging to find meaning and satisfaction in the reduced physical capacity and changed circumstances that naturally come with aging.

Marcus's trajectory points toward expanding influence and deepening satisfaction. His health practices have been maintained consistently over decades, providing a foundation of physical resilience that supports active engagement with life's opportunities. His financial disciplines have created security that allows focus on contribution rather than survival. His relationship investments have built social networks characterized by mutual support and genuine affection. His professional development has created expertise and a reputation that remains valuable regardless of specific employment circumstances.

The psychological patterns Marcus has developed support successful adaptation to aging rather than resistance to inevitable changes. His habit of taking responsibility creates openness to learning new approaches as circumstances evolve. His comfort with difficult conversations enables the kind of family planning that ensures dignity and support in later years. His orientation toward growth and contribution provides motivation and meaning that transcend physical limitations or professional achievements.

The Choice Point

The examination of these long-term consequences reveals that both Robert and Marcus reached subtle but critical choice points throughout their lives—moments where different responses might have created different trajectories. These weren't dramatic crossroads with obvious significance, but everyday decisions about how to interpret challenges, whether to invest in growth, and how to respond to feedback from others.

For Robert, many of these choice points involved the temptation to blame versus the opportunity to learn. When his supervisor criticized his approach to a project, Robert could have responded with curiosity about how to improve his performance rather than defensiveness about the unfairness of the criticism. When his marriage encountered difficulties, he could have sought counseling or committed to communication improvement rather than withdrawing emotionally. When financial pressures increased, he could have developed budgeting skills and strategic planning rather than simply working harder at the same ineffective approaches.

Each of these choice points offered the possibility of different patterns, different skills, and ultimately different outcomes. The tragedy isn't that Robert made conscious decisions to limit his possibilities but that he didn't recognize these moments as choices at all. His automatic responses, shaped by early experiences and reinforced by repetition, prevented him from seeing alternatives that might have been available with greater awareness and intentional effort.

Marcus faced similar choice points but responded differently. When criticism arose, he interpreted it as valuable feedback rather than a personal attack. When relationship challenges emerged, he invested in communication skills and conflict resolution rather than withdrawal or blame. When business difficulties occurred, he used them as opportunities to develop better systems and strategies rather than evidence that success was impossible. These different responses at critical moments created the compound effects that distinguish his current circumstances from Robert's limitations.

The hopeful implication of recognizing these choice points is that they continue to arise throughout life. Robert's patterns aren't permanently fixed; they represent accumulated responses to past choice points rather than inevitable destiny. New choice points emerge regularly—in how he responds to health challenges, financial pressures, relationship difficulties, and professional setbacks. Each moment offers the possibility of different responses that could begin to create different patterns and, ultimately, different outcomes.

The Possibility of Transformation

While the consequences of long-term patterns create significant momentum, human experience demonstrates that transformation remains possible at any stage of life. The key lies in recognizing that current circumstances reflect accumulated choices rather than external fate and that different choices can begin to create different outcomes even when change feels difficult or unlikely.

For someone in Robert's position, transformation doesn't require dramatic gestures or complete personality change. It begins with small shifts in attention and response that gradually create new patterns. Instead of immediately identifying what's wrong in each situation, he could practice identifying one element that's working well. Instead of explaining why suggestions won't work, he could experiment with implementing one small improvement. Instead of focusing exclusively on immediate pressures, he could invest even minimal time in considering longer-term possibilities.

These small shifts, maintained consistently over time, could begin to create the same kind of compound effects that created his current limitations—but in the opposite direction. One genuinely curious response to feedback could open a conversation that improves a relationship. One strategic financial decision could begin to build the kind of security that makes future decisions easier. One investment in skill development could create opportunities that currently seem impossible.

The thinker's approach offers a blueprint for such transformation, but not a rigid formula to be copied exactly. Marcus's patterns work for him because they align with his values, circumstances, and capabilities. Someone else's transformation might involve different specific choices while embodying the same underlying principles: taking responsibility for outcomes, investing in growth and development, maintaining a long-term perspective, and approaching challenges as opportunities for learning and improvement.

The mathematics of accumulated choice works equally powerfully in both directions. Just as limiting patterns compound over time to create increasing restrictions, growth-oriented patterns compound to create expanding possibilities. The key is beginning with awareness of current patterns, commitment to different responses, and patience with the gradual process through which new choices create new circumstances.

The ultimate message of examining these consequences isn't a judgment of either approach but a recognition of their power and possibility. We all make choices every day that either support or undermine the lives we claim to want. The consequences of these choices unfold over time with mathematical precision, creating the circumstances we experience as fate or fortune. By understanding this process, we gain the power to consciously influence it, creating through intentional choice the kinds of consequences we genuinely desire rather than those we unconsciously generate through patterns of reaction and avoidance.

The stories of Robert and Marcus remind us that our current circumstances, whatever they may be, represent accumulated choices rather than final destinations. New choices remain possible, new patterns can be established, and new consequences can be created through the patient's application of different responses to life's ongoing demands. The question isn't whether change is possible but whether we're willing to recognize our role in creating our current circumstances and invest in the consistent effort required to create different ones.

Chapter 8
Mental Effects on the Families

No individual exists in isolation, and the patterns that define our approach to life inevitably extend their influence far beyond personal boundaries into the most intimate spaces of human connection. The choices we make about how to respond to challenges, process disappointments, and engage with daily responsibilities create psychological atmospheres that permeate our homes, shape our children's understanding of what's possible, and determine whether family relationships become sources of mutual growth or persistent tension. The complainer and the thinker don't just create different outcomes for themselves; they create entirely different emotional and psychological environments for those who share their lives most closely.

Family systems operate according to their own form of psychological physics, where one person's consistent patterns of thought and behavior generate forces that influence every other member of the household. Children develop their earliest understanding of how the world works through observation of their parents' responses to life's demands. Spouses learn to adapt their own behaviors to accommodate the emotional climate created by their partner's habitual patterns. Extended family members adjust their expectations and interactions based on the psychological predictability of familiar relationship dynamics.

The mental effects of the complainer's patterns and the thinker's patterns on their families represent some of the most profound consequences of these contrasting approaches to life. Where the complainer's defensive, blame-focused orientation creates family environments characterized by tension, limitation, and emotional constriction, the thinker's responsible, growth-oriented approach generates family atmospheres marked by security, possibility, and emotional expansion. These differences compound over years of shared experience, creating family legacies that influence not just immediate relationships but the patterns that children carry forward into their own adult lives and relationships.

Part 1: The Complainer

The Atmospheric Pressure of Persistent Negativity

Robert's apartment feels smaller than its actual square footage suggests, not because of physical constraints but because of the psychological atmosphere that his patterns have created over years of cohabitation with his own defensive reactions to life's challenges. When family members visit or when he interacts with his adult daughter, Sarah, the space itself seems to contract around the emotional weight of unresolved grievances, unexpressed disappointments, and the perpetual sense that circumstances are fundamentally unfair and unlikely to improve.

This atmospheric pressure manifests in subtle but pervasive ways that affect everyone who spends extended time in Robert's presence. Conversations that begin with neutral topics gradually drift toward complaints about work, finances, health, or social relationships. Attempts to introduce positive developments or future possibilities are met with skeptical responses that focus on potential problems rather than potential benefits. Even moments of genuine enjoyment are shadowed by Robert's tendency to anticipate what will inevitably go wrong or to compare current circumstances unfavorably with past experiences or other people's apparent advantages.

The psychological atmosphere created by Robert's patterns affects his daughter Sarah most profoundly, as she has spent her entire life learning to navigate the emotional climate that his defensive worldview generates. From childhood through her current adult relationship with her father, Sarah has developed sophisticated strategies for managing interactions that might trigger his complaints or defensive responses. She has learned to avoid topics that reliably lead to lengthy monologues about life's unfairness, to limit sharing of her own successes to prevent comparisons that make him feel worse about his circumstances, and to offer support in ways that don't challenge his narrative of external victimization.

This careful navigation of her father's emotional landscape has required Sarah to develop what psychologists recognize as hypervigilance—a state of heightened awareness of other people's emotional states and potential reactions. She automatically scans conversations for signs that Robert is becoming frustrated or defensive, modifies her own communication to avoid triggering negative responses, and experiences chronic low-level anxiety about whether interactions will remain pleasant or devolve into familiar patterns of complaint and blame. This hypervigilance, developed as a survival strategy for managing a difficult family relationship, has become a generalized pattern that affects Sarah's interactions with colleagues, friends, and romantic partners.

The impact on Sarah's own emotional development has been profound and lasting. Growing up in an environment where problems were consistently framed as external impositions rather than challenges to be addressed has limited her own problem-solving capabilities and confidence in her ability to influence outcomes through personal agency. When she encounters difficulties in her career, relationships, or financial situation, her automatic response mirrors the patterns she observed throughout childhood: identify external factors to blame, focus on why solutions won't work, and accept limitations as evidence of life's inherent unfairness rather than opportunities for growth and learning.

Robert's ex-wife, Linda, represents another dimension of how the complainer's patterns affect family mental health. Their marriage dissolved not because of dramatic conflicts or betrayals but because of the gradual erosion that occurs when one partner's persistent negativity makes positive connections increasingly difficult to maintain. Linda describes the experience of living with Robert as "walking on eggshells," never knowing which ordinary life events would trigger extended complaints about unfairness, incompetence, or systemic problems beyond anyone's control.

The mental exhaustion that Linda experienced during their marriage illustrates how the complainer's patterns create a burden for others that extends far beyond the specific complaints themselves. Robert's tendency to process every challenge as evidence of external unfairness meant that Linda often found herself in the position of trying to provide perspective, encouragement, or practical suggestions that were inevitably rejected as not understanding the unique difficulties of his situation. Over time, these interactions created a dynamic where Linda felt simultaneously responsible for Robert's emotional state and powerless to influence it in a positive direction.

The Inheritance of Defensive Patterns

Perhaps the most tragic aspect of Robert's impact on his family lies in how his defensive patterns have been unconsciously transmitted to his daughter, creating limiting beliefs and response strategies that now constrain her own possibilities for happiness and success. Sarah has inherited not just genetic material from her father but psychological patterns that shape how she interprets challenges, processes feedback, and approaches relationships. These inherited patterns operate largely below conscious awareness, influencing her choices and responses in ways that recreate familiar limitations even when she consciously desires different outcomes.

Sarah's approach to romantic relationships exemplifies this inheritance of defensive patterns. She finds herself consistently attracted to partners who require careful emotional management, recreating the dynamic she learned in childhood, where love involves anticipating and accommodating another person's potential negative reactions. When conflicts arise in her relationships, her automatic response is to identify what she might have done wrong to trigger the problem rather than to engage in the kind of honest communication that might resolve underlying issues. This pattern, learned through years of managing her father's emotional reactions, prevents her from developing the relationship skills necessary for genuine intimacy and mutual growth.

The professional impact of inherited defensive patterns is equally significant in Sarah's life. In workplace situations, she exhibits the same hypervigilance that characterizes her family relationships, focusing more energy on avoiding potential conflicts than on pursuing opportunities for advancement or contribution. When supervisors provide feedback, her immediate internal response is defensive rather than curious, even when the feedback is genuinely constructive and well-intentioned. When projects encounter obstacles, she experiences them as evidence that circumstances are working against her rather than as normal challenges requiring creative problem-solving.

Financial patterns represent another area where Sarah has unconsciously absorbed her father's limiting approaches. Despite earning a reasonable income, she maintains the same reactive relationship with money that Robert modeled throughout her childhood. Unexpected expenses feel like emergencies rather than predictable life events requiring advance preparation. Investment opportunities seem risky and unrealistic rather than normal components of long-term financial planning. Conversations about money quickly devolve into complaints about costs, unfair economic systems, or the advantages that other people seem to possess rather than strategic discussions about how to create greater financial security and freedom.

The psychological inheritance extends to Sarah's relationship with her own potential and possibilities. Having grown up in an environment where dreams and aspirations were consistently met with a focus on obstacles and potential disappointments, she has developed what psychologists call "learned helplessness" disguised as realistic thinking. When opportunities for career advancement, relationship improvement, or personal growth arise, her automatic mental response emphasizes the reasons why such possibilities probably won't work out rather than strategies for making them successful. This isn't conscious pessimism but an unconscious protective mechanism designed to prevent the kind of disappointment that she witnessed her father experience repeatedly.

The most insidious aspect of this psychological inheritance is how it creates resistance to the very experiences that might break the limiting patterns. When Sarah encounters people who demonstrate different approaches to life's challenges—colleagues who respond to setbacks with strategic planning rather than complaints, friends who pursue ambitious goals with confidence and persistence, or romantic partners who approach conflicts with curiosity rather than defensiveness, she often experiences these differences as evidence that such people don't understand "real life" rather than as examples of alternative possibilities. This resistance protects her from the discomfort of recognizing how her inherited patterns might be limiting her own outcomes while ensuring their continuation.

The Ripple Effects on Extended Family

Robert's patterns create mental health impacts that extend beyond his immediate relationship with Sarah to affect extended family members who must navigate the complex dynamics that his defensive worldview generates at family gatherings, celebrations, and crisis situations. His siblings, parents, and other relatives have learned to modify their own behavior and expectations to accommodate his tendency to interpret neutral situations as personal slights and ordinary challenges as evidence of systematic unfairness.

Family celebrations provide particularly clear examples of how Robert's patterns affect group dynamics and individual family members' enjoyment of shared experiences. Birthday parties, holiday gatherings, and family reunions that should represent opportunities for connection and joy instead become exercises in careful management of topics, expectations, and interactions to prevent Robert's complaints from dominating conversations or creating tension that affects everyone's experience. Other family members find themselves automatically editing their own sharing of positive developments, career successes, or exciting plans to avoid triggering comparisons that will lead to extended monologues about Robert's own challenges and disappointments.

The mental exhaustion experienced by family members who love Robert but struggle to maintain positive connections with him represents a particularly painful consequence of his patterns. His sister Margaret describes feeling "drained" after family gatherings where she's spent significant energy trying to redirect conversations away from complaints, provide encouragement that's consistently rejected, and maintain optimism in the face of persistent negativity. This emotional labor, repeated across years of family interactions, has created a relationship characterized more by duty and guilt than by genuine enjoyment and mutual support.

The impact on family decision-making processes illustrates another dimension of how the complainer's patterns affect group mental health. When an extended family faces challenges requiring a collective response—caring for aging parents, managing family property, or addressing crisis situations—Robert's tendency to focus on obstacles rather than solutions creates additional complexity that other family members must navigate. His automatic response to proposed solutions emphasizes potential problems, legal complications, or unfair distribution of responsibilities rather than contributing constructive alternatives or collaborative problem-solving energy.

This dynamic has gradually led to a family pattern where important decisions are often made without including Robert in initial discussions, not out of malice but as a practical strategy for maintaining forward momentum and positive group dynamics. Family members have learned that including him from the beginning of planning processes reliably leads to extended focus on why various approaches won't work, rather than the creative development of workable solutions. While this exclusion protects group effectiveness, it also reinforces Robert's sense of being unfairly treated and misunderstood, creating additional grievances that further strain family relationships.

The psychological impact on family members extends to their own relationships with possibility and problem-solving. Spending significant time around Robert's consistent negativity and blame-focused responses gradually influences other family members' own mental patterns, making them more likely to focus on potential problems, anticipate disappointing outcomes, and approach challenges with decreased confidence in positive resolutions. This psychological contagion doesn't completely transform their worldviews but creates subtle shifts toward more defensive, reactive approaches that limit their own effectiveness and satisfaction.

The Cycle of Enabling and Resentment

One of the most complex psychological dynamics that Robert's patterns create within his family involves the alternating cycle of enabling and resentment that characterizes many of his closest relationships. Family members who love him genuinely want to provide support and encouragement, but their well-intentioned efforts to help often inadvertently reinforce the very patterns that create his ongoing difficulties while generating frustration and resentment when their assistance fails to produce positive change.

Sarah's relationship with her father exemplifies this cycle most clearly. When Robert faces financial difficulties, health challenges, or relationship problems, her natural impulse is to offer practical assistance, emotional support, or helpful suggestions. However, her attempts to help consistently encounter his defensive explanations of why external factors make improvement impossible, why her suggestions don't apply to his unique circumstances, or why her concern represents a misunderstanding of his situation rather than genuine care. These interactions leave Sarah feeling frustrated with her father's resistance to help, while also feeling guilty about her frustration with someone she knows is genuinely struggling.

The enabling component of this cycle occurs when family members, exhausted by Robert's resistance to constructive assistance, begin providing support that requires no change on his part while temporarily alleviating some consequences of his limiting patterns. Financial gifts that cover emergencies he hasn't prepared for, emotional labor that manages relationships he's damaged through defensive responses, or practical assistance that addresses problems his avoidance has created—all of these forms of support provide short-term relief while inadvertently reinforcing the very patterns that create ongoing difficulties.

The resentment component emerges when family members recognize that their well-intentioned assistance hasn't contributed to positive change but has instead enabled continued limitation while creating a burden for themselves. Sarah finds herself feeling angry about the time and energy she invests in trying to help her father while seeing no movement toward greater self-sufficiency or improved circumstances. This anger conflicts with her genuine love and concern for him, creating internal emotional turmoil that affects her own mental health and relationships.

The psychological complexity of this cycle lies in how it creates guilt and confusion for family members who want to be supportive but gradually recognize that their efforts may be counterproductive. They experience themselves as caring, responsible family members while simultaneously feeling frustrated with the lack of progress and resentful about the ongoing demands on their emotional and practical resources. This internal conflict affects their own decision-making, relationship satisfaction, and sense of effectiveness in other areas of their lives.

Extended family members caught in this cycle often find themselves walking a difficult line between providing the necessary support during genuine crises and avoiding assistance that enables continued dependence on external rescue rather than internal development. Robert's brother Tom describes the challenge of wanting to help during legitimate emergencies while recognizing that consistent rescue prevents Robert from developing the planning and problem-solving skills that might prevent future emergencies. This awareness creates difficult decisions about when to provide assistance and when to allow natural consequences to occur, decisions that generate their own stress and uncertainty.

The mental health impact of this cycle extends to family members' relationships with other people and situations in their lives. Having invested significant energy in trying to help someone who consistently resists change, family members often develop decreased confidence in their ability to provide effective support or influence positive outcomes in other relationships. The experience of failed attempts to help Robert creates learned helplessness about the possibility of making meaningful differences in others' lives, leading to either over-involvement in other relationships as compensation or under-involvement as protection against repeated disappointment.

The Development of Family Coping Strategies

Over the years of living with and loving someone whose patterns create persistent challenges, Robert's family members have developed sophisticated psychological coping strategies that allow them to maintain a connection while protecting their own mental health. These strategies represent genuine adaptations to difficult circumstances, but they also illustrate the ongoing mental health costs of prolonged exposure to defensive, blame-focused patterns of thinking and behavior.

Emotional compartmentalization represents one of the primary coping strategies that family members have developed. Sarah has learned to separate her love for her father from her frustration with his patterns, maintaining care and concern for his well-being while emotionally protecting herself from the disappointment that comes from hoping for change that doesn't occur. This compartmentalization allows her to continue the relationship without being constantly retraumatized by repeated experiences of offering help that's rejected or investing hope in improvement that doesn't materialize.

The development of realistic expectations represents another crucial coping strategy. Family members have gradually adjusted their expectations of interactions with

Robert to focus on what's actually possible rather than what they wish were possible. Instead of hoping for conversations that include mutual problem-solving, genuine curiosity about others' experiences, or collaborative planning for positive outcomes, they've learned to appreciate interactions that remain pleasant, avoid major conflicts, and provide opportunities for limited connection within the constraints of their defensive patterns.

Strategic topic management has become an automatic family skill, where members unconsciously steer conversations away from subjects that reliably trigger complaints and toward neutral territory that allows for positive interaction. This isn't conscious manipulation but learned behavior that emerges from years of discovering which topics lead to enjoyable exchanges and which lead to lengthy monologues about life's unfairness. While this strategy enables more pleasant visits, it also limits the depth and authenticity of family relationships by requiring constant monitoring of communication to avoid triggering negative responses.

Emotional support seeking from sources outside the family has become essential for family members' mental health maintenance. Sarah has learned to process her frustrations with her father's patterns through friendships and professional counseling rather than trying to address them directly within the family system. This external support provides perspective, validation, and coping strategies that help her maintain the relationship without being overwhelmed by its limitations. However, the need for external support to manage a family relationship also represents an ongoing mental health cost that affects her energy and resources available for other life areas.

Time and energy management has evolved into another necessary coping strategy. Family members have learned to limit the duration and frequency of interactions with Robert to levels that allow them to maintain care and connection without becoming emotionally depleted by exposure to persistent negativity. They've developed internal strategies for recharging after difficult conversations, processing their own emotional responses to his patterns, and maintaining their own positive momentum despite regular exposure to his limiting worldview.

The development of these coping strategies represents both resilience and loss within the family system. While family members have successfully adapted to maintain relationships despite challenging dynamics, the energy and attention required for such adaptation represent resources that might otherwise be invested in personal growth, other relationships, or life pursuits. The mental health impact of loving someone whose patterns require extensive management strategies affects family members' own capacity for spontaneous joy, unrestricted emotional expression, and confident engagement with their own possibilities.

Part 2: The Thinker

The Architecture of Emotional Security

Marcus's home environment reflects not just aesthetic choices but the psychological architecture of emotional security that his approach to life's challenges has created for his family over the years of consistent, responsible leadership. When family members return home each evening, they enter a space that feels emotionally as well as physically welcoming—a place where challenges are met with creative problem-solving rather than complaints, where individual growth is encouraged rather than threatened, and where the future is discussed with realistic optimism rather than defensive pessimism.

The psychological atmosphere that Marcus's patterns create within his family feels expansive rather than contractive, characterized by the sense that problems can be solved, goals can be achieved, and relationships can deepen through honest communication and mutual investment. Conversations at the dinner table naturally include sharing of both challenges and victories, collaborative problem-solving for difficulties that family members encounter, and strategic planning for opportunities that align with individual interests and family values. This isn't forced positivity but the natural result of a family environment where difficulties are framed as normal life experiences requiring thoughtful responses rather than evidence of systematic unfairness.

Marcus's wife, Jennifer, experiences their relationship as a source of genuine partnership in navigating life's complexities rather than a burden requiring constant emotional management. When challenges arise in her career, health, or family relationships, she knows that sharing these concerns with Marcus will result in supportive listening, collaborative brainstorming, and practical assistance that honors both her autonomy and mutual commitment. This predictable supportiveness creates psychological safety that allows her to take appropriate risks, pursue meaningful goals, and maintain confidence in her ability to handle whatever circumstances might emerge.

The impact on their children—sixteen-year-old David and fourteen-year-old Emma—illustrates how the thinker's patterns create family environments that support rather than constrain individual development. Both children have grown up experiencing challenges as normal parts of life that can be addressed through appropriate effort and strategy rather than as evidence that circumstances are fundamentally unfair or beyond personal influence. When David encounters academic difficulties, his automatic response is to consider study strategies, seek additional help, or modify his approach rather than to blame teachers, curriculum, or external factors for his struggles.

Emma's response to social challenges at school demonstrates the same pattern of personal agency and constructive problem-solving that she's observed throughout her childhood. When friendship conflicts arise, she approaches them with curiosity about different perspectives and commitment to honest communication rather than with defensive blame or resigned acceptance of social drama as inevitable. Her confidence in her ability to influence outcomes through thoughtful choices reflects the psychological foundation that Marcus's leadership has provided throughout her developmental years.

The emotional security that Marcus's patterns create extends to the family's financial psychology as well. Money is discussed openly and strategically rather than being a source of persistent anxiety or conflict. Children understand the family's financial goals, participate in age-appropriate planning discussions, and develop their own money management skills within a framework of abundance thinking rather than scarcity consciousness. When unexpected expenses arise, they're addressed through established emergency planning rather than creating crisis reactions that destabilize family emotional dynamics.

This financial security creates psychological freedom for family members to pursue interests, education, and opportunities without the constant anxiety about basic survival that characterizes many family environments. Jennifer can consider career transitions that align with her values and interests rather than being limited to choices that provide immediate financial security. The children can explore academic subjects, extracurricular activities, and future possibilities with confidence that their family's financial foundation will support their development rather than constrain their options.

The Multiplication of Possibility

One of the most profound impacts of Marcus's approach on his family lies in how his growth-oriented mindset creates a family culture where individual possibilities are multiplied rather than limited by family dynamics. Instead of family relationships requiring careful management to avoid triggering negative responses, family interactions naturally support and amplify each member's personal development, career aspirations, and relationship goals. This multiplication of possibility occurs through both direct support and indirect modeling of approaches that create expanding rather than contracting life experiences.

Jennifer's career development exemplifies this multiplication effect. When she expressed interest in transitioning from accounting to nonprofit management, Marcus's response focused immediately on how to make such a transition successful rather than on the risks, obstacles, or potential problems involved. His approach included researching educational requirements, identifying networking opportunities, and developing financial strategies that would support the transition period. More importantly, his confidence in her capability and his commitment to collaborative problem-solving provided psychological support that allowed her to pursue the transition with energy and optimism rather than anxiety and self-doubt.

The practical assistance that Marcus provided during Jennifer's career transition—managing additional household responsibilities while she completed certification programs, connecting her with professional contacts who could provide guidance, and maintaining family financial stability during a period of reduced and uncertain income—demonstrated the kind of partnership that makes ambitious goals achievable rather than overwhelming. His investment in her success created compound benefits not just for Jennifer individually but for their entire family, as her increased professional satisfaction and earning potential contributed to overall family security and satisfaction.

David's academic and athletic development illustrates how Marcus's approach creates expanding possibilities for children as well. When David expressed interest in competitive swimming, Marcus's response included not just enrollment in programs and transportation to practices but strategic thinking about how to optimize training, nutrition, and academic balance to support David's goals. His approach to David's swimming career demonstrates the same long-term thinking and comprehensive support that characterizes his business leadership, creating conditions where David's natural abilities can develop fully rather than being limited by inadequate resources or strategic planning.

The psychological impact on David extends far beyond swimming performance to encompass his overall approach to goal achievement and challenge navigation. Having experienced consistent parental support that focuses on strategic problem-solving rather than obstacle identification, David has developed confidence in his ability to achieve ambitious goals through appropriate planning and persistent effort. This confidence affects his academic performance, social relationships, and future planning in ways that create expanding rather than contracting possibilities throughout his adolescent development.

Emma's creative and academic interests receive the same multiplicative support. When she expressed fascination with environmental science, Marcus's response included researching summer programs, connecting her with family and friends who worked in environmental fields, and supporting school projects that allowed her to explore her interests more deeply. His approach transforms a child's passing interest into genuine learning opportunities that might influence future academic and career directions. More importantly, his responsiveness to her interests communicates that her curiosities and aspirations are valued and worth investing in, creating psychological foundations for continued growth and exploration.

The family's approach to challenges illustrates how Marcus's patterns create a proliferation of problem-solving capabilities rather than piling up stress and limitations. When Emma struggled with anxiety about social situations, the family's response included research about anxiety management techniques, consultation with appropriate professionals, and collaborative development of strategies that honored Emma's personality while building her social confidence. This comprehensive approach addressed not just immediate symptoms but underlying patterns, creating learning that will benefit Emma throughout her life while strengthening family bonds through successful collaborative problem-solving.

The Heritage of Competence

Perhaps the most significant long-term impact of Marcus's approach on his family lies in the heritage of competence that his children are developing through daily observation of effective leadership, strategic thinking, and collaborative problem-solving. Unlike Robert's children, who inherit defensive patterns and limiting beliefs, Marcus's children are developing psychological frameworks and practical capabilities that will support their own success and contribution throughout their adult lives.

David's approach to academic challenges demonstrates this inheritance of competence clearly. When he encounters difficult material in advanced mathematics, his automatic response mirrors the strategic thinking he's observed throughout childhood: identify specific areas of confusion, seek appropriate help from teachers or tutors, develop practice strategies that address his learning style, and maintain persistence through temporary frustration until understanding emerges. This approach to learning challenges reflects not just good study habits but fundamental beliefs about his own capability and the possibility of overcoming obstacles through appropriate effort.

The social confidence that both children display reflects their inheritance of Marcus's approach to relationship building and conflict resolution. They've learned through observation that disagreements can be addressed through honest communication, that different perspectives can coexist within respectful relationships, and that conflicts often contain opportunities for deeper understanding and stronger connections. These social skills, developed through family modeling rather than formal instruction, provide foundations for leadership capability and relationship satisfaction that will benefit them throughout their personal and professional lives.

Emma's entrepreneurial interests illustrate another dimension of inherited competence. At fourteen, she's already demonstrated the same strategic thinking that characterizes Marcus's business approach by developing a small tutoring service for younger students in her school. Her approach includes identifying market needs, developing service offerings that match her capabilities, setting appropriate prices, and managing client relationships professionally. This isn't precocious business development but a natural application of problem-solving frameworks and growth mindsets that she's absorbed through years of family discussions about challenges and opportunities.

The financial literacy that both children are developing represents a particularly valuable component of their inherited competence. They understand concepts like compound interest, strategic investing, and long-term financial planning not through formal education but through participation in family discussions about financial decisions and observation of how strategic financial thinking creates security and opportunity. This early foundation in financial competence will prevent the kind of reactive money management that creates persistent stress and limitations in many adult lives.

Professional development concepts have become natural parts of the children's thinking about their own futures. They understand that career success results from continuous learning, relationship building, and strategic positioning rather than from luck or external circumstances. David's approach to summer job opportunities reflects this understanding—he evaluates positions not just for immediate income but for skill development, relationship building, and learning experiences that might support future goals. Emma's academic choices reflect similar strategic thinking about how current investments in learning will create future opportunities and capabilities.

The psychological inheritance extends to the children's relationship with challenge and uncertainty. Having grown up in an environment where difficulties are framed as normal parts of life requiring thoughtful responses, both children approach new situations with confidence and curiosity rather than anxiety and avoidance. When David faces the uncertainty of college applications and future career choices, his predominant emotional experience is excitement about possibilities rather than worry about potential problems.

When Emma encounters social or academic challenges, her default assumption is that appropriate strategies can address whatever difficulties emerge.

The Ripple Effects of Positive Leadership

Marcus's patterns create positive mental health impacts that extend beyond his immediate family to affect extended family relationships, community connections, and the broader social networks that intersect with his family's life. His approach to leadership and problem-solving creates ripple effects that strengthen rather than strain the relationships surrounding his family, contributing to social environments characterized by mutual support, collaborative problem-solving, and shared investment in positive outcomes.

Extended family gatherings in Marcus's family feel fundamentally different from similar gatherings in Robert's family. Instead of requiring careful topic management to avoid triggering complaints or defensive responses, family conversations naturally include sharing of both challenges and successes, collaborative brainstorming about difficulties that family members face, and celebration of achievements and milestones. Marcus's presence at family events contributes positive energy and practical problem-solving capability that enhances rather than constrains group dynamics.

When extended family members face significant challenges—health crises, financial difficulties, or relationship problems—Marcus's response typically includes both emotional support and practical assistance that honors others' autonomy while providing genuine help. His approach to family crisis situations demonstrates the same strategic thinking and comprehensive support that characterizes his business leadership, creating confidence among family members that challenges can be addressed effectively through collaborative effort and appropriate resources.

The impact on his siblings' relationships with their own children illustrates another dimension of positive ripple effects. Marcus's approach to parenting provides a model that his siblings can observe and adapt to their own family circumstances. His children's confidence, competence, and positive relationships with adults provide evidence that children can develop successfully within family environments characterized by high expectations combined with consistent support. This modeling effect contributes to improved parenting practices throughout the extended family system.

Community involvement represents another area where Marcus's patterns create positive mental health effects for his family and others. His participation in school board meetings, youth sports organizations, and community development initiatives demonstrates active citizenship and contribution that his children observe and that benefits other families in their community. His approach to community challenges focuses on collaborative problem-solving and resource development rather than complaints about inadequate leadership or systematic problems, contributing to community cultures characterized by possibility and proactive engagement.

The psychological impact on Jennifer extends to her own professional and community relationships. Being married to someone whose patterns create expanding rather than contracting possibilities provides psychological freedom for her own growth and contribution. She can pursue ambitious professional goals, invest energy in community organizations, and maintain extensive friendships without worrying that family dynamics will undermine her efforts or create additional stress that limits her capacity for outside engagement.

The children's social development reflects the positive modeling they receive at home in their interactions with peers, teachers, and community adults. Their confidence in approaching new relationships, comfort with diverse perspectives, and skills in collaborative problem-solving make them attractive friends and reliable team members in various academic and extracurricular contexts. These social capabilities create expanding networks of positive relationships that provide support, opportunities, and learning experiences throughout their development.

The Sustainable Satisfaction of Mutual Growth

One of the most profound mental health benefits that Marcus's patterns create for his family lies in the sustainable satisfaction that emerges when family relationships become vehicles for mutual growth rather than sources of persistent stress or careful management. Each family member experiences genuine support for their individual development while contributing to collective family success, creating reinforcing cycles of investment and satisfaction that strengthen over time rather than requiring increasing energy to maintain.

Jennifer's experience of marriage clearly illustrates this sustainable satisfaction. Instead of feeling burdened by the emotional labor of managing a partner's defensive patterns or limited by a spouse's resistance to growth and change, she experiences marriage as amplifying her own possibilities while providing meaningful opportunities to support Marcus's continued development. Their relationship conversations include strategic planning for both individual and shared goals, honest feedback that supports rather than threatens each person's growth, and collaborative problem-solving that strengthens their partnership while addressing whatever challenges emerge.

The absence of chronic relationship tension creates psychological space for Jennifer to invest energy in personal development, professional advancement, and community contribution that might otherwise be consumed by relationship management or emotional recovery from difficult family dynamics. This freedom translates into career satisfaction, friendship development, and personal fulfillment that contribute to her overall life satisfaction while strengthening her capacity to be a supportive partner and mother.

David and Emma's experience of family life creates psychological foundations for their own future relationships and parenting. They're learning that family relationships can provide consistent support without limiting individual growth, that honest communication strengthens rather than threatens connections, and that collaborative problem-solving creates better outcomes than individual struggle. These relationship skills and expectations will influence their choice of romantic partners, their approach to friendship development, and their own future parenting in ways that perpetuate positive family dynamics across generations.

The sustainable aspect of family satisfaction in Marcus's household results from the alignment between individual growth and family welfare. Jennifer's career development contributes to the family's financial security while providing personal fulfillment. David's academic and athletic achievements create pride and joy for the entire family while building his own confidence and capabilities. Emma's creative and entrepreneurial interests add energy and excitement to family life while developing skills that will serve her throughout adulthood. Each person's individual success contributes to collective family satisfaction, creating reinforcing cycles that make continued investment feel natural and rewarding.

The mental health benefits extend to the family's approach to future planning and goal setting. Instead of anxiety about uncertain outcomes or resignation about limited possibilities, family discussions about the future are characterized by realistic optimism and strategic thinking. College planning for David includes consideration of academic interests, career possibilities, and financial strategies that make ambitious educational goals achievable rather than stressful. Emma's exploration of various interests receives support that allows her to discover genuine passions rather than pressure to make premature commitments.

Financial discussions within the family exemplify the sustainable satisfaction of aligned goals and mutual support. Money conversations include both practical planning and value-based decision-making that honors individual interests while supporting family security and opportunity. Investment in children's education, family experiences, and long-term security feels natural and sustainable because it reflects shared values and strategic thinking rather than competing individual interests or financial anxiety.

The emotional climate of Marcus's family creates conditions where genuine intimacy and authentic self-expression can develop naturally. Family members feel safe to share struggles, dreams, and uncertainties without fear of triggering defensive responses or overwhelming others with emotional burdens. This emotional safety creates opportunities for the kind of deep connection and mutual understanding that makes family relationships sources of strength and joy rather than obligation and stress.

The Legacy of Emotional Intelligence

The long-term mental health impact of Marcus's approach on his family extends to the development of emotional intelligence and interpersonal skills that will influence his children's success and satisfaction throughout their adult lives. Unlike Robert's children, who inherit defensive patterns and limited relationship skills, Marcus's children are developing sophisticated capabilities for emotional awareness, communication effectiveness, and collaborative problem-solving that will serve them in all areas of future relationships and career development.

David's emotional intelligence development is evident in his approach to peer relationships and academic challenges. He demonstrates a sophisticated awareness of his own emotional responses and those of others, allowing him to navigate social complexities with both sensitivity and confidence. When conflicts arise with friends, his approach includes perspective-taking, honest communication, and creative problem-solving that typically strengthens rather than damages relationships. These skills, developed through family modeling and practice, provide foundations for leadership capability and relationship satisfaction that will benefit him throughout his personal and professional life.

The communication skills that both children are developing represent another crucial component of their emotional intelligence inheritance. They've learned through family practice that difficult conversations can strengthen rather than threaten relationships, that different perspectives can coexist within respectful dialogue, and that honest feedback represents care rather than criticism. These communication capabilities will influence their success in future romantic relationships, friendships, professional collaborations, and their own eventual parenting.

Emma's developing emotional intelligence manifests in her approach to academic and social challenges. She demonstrates a sophisticated understanding of how emotional states affect performance and relationships, allowing her to manage her own anxiety and frustration while providing support for friends experiencing difficulties. Her ability to recognize and respond appropriately to others' emotional needs makes her a valued friend and reliable team member in various academic and extracurricular contexts.

The conflict resolution skills that both children are developing through family experience will prevent many of the relationship difficulties that plague adults who lack such capabilities. They understand that disagreements often contain opportunities for deeper understanding, that compromise can honor everyone's important interests, and that collaborative problem-solving typically produces better outcomes than winning or losing approaches to conflict. These skills will influence their choice of romantic partners, their approach to workplace challenges, and their own future family relationships.

Stress management represents another crucial component of the emotional intelligence that Marcus's children are developing. Having grown up in an environment where challenges are met with strategic planning rather than panic responses, they've learned to maintain perspective during difficult periods, seek appropriate help when needed, and maintain confidence in their ability to handle whatever circumstances might emerge. This stress resilience will protect their mental health while enabling sustained high performance throughout their adult lives.

The empathy and social awareness that both children demonstrate reflect their inheritance of Marcus's approach to understanding and supporting others. They naturally consider how their choices affect other people, seek to understand different perspectives before making judgments, and invest energy in supporting friends and family members without feeling overwhelmed by others' emotional needs. These social capabilities create expanding networks of positive relationships while contributing to community environments characterized by mutual support and collaborative problem-solving.

The psychological resilience that Marcus's children are developing represents perhaps the most valuable component of their emotional intelligence inheritance. Having grown up experiencing challenges as normal parts of life that can be addressed through appropriate strategies, they've developed what psychologists call "internal locus of control"—the belief that their choices significantly influence their outcomes. This orientation creates confidence in facing uncertainty, motivation for continued learning and development, and resistance to the kind of learned helplessness that constrains many adults' possibilities for growth and contribution.

The Mathematics of Family Mental Health

The contrast between the mental health impacts created by Robert's and Marcus's patterns illustrates a fundamental truth about family systems: individual psychological patterns don't simply affect the person who holds them but create mathematical progressions of mental health consequences that multiply across relationships and generations. The complainer's defensive, blame-focused approach creates compound negative effects that diminish family members' confidence, limit their problem-solving capabilities, and constrain their own possibilities for satisfaction and success. The thinker's responsible, growth-oriented approach creates compound positive effects that enhance family members' capabilities, expand their possibilities, and strengthen their resilience in navigating life's inevitable challenges.

The psychological mathematics of Robert's impact on his family operates through what systems theorists call "negative feedback loops"—patterns where one person's limitations create conditions that reinforce similar limitations in others. Robert's focus on external blame teaches his daughter to avoid responsibility for outcomes, which limits her problem-solving development and creates more situations requiring external blame, which reinforces the original pattern while extending it to the next generation. His defensive responses to feedback prevent relationship improvement, which creates more relationship difficulties, which provides more evidence for his defensive worldview while teaching family members to avoid honest communication that might trigger defensiveness.

The financial impact of these negative feedback loops extends beyond Robert's personal circumstances to affect his family's economic possibilities across generations. Sarah's inheritance of reactive money management patterns creates the same kind of financial instability that characterized her childhood, ensuring that her own children will grow up with similar economic anxiety and limited models for strategic financial planning. The psychological patterns that prevent Robert from building financial security also prevent Sarah from developing the financial discipline and strategic thinking necessary for breaking cycles of economic limitation.

Marcus's impact on his family demonstrates the opposite mathematical progression—positive feedback loops where one person's growth-oriented patterns create conditions that support similar development in others. His strategic thinking and problem-solving capabilities provide models that his children naturally absorb and apply to their own challenges, creating expanding capabilities that will serve them throughout their lives. His approach to financial planning and investment creates not just immediate family security but generational wealth-building patterns that will benefit his children and grandchildren for decades to come.

Psychological mathematics extends to social and community relationships as well. Robert's defensive patterns create social isolation that limits his family's access to the kind of community support and networking opportunities that facilitate individual success and family resilience. Sarah's inherited patterns of hypervigilance and conflict avoidance limit her own social development and professional networking, perpetuating cycles of limitation across multiple life areas. The family's approach to problems as external impositions rather than solvable challenges prevents the kind of community engagement and mutual support that creates expanding possibilities for all family members.

Marcus's family demonstrates how positive patterns create expanding social mathematics that benefits multiple generations. His community involvement and professional success create networking opportunities and social capital that his children can access throughout their development. Jennifer's professional advancement, supported by family stability and partnership, creates additional career and educational opportunities for their children. The family's reputation for competence, integrity, and collaborative problem-solving attracts other families with similar values, creating social environments that reinforce positive patterns while providing mutual support during challenging periods.

The Intergenerational Transmission of Mental Health Patterns

Perhaps the most profound consequence of these contrasting approaches to family mental health lies in how psychological patterns transmit across generations, creating family legacies that influence not just immediate relationships but the mental health and life possibilities of children, grandchildren, and future family members who will inherit either limiting or expanding frameworks for understanding life's challenges and possibilities.

Robert's psychological inheritance to his family includes patterns that will likely persist across multiple generations unless consciously recognized and addressed. Sarah's children are already showing signs of the same hypervigilance, defensive communication, and external blame patterns that characterized their grandfather and mother. When faced with academic challenges, they tend to focus on unfair teacher expectations rather than study strategy improvements. When social conflicts arise, they seek external validation rather than examining their own contribution to relationship difficulties. When family financial pressures emerge, they experience them as evidence of systematic unfairness rather than as predictable challenges requiring a strategic response.

The most insidious aspect of this intergenerational transmission lies in how limiting patterns disguise themselves as wisdom gained through experience. Sarah genuinely believes that her focus on obstacles and potential problems represents realistic thinking based on life experience rather than inherited pessimism that prevents recognition of genuine opportunities. Her children are learning to interpret her protective warnings about disappointment and difficulty as mature guidance rather than as projections of limiting beliefs that constrain their own willingness to pursue ambitious goals or invest energy in challenging relationships.

The psychological patterns that Robert's family has inherited affect not just individual mental health but family relationship dynamics across generations. Sarah's approach to parenting mirrors her father's defensive patterns in subtle but significant ways. She focuses more energy on protecting her children from potential disappointments than on building their confidence and problem-solving capabilities. Her communication style emphasizes potential problems with their plans rather than collaborative strategizing that might make their goals more achievable. Her financial anxiety creates household tension that teaches her children to experience money as a source of stress rather than as a tool for creating security and opportunity.

Marcus's psychological inheritance to his family demonstrates how positive patterns compound across generations to create expanding possibilities and strengthen mental health foundations. His children are developing psychological frameworks and practical capabilities that they will naturally transmit to their own children, creating generational patterns of competence, confidence, and collaborative problem-solving that will benefit family members for decades to come.

David's approach to challenges already demonstrates the same strategic thinking and growth orientation that characterizes his father's leadership. When he encounters academic difficulties, his automatic response includes assessment of learning strategies, seeking appropriate help, and maintaining confidence in his ability to improve performance through appropriate effort. These patterns will influence his own future parenting, creating conditions where his children develop similar confidence and problem-solving capabilities. The psychological inheritance extends beyond specific skills to encompass fundamental beliefs about personal agency, the possibility of positive change, and the value of persistent effort directed toward meaningful goals.

Emma's developing emotional intelligence and social capabilities represent another component of positive intergenerational transmission. Her sophisticated understanding of relationship dynamics, communication effectiveness, and collaborative problem-solving will influence her choice of romantic partners, her approach to friendship development, and her own future family relationships. The social skills she's developing through family modeling will create expanding networks of positive relationships throughout her life while contributing to community environments characterized by mutual support and shared investment in positive outcomes.

The financial inheritance that Marcus's children are receiving extends far beyond material resources to encompass psychological frameworks and practical capabilities for wealth building and strategic resource management. They understand concepts like compound interest, strategic investing, and long-term financial planning not as abstract theories but as practical tools for creating security and opportunity. This financial literacy, combined with the confidence and strategic thinking capabilities they're developing, will enable them to build generational wealth that provides security and possibility for their own children and grandchildren.

The Healing Potential of Recognition and Change

While the mental health impacts of contrasting family patterns create significant momentum across generations, human psychological development also demonstrates a remarkable capacity for healing and transformation when limiting patterns are recognized and consciously addressed. The hopeful aspect of understanding these family dynamics lies in recognizing that inherited patterns, however deeply ingrained, remain changeable through awareness, commitment, and appropriate strategies for personal development.

Sarah's journey toward greater psychological health illustrates this healing potential clearly. Through professional counseling and personal development work, she has begun to recognize how her inherited patterns of defensive thinking and external blame have limited her own possibilities for satisfaction and success. This recognition hasn't eliminated the patterns immediately, but it has created awareness that allows her to make different choices in specific situations, gradually building new response patterns that support rather than undermine her goals.

The most significant aspect of Sarah's healing journey lies in her growing ability to interrupt automatic defensive responses and consider alternative interpretations of challenging situations. When her supervisor provides feedback about her work performance, she's learning to experience this information as potentially helpful guidance rather than automatically interpreting it as unfair criticism. When financial pressures arise, she's developing the capability to consider strategic responses rather than immediately focusing on external factors beyond her control. These changes represent genuine psychological development that creates expanding possibilities for professional advancement, relationship improvement, and financial stability.

The impact of Sarah's healing on her own children demonstrates how positive change can interrupt the intergenerational transmission of limiting patterns. As she develops greater emotional awareness and communication skills, her interactions with her children naturally become more supportive and less protective. Instead of focusing conversations on potential problems with their plans, she's learning to engage in collaborative problem-solving that builds their confidence while addressing legitimate concerns. Her developing financial literacy and strategic thinking create opportunities to teach her children different approaches to money management and goal achievement.

The therapeutic process that supports such healing typically involves several crucial components that address both individual psychological patterns and family system dynamics. Recognition of inherited patterns represents the essential first step—developing awareness of how childhood experiences create automatic response patterns that continue to influence adult choices and outcomes. This recognition often feels uncomfortable initially because it challenges familiar narratives about external causation while highlighting personal responsibility for continuing patterns.

Skill development represents another crucial component of healing from inherited limiting patterns. Sarah's therapeutic work has included learning new communication techniques, developing strategic thinking capabilities, and practicing emotional regulation skills that support different responses to challenging situations. These skills don't replace inherited patterns immediately but provide alternatives that become more natural and automatic through practice and repetition.

Relationship repair often emerges as both a component and a consequence of individual healing work. As Sarah develops different response patterns, her relationships with family members, colleagues, and friends naturally improve, creating positive feedback that reinforces continued growth and development. Her relationship with her father remains limited by his continued defensive patterns, but her own changes have allowed her to maintain a connection without being overwhelmed by his negativity or drawn into enabling dynamics that prevent his own potential growth.

The most profound aspect of healing from inherited family mental health patterns lies in how individual change creates expanding possibilities for future generations. Sarah's children are witnessing different approaches to challenge navigation, relationship management, and goal achievement that will influence their own psychological development and family relationships throughout their lives. The positive changes she's making today will compound across decades to create different outcomes for her children and grandchildren, demonstrating how conscious change can interrupt limiting patterns while establishing more supportive family legacies.

The Community Impact of Family Mental Health Patterns

The mental health effects that different family patterns create extend beyond individual households to influence community environments, social institutions, and the broader cultural contexts where families live and interact. Robert's and Marcus's contrasting approaches to family leadership create ripple effects that either strengthen or weaken the communities where their families participate, demonstrating how individual psychological patterns scale up to affect collective social and mental health outcomes.

Communities with high concentrations of families exhibiting Robert's patterns—defensive thinking, external blame, and resistance to collaborative problem-solving—tend to develop characteristics that reflect and reinforce these individual limitations. Community meetings focus more energy on identifying problems and assigning blame than on developing creative solutions and strategic planning. Local organizations struggle to maintain volunteer participation because residents approach community involvement with the same defensive patterns that characterize their family relationships. Economic development efforts encounter resistance based on a focus on potential problems rather than the strategic assessment of opportunities and challenges.

The educational institutions in such communities often reflect similar patterns, with parent-teacher interactions characterized by defensive responses to student challenges rather than collaborative problem-solving that supports student success. School board meetings focus disproportionate attention on complaints about inadequate resources or unfair policies rather than strategic planning for educational improvement within existing constraints. These dynamics create educational environments that constrain rather than expand student possibilities while perpetuating limiting patterns across generations of community residents.

Communities with higher concentrations of families exhibiting Marcus's patterns demonstrate opposite characteristics that support rather than constrain individual and collective flourishing. Community organizations benefit from volunteer participation that includes strategic thinking, collaborative problem-solving, and commitment to long-term positive outcomes rather than short-term complaint resolution. Economic development efforts attract investment and support because community leaders approach opportunities with realistic optimism and comprehensive planning rather than a defensive focus on potential problems.

The educational institutions in such communities typically demonstrate higher performance and student satisfaction because parent involvement includes strategic support for educational excellence rather than defensive reactions to student challenges. School board participation focuses on resource development and strategic planning that creates expanding educational opportunities rather than complaint-focused meetings that consume energy without producing improvement. These dynamics create educational environments that support student achievement while modeling positive approaches to challenge navigation and collaborative problem-solving.

The mental health resources and social services available in different communities also reflect the predominant family patterns among residents. Communities characterized by defensive, blame-focused family patterns typically require more crisis intervention services, conflict resolution resources, and remedial assistance programs. Communities characterized by growth-oriented, collaborative family patterns typically require more development-focused services, educational enrichment programs, and strategic planning resources that support expanding rather than constraining possibilities.

The long-term community development patterns demonstrate how family mental health approaches create compound effects across generations of residents. Communities that attract and retain families with growth-oriented patterns tend to develop expanding economic opportunities, strengthen educational institutions, and increase property values, creating positive feedback loops and attracting additional growth-oriented families. Communities that concentrate on families with limiting patterns tend to develop contracting economic opportunities, struggling educational institutions, and declining property values that create negative feedback loops, attracting additional families with similar patterns.

The Ultimate Choice: Legacy and Transformation

The examination of mental health effects on families ultimately reveals that each individual faces ongoing choices about the psychological legacy they create for those they love most deeply. These aren't one-time decisions but daily choices about how to respond to challenges, process disappointments, and engage with the opportunities and difficulties that characterize human experience. The accumulation of these choices over the years and decades creates family environments that either expand or constrain the mental health and life possibilities of children, spouses, and extended family members.

Robert's story illustrates how defensive patterns, while providing short-term emotional protection, create long-term mental health costs that extend far beyond the individual who maintains such patterns. His focus on external blame and resistance to personal responsibility has created family relationships characterized by careful management rather than genuine intimacy, limited possibilities rather than expanding growth, and inherited limitations rather than inherited capabilities. The mental health impact on his daughter and extended family members represents the ongoing consequences of choices he made decades ago, but continues to be reinforced through current behavioral patterns.

The hopeful aspect of Robert's situation lies in recognizing that these patterns remain changeable through conscious effort and appropriate support. Professional counseling, personal development work, and commitment to different response patterns could begin to create different outcomes for himself and his family members. The healing potential exists even after decades of limiting patterns, though the process requires genuine recognition of personal responsibility and sustained commitment to different approaches to life's challenges.

Marcus's story demonstrates how growth-oriented patterns create compound positive effects that strengthen family mental health across generations while contributing to community environments characterized by possibility and collaborative problem-solving. His approach to challenges, relationships, and personal development has created family dynamics that support rather than constrain individual growth while building psychological foundations that will benefit his children throughout their adult lives and family relationships.

The contrast between these approaches reveals that family mental health outcomes aren't determined by external circumstances but by the accumulated effect of individual choices about how to interpret and respond to life's inevitable challenges and opportunities. Both Robert and Marcus have faced difficulties, setbacks, and uncertainties throughout their lives. The difference in family mental health outcomes reflects their contrasting approaches to processing such experiences and the patterns they've established for navigating complexity and change.

The ultimate message about family mental health effects emphasizes both the profound responsibility and the tremendous opportunity that each individual holds for influencing the psychological well-being of those they love most. The choices we make about how to approach challenges, communicate about difficulties, and respond to opportunities create psychological atmospheres that shape our children's understanding of what's possible, influence our spouses' confidence and satisfaction, and determine whether family relationships become sources of mutual growth or persistent limitation.

The good news lies in recognizing that these choices remain available regardless of current circumstances or past patterns. Each conversation with family members represents an opportunity to model different approaches to challenge navigation. Each response to unexpected difficulties demonstrates either limiting or expanding ways of thinking about problems and possibilities. Each interaction with children provides chances to communicate either that life is fundamentally unfair and beyond personal control or that challenges represent normal parts of existence that can be addressed through strategic thinking and persistent effort.

The family mental health legacy that we create through our daily choices will influence not just our immediate relationships but generations of family members who will inherit either psychological frameworks that support their flourishing or patterns that constrain their possibilities. This recognition transforms everyday interactions from routine exchanges into opportunities for creating positive change that extends far beyond our own experience to encompass the mental health and life satisfaction of those we love most deeply. The choice between creating, expanding, or contracting psychological environments for our families remains available at each moment, waiting for our conscious recognition and intentional response.

Chapter 9
The Silent Witnesses

How Children Interpret Parental Actions

Part 1: The Complainer's Legacy

Children are extraordinary observers, absorbing patterns and meanings with an intensity that adults often underestimate. In households shaped by parental evasion, they become silent anthropologists, studying behaviors that will unconsciously guide their own life choices for decades to come. Their young minds work like sophisticated recording devices, capturing not just words and actions but the underlying emotional currents that flow beneath family interactions.

In a home where financial responsibility is consistently deflected, children develop a peculiar form of hypervigilance. They learn to read the subtle signs of impending financial crisis, the tightening around their father's eyes when bills arrive, the careful modulation of their mother's voice when discussing expenses, and the unspoken tension that fills rooms when credit card statements appear on the kitchen counter. These children become emotional meteorologists, constantly monitoring the atmospheric pressure of household stress.

Ten-year-old Jessica has become an expert at interpreting these emotional weather patterns. She notices how her father's complaints about "predatory banks" and "impossible interest rates" always follow certain patterns. The more serious the financial situation becomes, the more elaborate his explanations of external persecution. She doesn't understand the adult complexities of compound interest or credit utilization, but she absorbs something far more fundamental: problems are things that happen to you, not things you create or solve.

Her younger brother, Michael, approaches these household dynamics differently. Where Jessica becomes hypervigilant, Michael retreats into elaborate fantasy worlds where heroes face challenges through cleverness rather than accountability. His bedroom becomes a fortress of imagination, filled with stories where protagonists overcome obstacles through luck, magic, or the intervention of powerful allies, never through patient, systematic effort.

The children's interpretation of their father's behavior isn't a conscious analysis. They don't sit down and decide that personal responsibility is dangerous or that external blame is preferable to self-examination. Instead, these lessons seep into their understanding like water into the soil, creating the foundational assumptions upon which they'll build their adult lives. Every dinner table conversation, every overheard phone call about bills, and every moment of tension around money becomes part of their unconscious education about how the world works.

The Language of Deflection

The vocabulary of deflection becomes their native tongue. When Jessica struggles with a math assignment, her first instinct isn't to examine her study methods or seek additional help. Instead, she's learned to identify external factors that might explain her difficulties. "The teacher goes too fast," she'll say, unconsciously mimicking her father's tendency to locate problems outside himself. "These problems are harder than what we did in class."

This linguistic pattern represents more than simple excuse-making. It's a fundamental orientation toward personal agency. Jessica is learning that she is acted upon rather than acting, a passive recipient of circumstances rather than an active creator of outcomes. The math assignment becomes something that happens to her rather than a challenge she can systematically address.

The sophistication of this learned helplessness is remarkable. Jessica doesn't simply make excuses; she develops elaborate analytical frameworks for understanding why external circumstances make success impossible. She becomes skilled at identifying the flaws in systems, the unfairness in expectations, and the impossibility of standards. Her intelligence, considerable though it is, becomes channeled into creating bulletproof explanations for why she shouldn't be held accountable for outcomes.

Michael's interpretation takes a different form. He becomes fascinated by stories of sudden transformation, fairy tales where ordinary people become extraordinary through magical intervention. His play patterns reflect this fascination. He doesn't practice skills or work toward gradual improvement; instead, he waits for moments of revelation or external rescue. This isn't laziness but a logical response to the household pattern he observes.

When Michael plays with building blocks, his approach is telling. He doesn't start with simple structures; he gradually builds complexity through practice and patience. Instead, he attempts elaborate constructions immediately, becomes frustrated when they collapse, and then abandons the project while blaming the blocks themselves. "These don't fit right," he'll say, unconsciously echoing his father's approach to financial challenges. "They're not made properly."

The children watch their mother navigate around their father's defensive patterns with the careful attention of wildlife biologists studying a dangerous species. They learn that direct communication about problems is risky and that approaching certain topics requires elaborate diplomatic strategies. This lesson in emotional management creates a particular kind of intelligence, the ability to read unstated tensions and manage other people's emotions, but it comes at the cost of learning direct, honest communication.

Jessica becomes particularly skilled at this emotional navigation. She learns to phrase requests carefully, to time conversations strategically, and to avoid topics that might trigger her father's defensive responses. This creates a precocious emotional sophistication that adults often mistake for maturity. In reality, she's developing survival skills for living in an emotionally unpredictable environment.

The sophistication of these children's adaptive strategies is both impressive and heartbreaking. They become experts at managing adult emotions, predicting and preventing conflicts, and navigating complex family dynamics. These skills serve them well within the dysfunction of their household, but they create profound challenges when they encounter environments where direct communication and honest accountability are expected and valued.

The Classroom as Laboratory

School becomes a laboratory where these absorbed patterns are tested and refined. Jessica's academic experience becomes a series of experiments in deflection and external blame. When she receives feedback on writing assignments, her first response isn't to consider how she might improve her work. Instead, she analyzes the teacher's biases, the unfairness of the grading criteria, and the impossibility of the assignment parameters.

Her teachers, well-meaning but often unprepared for such sophisticated deflection, find themselves drawn into complex discussions about fairness and expectation rather than focusing on skill development. Jessica learns that adults can be manipulated through appeals to justice and equality, that emotional arguments can substitute for academic improvement, and that problems can be made to disappear through sufficient analysis of external factors.

This pattern creates a peculiar academic trajectory. Jessica excels in subjects where her natural abilities align with requirements, creating evidence that she's "smart" and "capable." However, she struggles profoundly in areas where sustained effort and gradual skill development are required. Her academic record becomes a series of highs and lows, with no middle ground where steady work leads to steady improvement.

Michael's school experience follows a different pattern but reflects the same underlying orientation. He approaches academic challenges with the expectation that solutions should arrive through inspiration rather than effort. When faced with multiplication tables, he doesn't develop systematic study strategies. Instead, he hopes that the patterns will suddenly become clear, that a teacher will provide a magical explanation, or that the requirement will somehow disappear.

His attention during lessons becomes highly selective. He engages intensely when topics feel immediately accessible or personally interesting, but mentally checks out when sustained effort is required. Teachers describe him as "bright but inconsistent," not understanding that his inconsistency reflects a learned approach to challenge rather than attention or ability deficits.

The social dynamics of school provide another arena where these patterns play out. Jessica becomes skilled at forming alliances with other students who share her approach to external blame. Together, they create micro-communities where mutual validation of victimhood becomes a form of bonding. They develop elaborate analyses of teacher unfairness, systemic problems in the educational system, and the impossibility of meeting unrealistic expectations.

These friendships feel supportive and validating, but they actually reinforce the patterns that limit growth. Jessica and her friends become increasingly skilled at identifying problems while becoming less capable of implementing solutions. Their social interactions center around shared complaints rather than collaborative problem-solving or mutual encouragement toward improvement.

Michael's social patterns reflect his absorbed expectation that problems should solve themselves or be solved by others. He becomes the friend who generates enthusiasm for group projects but contributes minimally to their completion. His natural charisma and creativity make him popular in the early stages of social interactions, but his reliability issues create ongoing tensions in longer-term friendships.

The Emotional Inheritance

The impact of growing up in an environment of deflected responsibility extends far beyond academic performance or financial literacy. These children are absorbing a comprehensive worldview about human agency, personal power, and the nature of problems themselves. They're learning that vulnerability is dangerous, that admitting mistakes invites criticism rather than support, and that the safest approach to life's challenges is to identify external causes rather than internal solutions.

Jessica develops what psychologists might recognize as an external locus of control, a deep-seated belief that the important outcomes in her life are determined by forces beyond her influence. This isn't a conscious philosophy but an unconscious operating system that will guide countless future decisions. When she eventually enters the workforce, she'll struggle with performance reviews that require self-assessment. The very concept of taking credit for successes or responsibility for failures will feel foreign and threatening.

The depth of this programming is remarkable. Jessica doesn't simply blame others for her failures; she genuinely cannot see her own role in creating outcomes. Her psychological architecture has been constructed around the principle that agency belongs to external forces, teachers, employers, systems, and circumstances, while she remains a relatively powerless observer of her own life.

This learned helplessness extends to her relationship with her own emotions. Jessica learns that feelings are things that happen to her rather than experiences she can influence through her choices and behaviors. When she feels anxious about a test, frustrated with a friend, or disappointed about an outcome, her automatic response is to analyze the external circumstances that created these feelings rather than considering how her own thoughts, preparations, or actions might be contributing to her emotional experience.

Michael's response patterns point toward different but equally problematic adult challenges. His fascination with external rescue creates an unconscious expectation that solutions should arrive without sustained personal effort. As he grows older, this pattern will manifest as an attraction to get-rich-quick schemes, revolutionary diets that promise instant transformation, and relationships where he expects partners to solve problems he's unwilling to address himself.

The tragedy of Michael's developing pattern is that his creativity and enthusiasm are genuine strengths that could serve him well if channeled through sustained effort. But he's learning to trust inspiration over perspiration, magic over methodology, and external intervention over internal development. His considerable potential becomes trapped within a framework that makes systematic growth nearly impossible.

Both children develop a particular relationship with authority that will create challenges throughout their lives. Authority figures become either rescuers who should solve their problems or persecutors who create unfair obstacles. The possibility that authority relationships might be collaborative partnerships focused on mutual growth and development remains unexplored.

Jessica learns to approach teachers, supervisors, and mentors with a mixture of dependency and defensiveness.

She wants their help but resists their feedback. She seeks their validation but challenges their expectations. This creates exhausting relationships for everyone involved, as authority figures find themselves simultaneously needed and undermined.

Michael's relationship with authority develops around charm and deflection. He learns to be likable and engaging while avoiding genuine accountability. Authority figures often describe him as "having potential" while struggling to help him realize that potential. His approach creates temporary goodwill but undermines the sustained support necessary for long-term development.

The Peer Laboratory

The children's relationships with their peers become testing grounds for their absorbed patterns around responsibility and agency. Jessica gravitates toward friendships where shared victimhood becomes a bonding experience. She and her friends develop sophisticated analyses of why various authority figures, systems, and circumstances are unfair or unreasonable.

These friendships provide emotional validation and social connection, but they also reinforce the patterns that limit growth. Jessica becomes increasingly skilled at articulating problems while becoming less capable of implementing solutions. Her social circle becomes an echo chamber where external blame is normalized, and internal responsibility is viewed as either impossible or inadvisable.

The conversations within Jessica's peer group follow predictable patterns. When one friend struggles with a challenging class, the group response isn't to brainstorm study strategies or seek additional resources. Instead, they analyze the teacher's shortcomings, the unfairness of the curriculum, and the impossibility of the expectations. These discussions feel supportive and validating, but they actually train the participants to see themselves as powerless in the face of challenge.

Michael's peer relationships develop around his natural charisma and creativity, but they're undermined by his unreliability and tendency to avoid follow-through. He becomes skilled at generating enthusiasm for group activities and projects, but his friends learn not to depend on his contributions when sustained effort is required.

His social patterns create a particular kind of loneliness. While he's often popular and well-liked, his relationships lack the depth that comes from mutual reliability and shared accomplishment. His friends enjoy his company, but learn to work around his limitations rather than count on his strengths.

Both children begin to attract peers who either enable their patterns or exhaust themselves trying to change them. Jessica's closest friendships develop with other children who share her approach to external blame, creating social environments where deflection is normalized and accountability is viewed as unfair or unrealistic.

Michael attracts friends who are drawn to his enthusiasm and creativity, but who eventually become frustrated with his inconsistency. His peer relationships follow a predictable cycle—initial excitement and connection, followed by gradual disappointment as his pattern of avoiding sustained effort becomes apparent.

The sports and extracurricular activities these children participate in become additional arenas where their absorbed patterns play out. Jessica joined the debate team, where her skills at identifying flaws and constructing arguments served her well initially. But she struggles when the focus shifts to improving her own performance rather than critiquing her opponents' weaknesses.

Michael tries various activities, such as soccer, art class, and music lessons, but his pattern of initial enthusiasm followed by gradual disengagement repeats consistently. Coaches and instructors describe him as talented but inconsistent, not understanding that his inconsistency reflects a learned approach to challenge rather than natural ability fluctuations.

The Academic Implications

As these children progress through their educational journey, their absorbed patterns around responsibility create increasingly significant academic challenges. Jessica's approach to learning becomes highly strategic but ultimately self-limiting. She becomes an expert at identifying teachers who are susceptible to her deflection strategies and avoiding those who insist on accountability.

Her course selection begins to reflect this pattern. She gravitates toward subjects where her natural abilities allow for success without sustained effort while avoiding areas where gradual skill development through practice is required. This narrows the number of opportunities that will have long-term consequences for her academic and professional options.

Jessica's relationship with homework becomes particularly revealing. She approaches assignments not as opportunities for learning and skill development but as obstacles to be navigated with minimal effort. She becomes skilled at identifying the minimum requirements for acceptable performance while avoiding the sustained engagement that would lead to actual mastery.

Her study strategies reflect her external orientation. Rather than developing systematic approaches to learning and retention, she focuses on predicting what teachers want, identifying shortcuts through a material, and finding ways to demonstrate competence without developing genuine understanding. These strategies create short-term academic success but undermine long-term learning and development.

Michael's academic trajectory follows a different pattern but reflects the same underlying orientation toward external solutions. He approaches challenging material with the expectation that understanding should arrive through inspiration rather than effort. When concepts don't come immediately, he becomes frustrated and disengaged, waiting for a teacher or tutor to provide the magical explanation that will make everything clear.

His attention patterns in class become highly selective. He engages intensely when material feels immediately accessible or personally interesting, but mentally checks out when a sustained effort is required. Teachers learn to capture their attention through entertainment and engagement rather than helping them develop the capacity for sustained focus on challenging material.

Both children begin to show signs of what educators call "learned helplessness" in academic settings. When faced with challenging material, their first response isn't to analyze what additional effort or resources might be helpful. Instead, they focus on external factors that make success impossible or unfair.

This learned helplessness becomes self-reinforcing. Because they avoid situations where sustained effort leads to gradual improvement, they never develop confidence in their ability to overcome challenges through persistence. Each avoided challenge reinforces their belief that difficult tasks are either immediately solvable or permanently impossible.

The Technology Generation

Growing up in an era of digital technology, these children's absorbed patterns around responsibility and instant gratification are amplified by their relationship with digital devices and online environments. Jessica became skilled at using technology to support her deflection patterns. She can quickly research arguments that support her position in any conflict, find online communities that validate her perspective, and locate information that reinforces her belief in external causation.

The internet became a powerful tool for avoiding personal responsibility. When she struggles with an assignment, Jessica can quickly find articles about how the educational system is flawed, how standardized testing is unfair, or how her particular learning style isn't being accommodated. This information isn't necessarily inaccurate, but it becomes another layer of sophisticated deflection that prevents genuine engagement with her own learning process.

Social media provides additional validation for Jessica's external orientation. She can connect with others who share her perspectives on unfairness and systemic problems, creating echo chambers where external blame is normalized, and personal responsibility is viewed as victim-blaming or unrealistic expectations.

Michael's relationship with technology reflects his pattern of seeking external solutions and instant gratification. He becomes drawn to apps and programs that promise quick fixes; study aids that claim to make learning effortless, games that provide immediate rewards without sustained effort, and social platforms where attention and validation come through performance rather than authentic relationship building.

His attention span, already challenged by his expectation that solutions should arrive without effort, becomes further fragmented by the rapid-fire stimulation of digital environments. The patience required for sustained learning and skill development becomes increasingly elusive as he becomes accustomed to immediate feedback and constant stimulation.

Both children develop relationships with technology that reinforce their absorbed patterns around agency and responsibility. Rather than using digital tools to enhance their capacity for learning, planning, and sustained effort, they use technology to avoid these challenges while maintaining the illusion of productivity and engagement.

The Long Shadow of Childhood Patterns

As these children move toward adolescence, the patterns established in childhood begin to crystallize into more permanent personality structures. Jessica develops what appears to be a strong sense of justice; she's always fighting against unfairness, but this justice is selective, applying primarily to circumstances that affect her while remaining blind to her own impact on others.

Her teenage years are marked by conflicts with teachers, employers, and, eventually, romantic partners who expect her to take responsibility for her choices. Each of these conflicts reinforces her learned worldview that the world is fundamentally unfair and that her problems stem from other people's unreasonable expectations rather than her own areas for growth.

The sophistication of Jessica's deflection strategies increases dramatically during adolescence. She becomes skilled at using sophisticated psychological and social justice language to frame her avoidance of responsibility. Her arguments become increasingly elaborate and intellectually impressive while remaining fundamentally evasive.

Her academic performance during high school reflects these patterns in increasingly consequential ways. Jessica gravitates toward subjects where she can critique systems and analyze problems rather than develop her own skills and capabilities. She excels in classes that involve social analysis and criticism while struggling in areas that require sustained skill development and personal accountability.

Michael's adolescence takes a different trajectory. He becomes charming and creative, skilled at generating enthusiasm for new projects and possibilities. But follow-through becomes his perpetual challenge. He starts and abandons hobbies, begins and never finishes projects, and makes commitments he can't keep. The pattern isn't conscious manipulation but the logical extension of a childhood spent watching problems get explained away rather than solved.

His teenage years are characterized by a series of exciting beginnings and disappointing middles. He joins clubs with enthusiasm, starts creative projects with passion, and makes social commitments with genuine intention. However, the sustained effort required to see these endeavors through to completion proves consistently challenging.

Michael's relationships with romantic partners begin to reflect his absorbed patterns around external rescue and instant transformation. He's drawn to relationships where intense emotion substitutes for sustained commitment, where dramatic gestures replace consistent effort, and where the excitement of new connection distracts from the work of building genuine intimacy.

Both children begin to make choices about their futures, college applications, career considerations, and relationship commitments based on their absorbed understanding of personal agency and responsibility. These choices will have consequences that extend far into their adult lives.

The Transition to Adult Relationships

The transition to adult relationships proves particularly challenging for both children. Jessica attracts partners who either enable her deflection patterns or exhaust themselves trying to break through her defensive structures. Her relationships follow a predictable pattern—initial attraction based on shared complaints about external circumstances, followed by growing tension as partners expect her to take responsibility for her role in relationship dynamics.

Jessica's romantic relationships become laboratories where her patterns around responsibility and agency play out in intimate settings. She's drawn to partners who either share her external orientation or who initially find her analytical skills and social consciousness attractive. However, the sustained intimacy required for a long-term partnership requires exactly the kinds of vulnerability and accountability that Jessica has learned to avoid.

Her relationship conflicts follow predictable patterns. When tensions arise, Jessica's first response is to analyze her partner's shortcomings, the unfairness of their expectations, or the external pressures that are creating stress in the relationship. The possibility that she might need to change her own behavior or acknowledge her own contributions to problems remains largely unexplored.

Partners often report feeling like they're in a relationship with someone who can expertly analyze everyone else's flaws but cannot see their own. This creates a particular kind of loneliness and frustration, as Jessica's considerable intelligence and analytical skills are focused outward rather than inward.

Michael's romantic relationships are characterized by intense beginnings and disappointing middles. He's excellent at the courtship phase, where enthusiasm and possibility are more important than sustained effort. However, the daily work of maintaining relationships and the unglamorous consistency required for a long-term partnership proves challenging. His partners often report feeling like they're in a relationship with someone who's always about to become the person they could be, but never quite arrives at that destination.

Michael's pattern of initial enthusiasm followed by gradual disengagement creates particular challenges in romantic relationships. His partners are initially drawn to his creativity, charm, and apparent potential. However, as the relationship deepens and requires sustained effort, consistency, and mutual accountability, Michael's limitations become apparent.

His relationships often end not with dramatic conflicts but with gradual disappointment as partners realize that Michael's considerable strengths- his creativity, his enthusiasm, his charm- are not accompanied by the reliability and follow-through that intimate partnership requires.

Both children carry their absorbed patterns of responsibility into their adult relationships, creating cycles of connection and disappointment that reflect their childhood learning rather than their conscious intentions or desires.

The Professional Consequences

The work lives these children eventually build reflect their absorbed childhood patterns in profound ways. Jessica gravitates toward careers where she can advocate against unfairness in social work, journalism, and activism, but struggles in roles that require consistent self-evaluation and personal development. Her professional growth stagnates not because she lacks ability but because she's never learned to examine her own contribution to workplace challenges.

Jessica's career path becomes a series of positions where she initially excels, then encounters conflicts with supervisors or colleagues who expect accountability. Each job change is accompanied by elaborate narratives about workplace politics, unreasonable expectations, or impossible circumstances. The common denominator, her own patterns, remains invisible to her.

Her professional relationships follow predictable patterns. Jessica attracts supervisors and colleagues who either enable her deflection or exhaust themselves, trying to provide feedback that she can hear and integrate. Her considerable skills and intelligence make her valuable in many contexts, but her inability to engage in honest self-evaluation limits her advancement and creates ongoing workplace tensions.

The performance review process becomes particularly challenging for Jessica. Rather than viewing feedback as information that could help her improve and advance, she experiences it as criticism to be defended against. She becomes skilled at constructing elaborate explanations for why performance metrics are unfair, why expectations are unreasonable, or why circumstances beyond her control are affecting her work.

Michael's professional life follows a different trajectory. He's drawn to entrepreneurial ventures, creative projects, and roles that promise rapid advancement. His resume becomes a collection of exciting beginnings, startups launched, creative projects initiated, ambitious goals announced, but few sustained successes. Each professional transition is explained through external factors: market conditions, timing, and other people's failures to recognize his contributions.

Michael's natural creativity and enthusiasm initially make him attractive to employers. He interviews well, generates excitement about possibilities, and brings energy to new projects. However, the sustained effort required for long-term professional success proves consistently challenging.

His work patterns reflect his absorbed expectation that solutions should arrive through inspiration rather than effort. He excels during brainstorming sessions and strategic planning meetings but struggles with implementation, follow-through, and the detailed work required to transform ideas into successful outcomes.

Both children's professional lives become expressions of their absorbed childhood patterns around responsibility and agency. Their careers become a series of unrealized potential rather than sustained accomplishment, not because they lack ability but because they've never learned the fundamental skills of honest self-assessment and sustained effort toward improvement.

Part 2: The Thinker's Children

In stark contrast, children raised in households where accountability is modeled and mistakes are treated as learning opportunities develop fundamentally different interpretations of human agency and personal power. These children grow up in environments where problems are approached systematically, effort is valued over outcome, and taking responsibility is seen as a form of empowerment rather than punishment.

Fifteen-year-old Marcus sits at the kitchen table with his mother, reviewing his recent chemistry test results. The grade isn't what he hoped for, but the conversation that follows is markedly different from what might occur in a household shaped by deflection patterns. His mother doesn't immediately reassure him that the test is unfair or that the teacher is too demanding. Instead, she asks questions designed to help him analyze his own preparation and performance.

"What do you think worked well in your study approach?" she asks, her tone curious rather than judgmental. "What might you try differently next time?" These aren't rhetorical questions but genuine inquiries into his learning process. Marcus has grown up with these conversations, and he responds with the kind of self-analysis that would be remarkable in most teenagers.

"I think I understood the concepts but didn't practice enough problems," he admits without defensiveness. "I spent too much time reading and not enough time actually solving equations." This level of honest self-assessment isn't innate; it's a learned skill developed through years of family conversations where mistakes are treated as data rather than disasters.

His younger sister, Olivia, observes these interactions with the same intensity that children in deflection-based households study emotional weather patterns. But what she's learning is fundamentally different. She's absorbing the understanding that difficulties are temporary states that can be changed through focused effort, that mistakes are stepping stones rather than defining characteristics, and that taking responsibility increases rather than decreases personal power.

The household atmosphere in which Marcus and Olivia are growing up is characterized by what psychologists call "psychological safety," the confidence that one can express ideas, ask questions, admit mistakes, and seek help without fear of negative consequences. This safety creates the foundation for genuine learning and growth.

The Language of Agency

The vocabulary in this household creates a different foundation for understanding human potential. When Olivia struggles with a piano piece she's been practicing, the family conversation doesn't focus on the difficulty of the piece or the unreasonable expectations of her teacher. Instead, her parents help her break down the challenge into manageable components.

"Which measures are giving you the most trouble?" her father asks, sitting beside her on the piano bench. "Let's work on just those sections until they feel comfortable." This approach teaches Olivia that complex challenges can be systematically addressed and that improvement comes through focused effort rather than hoping circumstances will change.

The language patterns in this household are fundamentally different from those in deflection-based families. Problems are discussed in terms of strategies and solutions rather than complaints and blame. Challenges are viewed as puzzles to be solved rather than evidence of unfair treatment. Mistakes are analyzed for lessons rather than explained away through external factors.

Marcus and Olivia are learning what psychologists call an internal locus of control, the deep belief that their actions significantly influence their outcomes. This isn't taught through lectures about personal responsibility but absorbed through countless small interactions where their parents demonstrate systematic problem-solving and honest self-assessment.

The children observe their parents facing real challenges, work stress, financial decisions, and relationship tensions, and watch how these difficulties are approached with curiosity rather than defensiveness. They see their parents making mistakes, acknowledging them openly, and working systematically toward improvement. These observations create a powerful model for how capable adults handle the inevitable challenges of life.

Marcus's approach to academic challenges reflects this absorbed learning. When he encounters a difficult concept in his advanced placement history class, his first response isn't to blame the curriculum or the teacher's presentation. Instead, he analyzes what additional resources might help him understand the material. He seeks out supplementary readings, forms study groups with classmates, and schedules office hours with his teacher, not to complain about the difficulty but to get additional clarification.

This approach isn't about perfectionism or excessive self-criticism. The children have learned to distinguish between productive self-analysis and destructive self-judgment. They can honestly assess their performance without interpreting mistakes as fundamental character flaws. This nuanced relationship with failure creates remarkable resilience, and they can face setbacks without being devastated by them.

Olivia's approach to her art classes demonstrates this learned resilience in action. When she creates a painting that doesn't match her vision, her response reflects her absorbed understanding of mistakes as information. Rather than becoming discouraged or blaming her materials, she analyzes what techniques might improve future work. She seeks feedback from her teacher, experiments with different approaches, and views each attempt as part of a learning process rather than a final judgment on her abilities.

The contrast with children from deflection-based households is remarkable. Where those children learn to avoid challenges that might result in mistakes, Marcus and Olivia are learning to embrace challenges as opportunities for growth. They're developing what researchers call a "growth mindset," the belief that abilities can be developed through dedication and hard work.

The Emotional Education

Perhaps most significantly, these children are receiving an emotional education that will serve them throughout their adult lives. They're learning that vulnerability can be a strength, that asking for help is a sign of wisdom rather than weakness, and that admitting mistakes creates opportunities for growth rather than inviting punishment.

Olivia's relationship with her ballet class demonstrates this emotional learning in action. When she struggles with a particularly challenging combination, she doesn't hide her difficulties or blame external factors. Instead, she approaches her instructor directly. "I'm having trouble with the third section," she says. "Could you show me again?" This simple request represents profound learning; she's internalized the understanding that difficulty is a normal part of learning and that seeking help is an effective problem-solving strategy.

The emotional vocabulary available to these children is remarkably sophisticated. They learn to distinguish between temporary frustration and permanent limitation, between productive challenge and overwhelming stress, and between healthy self-evaluation and destructive self-criticism. These distinctions allow them to navigate difficulties with emotional intelligence rather than reactive defensiveness.

Marcus's response to social challenges reflects this emotional sophistication. When he experiences conflict with friends, his approach demonstrates learned skills in communication and problem-solving. Rather than immediately blaming others or avoiding the situation, he analyzes his own contributions to the problem and seeks constructive solutions.

A recent incident with his closest friend illustrates this approach. When a misunderstanding created tension between them, Marcus's first response was self-reflection. "I think I might have been unclear about my expectations," he told his parents during a family discussion. "I want to talk with him about how we can prevent this kind of confusion in the future." This response reflects years of learning that relationships require ongoing attention and that problems are opportunities for deeper understanding rather than evidence of incompatibility.

The family's financial conversations provide another layer of this emotional education. Unlike households where money is either ignored or discussed in terms of external persecution, this family treats financial decisions as collaborative learning opportunities. When they face a significant expense, a needed car repair, a medical bill, or a home maintenance issue, the parents include the children in age-appropriate discussions about how to address the challenge.

"Our car repair is going to cost more than we budgeted this month," the mother explains during a family meeting.

"Let's talk about how we might adjust our spending to accommodate this expense." This conversation isn't about creating anxiety in the children but about demonstrating that financial challenges are problems to be solved rather than disasters to be endured.

Marcus and Olivia watch their parents analyze options, consider trade-offs, and make decisions based on their family's priorities and values. They're learning that financial stability comes through conscious choice-making rather than luck or external circumstances. They're absorbing lessons about delayed gratification, priority-setting, and the relationship between current choices and future outcomes.

These financial conversations also teach important lessons about emotional regulation under stress. The children observe their parents facing real financial pressure while maintaining a problem-solving orientation rather than panic or blame. They learn that stress is a normal response to challenges, but that emotional reactivity doesn't have to determine decision-making quality.

The Academic Laboratory

School becomes a laboratory where these children's absorbed patterns around responsibility and growth are tested and refined. Marcus's academic experience demonstrates the profound advantages of approaching learning with an internal orientation and a growth mindset. When he receives feedback on assignments, his first response is curiosity about how he can improve rather than defensiveness about the evaluation.

His relationship with teachers reflects this orientation. Marcus approaches instructors as resources for learning rather than judges to be convinced or obstacles to be navigated. He asks clarifying questions about expectations, seeks additional help when concepts are challenging, and uses feedback to improve future performance rather than defending past work.

This approach creates a virtuous cycle in Marcus's academic life. Because he's focused on learning rather than protecting his self-image, he's willing to tackle challenging material and take intellectual risks. This willingness to stretch himself leads to genuine skill development, which creates confidence that allows him to take on even greater challenges.

Marcus's study strategies reflect his internal orientation and systematic approach to problem-solving. Rather than hoping for inspiration or trying to predict what teachers want, he develops consistent study routines based on what research suggests about effective learning. He uses techniques like spaced repetition, active recall, and deliberate practice, approaches that require sustained effort but produce genuine mastery.

Olivia's academic experience in elementary school provides a glimpse of how these patterns develop over time. When she encounters a challenging math concept, her response demonstrates absorbed learning about persistence and systematic problem-solving. Rather than becoming frustrated and giving up, she breaks the problem down into smaller components and works through each step methodically.

Her teachers consistently note Olivia's resilience and problem-solving approach. When she makes mistakes, she views them as information about what she needs to practice more rather than evidence of her limitations. This orientation allows her to tackle increasingly challenging material with confidence rather than anxiety.

Both children's relationships with homework reflect their absorbed understanding of effort and improvement. Rather than viewing assignments as obstacles to be minimized or avoided, they approach homework as opportunities for practice and skill development. This doesn't mean they always enjoy every assignment, but they understand the connection between current effort and future capability.

Their approach to group projects demonstrates learned skills in collaboration and shared accountability. Marcus naturally assumes responsibility for his contributions while also supporting his teammates' success. When group projects face challenges, his first response is to analyze how the team can work more effectively rather than identifying who's not doing their part.

Olivia's participation in science fair projects shows similar patterns. She chooses topics that genuinely interest her rather than ones that seem easy or impressive. When her experiments don't produce expected results, she treats these outcomes as data to be analyzed rather than failures to be hidden. Her projects often evolve significantly from initial conception to final presentation as she follows where the evidence leads rather than forcing predetermined conclusions.

The Social Development

The social relationships these children develop reflect their learned approach to personal responsibility and problem-solving. Marcus's friendships are characterized by a particular quality of mutual support and honest communication. When his friends face challenges, he doesn't immediately join in criticizing external circumstances. Instead, he asks questions that help them think through potential solutions.

"What do you think you could try differently?" becomes a natural part of his conversational repertoire. This isn't advice-giving or problem-solving for others but collaborative thinking that helps friends develop their own analytical skills. His peer relationships become vehicles for mutual growth rather than mutual validation of victimhood.

Marcus's social circle attracts other young people who share his orientation toward growth and improvement. Together, they create peer environments where challenges are discussed in terms of strategies and solutions rather than complaints and blame. Their conversations focus on what they're learning, what they want to improve, and how they can support each other's development.

This doesn't mean Marcus and his friends don't experience normal adolescent struggles with social dynamics, academic pressure, and identity development. However, their approach to these challenges reflects learned skills in problem-solving and emotional regulation. They support each other through difficulties while maintaining focus on constructive responses rather than getting stuck in victimization narratives.

Olivia's approach to group projects at school demonstrates her absorbed learning about accountability and collaboration. When her team faces obstacles, she doesn't focus on assigning blame or identifying external factors that make success impossible. Instead, she helps the group analyze what's working, what isn't, and how they might adjust their approach.

This orientation makes her a valued team member, not because she's always right or never makes mistakes, but because she approaches challenges constructively. Her classmates learn to trust her contributions because she's reliable in both her effort and her honesty about areas where improvement is needed.

The children's relationships with authority figures, teachers, coaches, and mentors are characterized by openness and genuine engagement. They approach these relationships without the defensive patterns that characterize children from deflection-based households. They can receive feedback without interpreting it as a personal attack, and they can ask for help without feeling diminished.

Marcus's relationship with his cross-country coach exemplifies this healthy approach to authority. When the coach provides feedback about his running form or training strategy, Marcus listens with genuine curiosity rather than defensiveness. He asks clarifying questions, experiments with suggested changes, and reports back on what he observes. This collaborative approach creates a relationship where the coach becomes invested in Marcus's development because his efforts produce visible results.

Olivia's interactions with her art teacher demonstrate similar patterns. When she receives critiques of her work, she responds with questions that help her understand how to improve rather than explanations of why the current work should be considered acceptable. Her teacher finds these interactions rewarding because Olivia's openness to feedback creates opportunities for meaningful instruction and visible growth.

Both children develop what researchers call "help-seeking behavior," the ability to identify when they need assistance and to request it effectively. This skill serves them well academically, socially, and emotionally. They're learning that independence doesn't mean never needing help, but rather knowing how to get the support necessary for success.

Their approach to extracurricular activities reflects their learned orientation toward improvement and challenge. Marcus chooses activities that stretch his abilities rather than ones where he's already competent. He joins the debate team despite initial anxiety about public speaking, recognizing that discomfort often signals growth opportunities.

Olivia's participation in competitive swimming demonstrates her absorbed understanding of effort and improvement. She doesn't expect immediate success but focuses on gradual progress toward her goals. When she doesn't qualify for a championship meet, her response reflects learned resilience and problem-solving orientation. Rather than blaming external factors, she analyzes her training regimen with her coach and develops specific strategies for improvement.

The Technology Integration

Growing up as digital natives, Marcus and Olivia's relationship with technology reflects their absorbed patterns around responsibility and systematic improvement. Rather than using digital tools to avoid effort or seek instant gratification, they leverage technology to enhance their learning and development.

Marcus uses educational apps and online resources strategically, seeking out materials that challenge him rather than ones that make learning effortless. He's drawn to programs that require sustained engagement and provide feedback that helps him identify areas for improvement. His screen time reflects intentional choices rather than passive consumption.

His social media usage demonstrates learned skills in digital citizenship and personal branding. Marcus understands that his online presence reflects his character and choices, so he curates content that aligns with his values and goals. He uses social platforms to connect with others who share his interests in learning and improvement rather than seeking validation or entertainment.

Olivia's relationship with technology shows similar intentionality. She uses digital art tools to experiment with techniques and styles, viewing technology as a means of expanding her creative capabilities rather than shortcuts to finished products. Her engagement with online content reflects curiosity and critical thinking rather than passive consumption.

Both children develop healthy boundaries around technology use, understanding that digital tools should enhance rather than replace real-world engagement and effort. They've learned to use technology as a resource for learning and connection while maintaining focus on the sustained effort required for genuine skill development and meaningful relationships.

Their parents' modeling of intentional technology use provides a framework for these healthy digital habits. The children observe their parents using technology strategically for research, communication, and problem-solving rather than as an escape from reality or a substitute for genuine engagement with challenges.

The Foundation for Adult Success

As these children move toward adolescence and young adulthood, the patterns established in childhood create a fundamentally different trajectory for their lives. Marcus's approach to academic challenges in high school reflects years of absorbed learning about systematic problem-solving and personal agency.

When he faces his first significant academic setback, a poor performance on a standardized test that affects his college applications, his response demonstrates the emotional resilience that comes from years of treating mistakes as learning opportunities. Rather than catastrophizing the result or blaming external factors, he analyzes his preparation, identifies areas for improvement, and develops a systematic approach to retesting.

"I think I spent too much time on practice tests and not enough time reviewing the underlying concepts," he tells his parents during a family conversation about the results. "I want to work with a tutor for a few months and then retake the test." This response isn't about perfectionism but about maintaining agency in the face of disappointment.

Marcus's approach to college applications reflects his learned understanding of persistence and systematic effort. Rather than applying only to schools where he's confident of acceptance or dreaming only of institutions beyond his reach, he develops a strategic approach based on a realistic assessment of his qualifications and a clear understanding of his goals.

His application essays demonstrate authentic self-reflection and genuine growth orientation. Instead of trying to present himself as perfect or making excuses for limitations, he writes honestly about challenges he's faced and what he's learned from them. Admissions officers respond positively to this authenticity and evidence of genuine learning.

Olivia's transition into her teenage years is marked by increasingly sophisticated decision-making skills. When she faces social pressures around drinking and experimentation, common challenges for adolescents, she approaches these situations with the analytical skills she's been developing since childhood.

Rather than making decisions based purely on peer pressure or rebellion against authority, she considers the potential consequences of various choices and makes decisions aligned with her long-term goals and values. This isn't about rigid rule-following but about conscious choice-making based on systematic thinking.

Her approach to dating and romantic relationships reflects learned skills in communication and boundary-setting. Olivia understands that healthy relationships require mutual respect, honest communication, and shared accountability. She's attracted to partners who share her orientation toward growth and improvement rather than those who either enable avoidance or create drama.

Both children develop what psychologists call "emotional intelligence," the ability to understand and manage their own emotions while effectively navigating social relationships. This intelligence serves them well as they face the increasing complexity of adolescent social dynamics.

Their approach to risk-taking reflects learned skills in analysis and decision-making. Rather than avoiding all risks or engaging in reckless behavior, they learn to evaluate potential outcomes and make informed choices. They understand that growth often requires stepping outside their comfort zones, but they approach challenges strategically rather than impulsively.

The Family Legacy

The household patterns that shaped Marcus and Olivia create a legacy that will extend far beyond their individual lives. They're learning skills and orientations that they'll eventually pass on to their own children, creating positive cycles of accountability and growth that can span generations.

Family traditions in this household center around learning and improvement rather than consumption or entertainment. Annual family goals include both individual development objectives and collective projects that require collaboration and sustained effort. These traditions teach the children that growth is a lifelong process and that families can support each other's development.

The financial literacy education these children receive extends far beyond practical money management skills. They're learning to think systematically about long-term goals, to understand the relationship between current choices and future outcomes, and to make decisions based on values rather than impulses.

Marcus's part-time job during high school demonstrates his absorbed understanding of work ethic and responsibility. Rather than viewing employment as simply a way to earn spending money, he approaches his job as an opportunity to develop professional skills and work habits. His supervisors consistently note his reliability, initiative, and willingness to learn.

Olivia's approach to saving and spending reflects learned skills in delayed gratification and priority-setting. When she wants to purchase art supplies or equipment, she develops a savings plan and often takes on additional chores or small jobs to earn the money. This approach teaches her the connection between effort and reward while building confidence in her ability to achieve goals through systematic action.

Both children develop what researchers call "future orientation," the ability to think beyond immediate circumstances and make choices based on long-term consequences. This skill serves them well in academic planning, relationship decisions, and personal development goals.

Their family's approach to celebrating successes reflects the household emphasis on effort and improvement rather than innate ability or luck. Achievements are acknowledged and celebrated, but the focus remains on the work that led to success and what can be learned for future challenges.

The Peer Influence Network

As these children develop into adolescents, they naturally attract peers who share their orientation toward growth and responsibility. Their social circles become networks of mutual support and positive influence rather than environments that reinforce limitation or blame.

Marcus's closest friendships develop with other young people who are serious about their academic and personal development. Together, they create study groups, support each other through challenges, and celebrate each other's achievements. Their conversations focus on goals, strategies, and lessons learned rather than complaints about unfair treatment or impossible circumstances.

These friendships provide emotional support during difficult times while maintaining focus on constructive responses to challenges. When Marcus faces disappointment or setbacks, his friends offer both empathy and practical suggestions for moving forward. They've learned to balance emotional support with encouragement toward action and improvement.

Olivia's social relationships reflect similar patterns. She's drawn to friends who share her interests in creative pursuits and personal development. Together, they attend art shows, participate in community service projects, and support each other's creative endeavors. Their relationships center around shared activities and mutual growth rather than drama or conflict.

Both children develop skills in choosing positive peer influences while maintaining their own sense of direction and values. They're not easily swayed by negative peer pressure because they have clear goals and strong internal motivation. When they encounter peers who engage in destructive behaviors, they can maintain friendly relationships without compromising their own standards.

Their approach to peer conflicts demonstrates learned skills in communication and problem-solving. Rather than avoiding disagreements or allowing them to escalate into permanent damage, they address issues directly and work toward resolution. They understand that healthy relationships require ongoing attention and that conflicts can actually strengthen relationships when handled constructively.

The Professional Promise

The career paths these children eventually pursue reflect their absorbed learning about personal agency and systematic problem-solving. Marcus gravitates toward fields that require sustained effort and continuous learning, engineering, medical research, and complex project management, and excels not just because of his technical abilities but because of his approach to challenges and setbacks.

His undergraduate studies demonstrate his learned approach to academic challenge and intellectual growth.

Rather than choosing classes based on ease or guaranteed success, Marcus selects courses that stretch his abilities and contribute to his long-term goals. He approaches difficult material with systematic study strategies and seeks help when needed rather than struggling in isolation.

Marcus's research projects during college reflect his absorbed understanding of persistence and methodology. He chooses topics that genuinely interest him rather than ones that promise quick results or easy publication. When his experiments produce unexpected results, he treats these outcomes as valuable data rather than failures, often leading to insights that advance his field of study.

His relationships with professors and mentors demonstrate learned skills in professional networking and development. Marcus approaches these relationships with genuine curiosity and respect, seeking guidance and feedback rather than simply trying to impress or gain favor. Faculty members consistently note his reliability, initiative, and thoughtful approach to learning.

Olivia's career development follows a different path but reflects the same fundamental orientation toward personal agency. She pursues work in education and organizational development, drawn to roles where she can help others develop the same analytical and emotional skills she learned in childhood.

Her undergraduate studies in psychology and education reflect her genuine interest in understanding how people learn and grow. Rather than approaching these subjects as abstract academic disciplines, she connects coursework to real-world applications and seeks opportunities for practical experience through internships and volunteer work.

Olivia's senior thesis project demonstrates her absorbed approach to systematic inquiry and improvement. She designs and implements a study of teaching methods that help elementary students develop a growth mindset orientation. Her research contributes meaningful findings to the educational literature while reflecting her personal commitment to helping others develop the skills she learned in childhood.

Her professional relationships during internships and early career positions reflect learned skills in collaboration and accountability. Supervisors consistently note her reliability, initiative, and ability to receive and implement feedback. She approaches workplace challenges with a problem-solving orientation rather than defensiveness or blame.

Both children develop professional reputations based on competence, reliability, and growth orientation. They become the colleagues that others seek out for difficult projects because they can be trusted to approach challenges systematically and to learn from both successes and setbacks.

The Relationship Revolution

Perhaps most significantly, the adult relationships these children eventually build are characterized by a quality of mutual accountability and growth that creates profound satisfaction and stability. Marcus's romantic relationships develop around a shared commitment to personal development rather than mutual validation of unchanging characteristics.

He attracts partners who share his orientation toward growth and change, and together, they create relationships where challenges are approached collaboratively rather than defensively. Their conflicts become opportunities for deeper understanding rather than battles for who's right or wrong.

Marcus's approach to relationship building reflects his learned understanding of sustained effort and continuous improvement. He doesn't expect relationships to be effortless or assume that compatibility means never having disagreements. Instead, he approaches romantic partnership as an ongoing collaborative project that requires attention, communication, and mutual support for individual growth.

His marriage, when it occurs, becomes a partnership focused on supporting each other's development while building shared goals and values. Financial decisions are made collaboratively, with both partners contributing their perspectives and expertise. Conflicts are addressed directly and constructively, with a focus on finding solutions rather than determining fault.

Olivia's approach to adult relationships reflects her learned understanding that vulnerability and accountability create intimacy rather than threaten it. Her friendships and romantic partnerships are characterized by honest communication, mutual support for growth, and the kind of deep trust that comes from knowing that both people are committed to continuous improvement.

Her romantic relationships develop with partners who share her values around personal responsibility and mutual support. Together, they create relationships where both people feel safe to be vulnerable, to admit mistakes, and to ask for help. Their conflicts become opportunities for deeper understanding and stronger connections.

Olivia's approach to marriage and family building reflects her absorbed understanding of accountability and systematic planning. She and her partner make conscious choices about their relationship structure, financial goals, and approach to potential parenting. They plan for challenges while maintaining optimism about their ability to handle whatever arises.

The financial lives both children eventually build reflect the lessons they have absorbed about systematic thinking and personal agency. They approach money as a tool for creating the lives they want rather than a source of anxiety or resentment. Their budgeting, investing, and spending decisions reflect long-term thinking and conscious value alignment.

Marcus develops sophisticated financial management skills, but more importantly, he maintains the analytical and systematic approach to money that he learned in childhood. He makes financial decisions based on clear goals and careful analysis rather than emotion or impulse. His investment strategy reflects patience, long-term thinking, and willingness to make current sacrifices for future benefits.

Olivia's financial approach reflects her learned understanding of conscious choice-making and accountability. She develops budgeting systems that align her spending with her values and goals. Her approach to debt, savings, and investment reflects the systematic thinking and future orientation she learned in childhood.

Both children become financially successful not because they avoid mistakes but because they approach financial challenges with the problem-solving skills and emotional resilience they developed through years of taking responsibility for their choices and learning from outcomes.

The Generational Impact

Most importantly, when they eventually become parents themselves, they're equipped to continue the cycle of accountability and growth rather than perpetuating patterns of deflection and blame. They've learned not just financial literacy but emotional literacy—the understanding that taking responsibility is a form of self-respect and that teaching children to do the same is one of the greatest gifts parents can provide.

Marcus's approach to parenting reflects his absorbed understanding of the growth mindset and systematic problem-solving. He creates household environments where mistakes are treated as learning opportunities, where effort is valued over outcome, and where children develop confidence through genuine competence rather than false praise.

His children grow up with the same kind of psychological safety that Marcus experienced—the confidence that they can express ideas, ask questions, admit mistakes, and seek help without fear of negative consequences. This safety creates the foundation for genuine learning and development.

Olivia's parenting style reflects her learned skills in emotional intelligence and communication. She helps her children develop vocabulary for discussing feelings and challenges while maintaining focus on constructive responses and personal agency. Her children learn that emotions are information to be understood rather than forces that determine behavior.

Both Marcus and Olivia create family financial practices that teach their children practical money management skills while also developing the analytical and emotional capabilities that underlie financial success. Their children learn not just how to balance checkbooks but how to think systematically about goals, make decisions based on values, and take responsibility for outcomes.

The household traditions they establish center around learning, improvement, and mutual support rather than consumption or entertainment. Family meetings include discussions of individual goals, collaborative projects, and lessons learned from both successes and setbacks.

The Ripple Effect

The contrast between these two approaches to childhood development extends far beyond individual success or failure. These different orientations toward responsibility and agency create ripple effects that shape entire communities and cultures.

Children raised with deflection patterns become adults who contribute to cultures of blame and victimization. They create workplaces where problems are discussed in terms of external causation rather than a systematic solution. They form relationships where conflicts center around fault-finding rather than collaborative problem-solving. They participate in civic life through complaint rather than constructive engagement.

Children raised with accountability patterns become adults who contribute to cultures of agency and improvement. They create workplaces where challenges are approached systematically, and mistakes are treated as opportunities for organizational learning. They form relationships characterized by mutual support for growth and honest communication. They participate in civic life through constructive engagement and solution-focused collaboration.

The implications extend to social and political institutions. Communities populated by adults who learned accountability patterns in childhood are more likely to address challenges through collaborative problem-solving rather than blame and division. They create institutions focused on improvement and learning rather than protection and deflection.

The educational systems in these communities reflect this orientation toward growth and improvement. Schools become environments where mistakes are treated as learning opportunities, where effort is valued over innate ability, and where both students and teachers focus on continuous improvement rather than defending current performance.

The economic implications are equally significant. Communities populated by adults with strong accountability patterns create more resilient and adaptable economies. Businesses focus on innovation and improvement rather than the protection of existing practices. Workers approach challenges with a problem-solving orientation rather than resistance to change.

Marcus and Olivia, along with others raised with similar patterns, become the kinds of citizens capable of addressing complex societal challenges through systematic analysis and collaborative action. They contribute to social progress through sustained effort rather than dramatic gestures, and they maintain optimism about positive change because they've learned that persistent effort produces results.

The financial implications of these different childhood patterns extend beyond individual success to community and societal well-being. Adults who learn accountability patterns create more stable financial institutions, make more thoughtful economic decisions, and contribute to economic resilience through their approach to both personal and collective financial challenges.

The Long View

The silent witnesses—children absorbing patterns of responsibility or deflection eventually become the architects of future communities and cultures. Their absorbed learning about human agency and personal power shapes not just their individual lives but the texture of entire societies.

The children raised in households of deflection become adults who perpetuate cycles of blame and helplessness, creating cultures where problems persist because energy is focused on explanation rather than solution. Their considerable talents and intelligence are channeled into defending limitations rather than transcending them.

The children raised in households of accountability become adults who create cultures of growth and possibility, where challenges are approached as opportunities for development and where human potential is cultivated through systematic effort and mutual support.

The contrast isn't about perfection versus failure, success versus poverty, or happiness versus misery. It's about fundamentally different orientations toward human potential and personal agency. One approach creates individuals who see themselves as acted upon by forces beyond their control; the other creates individuals who see themselves as active agents in shaping their own lives and contributing to positive change in their communities.

In a world facing increasingly complex environmental, technological, social, and economic challenges, the children raised with accountability patterns are uniquely equipped to create positive change. They've learned that problems are opportunities for growth, that mistakes are data for improvement, and that taking responsibility is the foundation of genuine empowerment.

The architecture of their childhood homes becomes the blueprint for the lives they build as adults, structures founded on the solid ground of personal agency rather than the shifting sands of external blame. In their success, we see not just individual achievement but a model for how families and communities can cultivate the kinds of citizens capable of addressing the challenges of an increasingly complex world.

The silent witnesses eventually become the creators of the next generation's examples. Their absorbed patterns become the teaching tools for their own children, perpetuating either cycles of limitation or cycles of growth. In this way, the quiet lessons of childhood reverberate across generations, shaping the fundamental character of human communities and the trajectory of human development itself.

Chapter 10
Principles Or Guidelines To Follow

They say it takes a village to raise a child, in retrospect. It takes organization to create a family structure to withstand the test of time. Every single person has to take responsibility for the family as a whole. This book demonstrates the importance of understanding the principles as they teach us how families survive together. The proper understanding and respect for each other play a significant role in whether families stand strong or fall apart in time. We will demonstrate the strengths and weaknesses we experience mentally and how to educate each other throughout the process. Real bonds are indestructible when we understand each other and our roles as children and adults.

The final chapter of any life story isn't written in dramatic moments of triumph or failure but in the quiet accumulation of daily choices that either build toward a meaningful legacy or perpetuate cycles of confusion and limitation. The principles and guidelines that govern successful families emerge not from theory or wishful thinking but from observing where different approaches to responsibility, planning, and personal agency ultimately lead over the span of decades.

Part 1: The Complainer

The Autumn of Avoidance

Marcus Williams sat in his threadbare recliner on a gray Tuesday afternoon in November, the remote control balanced on the arm of the chair that had been his primary companion for the past three years. At sixty-two, his body told the story of a life lived in perpetual crisis mode—high blood pressure that required three different medications, diabetes that had developed from years of stress eating, and a heart condition that his cardiologist attributed directly to decades of financial anxiety and sleepless nights.

Upon old age, Marcus had no choice but to appreciate his life. The diagnosis had been clear and unforgiving: his body was breaking down from the cumulative stress of a lifetime spent in reactive mode, never planning ahead, always scrambling to address problems that could have been prevented. When the doctor showed him the test results and explained the connection between chronic stress and cardiovascular disease, Marcus felt something he'd never experienced before, a forced gratitude born not from wisdom but from the stark realization that time was running out.

"Well," he said to his empty apartment, his voice echoing off walls that needed paint he couldn't afford, "at least I made it this far." The words felt strange in his mouth, unfamiliar territory for a man who had spent six decades cataloging everything that was wrong with his circumstances, his employers, his family, and the world in general.

This newfound appreciation wasn't the peaceful acceptance of a man who had found contentment through reflection and growth. It was the desperate gratitude of someone who had run out of time to complain his way to a different outcome. Marcus appreciated his small Social Security check not because he'd learned to value what he had but because he finally understood it was all he was ever going to have. He appreciated his modest apartment not because he'd discovered the joy of simple living but because he knew he'd never again have the energy or opportunity to build anything better.

The stack of medical bills on his coffee table served as a daily reminder of the cumulative cost of his approach to life. Each prescription, each doctor's visit, each diagnostic test represented not just the price of treating his physical ailments, but the financial consequence of decades spent in stress-induced crisis mode. The irony wasn't lost on him. In his final years, when he most needed financial resources for healthcare, he had the least money available because he'd never learned to plan for the predictable challenges of aging.

The Viral Confusion

Even in this twilight appreciation, Marcus found himself unable to break the patterns that had defined his entire adult life. The rebuttal of confusion he implemented on the lives and family members around him had become so automatic, so deeply ingrained, that he continued spreading mixed messages and contradictory guidance without conscious awareness of the damage he was causing.

When his son Kevin called to discuss his own retirement planning, Charles would launch into elaborate lectures about the importance of saving money and being financially responsible. His voice would take on the authoritative tone of someone who had learned important lessons through hard experience, and he would speak with passionate conviction about the necessity of starting early, investing wisely, and preparing for the unexpected challenges that life inevitably presents.

"You need to be putting away at least fifteen percent of your income," Charles would insist, his voice carrying the weight of hard-earned wisdom. "Don't make the mistakes I made. The social security system won't be there for you the way it is for me. You need to take responsibility for your own financial future."

Kevin would listen respectfully, but both men knew the advice rang hollow. How could Charles teach financial responsibility when his own checking account rarely had more than two hundred dollars in it? How could he preach about planning for retirement when he was working part-time at a hardware store at age sixty-two because he had no other options? The contradiction between his words and his life created a particular kind of cognitive dissonance that left his son feeling confused about whether to take the advice seriously or dismiss it entirely.

But the confusion Charles spread extended far beyond financial advice. When his daughter Michelle brought her teenage children over for their monthly visits, Charles would hold forth on the importance of education, hard work, and persistence. He would tell stories about successful people he'd read about in magazines, weaving elaborate narratives about the value of setting goals and never giving up on your dreams.

"Your grandfather worked his whole life in the factory," he would tell his grandson, conveniently omitting the fact that his own father had achieved financial stability and owned his home outright by retirement age. "He understood that success comes from showing up every day and doing your best, no matter what obstacles you face."

His grandson, now sixteen and old enough to observe the contradictions, would listen politely while mentally noting that his grandfather was currently facing eviction notices because he couldn't consistently pay rent on his modest apartment. The boy was learning to decode the difference between the principles his grandfather espoused and the reality his grandfather lived, a skill that would serve him well but shouldn't have been necessary.

Marcus had planted a lifeline visioning only what he established, but that lifeline was built on quicksand rather than a solid foundation. The family legacy he was creating wasn't one of wisdom earned through experience but of confusion created by the gap between intention and execution. His children and grandchildren were inheriting not his dreams and aspirations, but his patterns of thinking that made achieving those dreams impossible.

The Unexamined Life

The fundamental tragedy of Marcus's story wasn't that he lacked intelligence or good intentions. He never really understood life because he had never taken the time to think clearly about the relationship between his choices and their consequences. He never calculated for pitfalls because calculating required a level of honest self-assessment that felt threatening and uncomfortable.

When Marcus was twenty-five and newly married, he had assumed that financial security would somehow emerge naturally from working hard and meaning well. He had never sat down with a calculator to figure out how much he would need to save each month to retire comfortably. He had never researched different career paths to understand which directions offered the best long-term prospects. He had never studied the basics of home maintenance, personal finance, or relationship building, which would have prevented many of the crises that came to define his adult life.

Upon not thinking things clearly, Charles had stumbled through six decades like a man walking through a dark house, bumping into furniture and cursing the obstacles instead of turning on the lights. When his car broke down, he was genuinely surprised, as if mechanical things weren't supposed to require maintenance and eventual replacement. When his credit cards reached their limits, he felt persecuted by the banking system rather than recognizing the predictable consequence of spending more than he earned for years at a time.

The pattern extended to every area of his life. Charles had never really thought about his career trajectory, assuming that showing up and doing his job would automatically lead to advancement and increased income. When promotions went to colleagues who had pursued additional education or developed specialized skills, Charles felt the sting of unfair treatment rather than recognizing opportunities he could have pursued himself.

He had never thought deeply about what kind of husband and father he wanted to be, operating instead on instinct and reaction. When conflicts arose in his marriage, his first impulse was to identify what his wife was doing wrong rather than examining his own contributions to the problems. When his children struggled with school or social challenges, he offered advice that reflected his own assumptions rather than taking time to understand their specific needs and circumstances.

Charles never thought about his life in systematic ways because systematic thinking required acknowledging areas where he could improve, and improvement implied that his current approach was inadequate. This level of self-examination felt like criticism rather than opportunity, so he avoided it instinctively, preferring to focus on external factors that explained his difficulties without requiring personal change.

The Feeling Chase

The deeper truth about Charles's approach to life was that he was so interested in wanting to feel something, whether it be love, acknowledgment, importance, or validation—that he made decisions based on immediate emotional needs rather than long-term practical consequences. This orientation toward feeling over building created a life that was emotionally chaotic and practically unsustainable.

When Charles wanted to feel successful, he would buy things he couldn't afford—a newer truck, expensive tools for projects he never completed, or clothes that projected an image of prosperity he hadn't actually achieved. These purchases provided temporary satisfaction and allowed him to present himself as someone who was doing well financially, but they contributed to the debt load that created ongoing stress and limited his future options.

When Charles wanted to feel generous and needed, he would lend money to relatives and friends who had poor track records of repayment. These loans made him feel important and helpful in the moment, creating a temporary sense of being valued and appreciated. But they consistently put his own family's financial security at risk and created ongoing tension when the money wasn't repaid as promised.

When Charles wanted to feel knowledgeable and wise, he would offer advice about topics he hadn't studied and make pronouncements about subjects he didn't really understand. This created momentary feelings of authority and expertise, but it often led to giving guidance that wasn't helpful and sometimes was actively harmful to the people who trusted him enough to ask for his opinion.

The pattern was consistent across every area of his life. Marcus made choices based on how they would make him feel in the moment rather than what they would create in the long term. He said yes to social commitments he couldn't afford because he wanted to feel included. He made promises he couldn't keep because he wanted to feel helpful. He avoided difficult conversations because he wanted to feel comfortable, even when those conversations could have prevented larger problems down the road.

This orientation toward immediate emotional gratification created a life that was always in motion but never made progress. Marcus was constantly busy managing the consequences of previous feeling-based decisions while making new feeling-based decisions that would create new consequences to manage. The cycle became self-perpetuating, creating a lifestyle that felt urgent and important but never actually moved him closer to the stability and satisfaction he genuinely wanted.

The Unacknowledged Cost

Marcus never thought about the health issues and stress he brought into his life, home, and loved ones because acknowledging this cost would have required admitting that his approach to life was fundamentally flawed. The physical toll of his lifestyle had accumulated slowly and subtly, making it easy to attribute his health problems to aging, genetics, or bad luck rather than the predictable consequences of living in perpetual crisis mode.

The sleepless nights Charles spent worrying about bills, relationship conflicts, and work problems had become so normal that he no longer recognized them as symptoms of a larger problem. He had learned to function on four or five hours of broken sleep, using caffeine and adrenaline to maintain energy during the day while never addressing the underlying issues that were keeping him awake at night.

The constant tension in his shoulders and back, which he attributed to getting older and working physical jobs, was actually the physical manifestation of carrying emotional and financial stress that could have been reduced through better planning and decision-making. The headaches he experienced several times a week weren't just random occurrences but stress responses to living in an environment where problems were never fully resolved, just temporarily managed.

Charles's weight gain over the years reflected not just aging or genetics, but stress eating patterns he had developed to cope with anxiety and frustration. Food became his primary comfort mechanism, a way to feel better temporarily when other areas of his life felt out of control. But the health consequences of this coping strategy created additional medical expenses and physical limitations that made his financial situation even more challenging.

The impact on his family was even more profound, though Charles remained largely unaware of the emotional and psychological toll his lifestyle imposed on the people closest to him. His wife had developed anxiety attacks during their marriage, lying awake at night wondering if they would have enough money to pay the mortgage or if Marcus would come home with another financial surprise that would throw their precarious budget into chaos.

His children had learned to read the signs of impending financial crisis, becoming hypervigilant about their father's moods and careful about making any requests that might trigger discussions about money. They developed premature emotional sophistication, learning to manage adult stress and anxiety that shouldn't have been their responsibility to handle.

Sarah still felt anxious about money in her own marriage, even though her husband was financially responsible and they had adequate savings. She found herself expecting disaster around every corner, unable to relax and enjoy financial stability because she had learned in childhood that security was always temporary and crisis was always lurking just beneath the surface.

Robert had gone in the opposite direction, becoming almost obsessively focused on financial planning and emergency preparedness. While this orientation served him well in many ways, it also created tension in his marriage when his wife felt that his approach to money was controlling and anxiety-driven rather than thoughtful and strategic.

The Ripple Effect of Dysfunction

Marcus's grandchildren were now absorbing the same patterns that had shaped their parents, creating a third generation affected by approaches to life that prioritized reaction over planning and emotion over strategy. His sixteen-year-old grandson had recently asked his mother why family gatherings always seemed to involve tension about money, and why his grandfather gave advice that contradicted the way his grandfather actually lived.

The boy was developing the same hypervigilance that had characterized his mother's childhood, learning to read adult moods and manage family emotional dynamics that should have been handled by the adults themselves. He was becoming prematurely sophisticated about dysfunctional family patterns while remaining naive about healthy approaches to money, relationships, and problem-solving.

His fourteen-year-old granddaughter had begun to associate family loyalty with accepting dysfunction and avoiding honest conversation about problems. She was learning that love meant not asking difficult questions and that caring for someone meant enabling their poor choices rather than encouraging growth and improvement.

Both grandchildren were developing assumptions about adult life that would shape their own future relationships and decision-making. They were learning that financial stress was normal, that conflict about money was inevitable, and that planning ahead was either impossible or ineffective. These lessons would influence their career choices, their approach to marriage and family, and their own financial decision-making for decades to come.

The family gatherings that should have been sources of connection and mutual support had become occasions that everyone endured rather than enjoyed. Conversations were carefully managed to avoid topics that might trigger Marcus's defensive responses or create conflict. Family members had learned to communicate around problems rather than addressing them directly, creating a culture of polite dysfunction that prevented genuine intimacy and mutual support.

The Medical Reckoning

The stack of medical bills on Marcus's coffee table represented more than just healthcare costs—they were a tangible manifestation of the cumulative toll that decades of stress and poor planning had taken on his physical body. Each prescription bottle on his kitchen counter told part of the story: blood pressure medication to address the cardiovascular impact of chronic stress, diabetes medication to manage a condition that had developed from years of poor diet and emotional eating, and heart medication to treat damage that his cardiologist directly attributed to sustained anxiety and worry.

The irony was inescapable. At the time in his life when Marcus most needed financial resources to address his health problems, he had the least money available because he had never learned to plan for the predictable costs of aging. The medical expenses that now consumed most of his modest income were largely preventable consequences of lifestyle choices that had seemed unimportant at the time but had compounded over decades into serious health conditions.

Marcus's doctor had been direct about the connection between his health problems and his approach to life. "Mr. Williams," the cardiologist had said during their last appointment, "your heart condition isn't primarily genetic or age-related. It's the result of chronic stress that has literally damaged your cardiovascular system over time. Managing your condition will require not just medication, but fundamental changes in how you handle stress and approach problems."

But changing fundamental approaches to life at sixty-two, especially when those approaches were deeply ingrained and had never been consciously examined, proved nearly impossible. Marcus understood intellectually that he needed to reduce stress, but he had no practical framework for addressing the underlying patterns that created stress in the first place.

Life Lessons from the Complainer

Marcus Williams's journey through life offers profound lessons about the cumulative impact of choices made without consideration for their long-term consequences. His story isn't unique; it's a pattern repeated in countless families where love and good intentions exist alongside confusion, poor planning, and reactive decision-making. The lessons from Marcus's experience serve as both a warning and guidance for anyone seeking to build a different kind of legacy for their families.

The first lesson Marcus teaches us is about the difference between appreciation forced by circumstance and gratitude chosen as a way of life. When Marcus finally began appreciating what he had, it wasn't because he had developed wisdom or gained perspective through reflection and growth. His appreciation was the desperate gratitude of someone who had run out of time to change his circumstances, forced to accept limitations because he no longer had the energy or opportunity to build something better.

True gratitude, by contrast, comes from recognizing abundance while we still have the power to build on it. It emerges from understanding that what we have today is the foundation for what we can create tomorrow, rather than the final verdict on what we'll ever achieve. This kind of gratitude motivates action and improvement rather than passive acceptance of limitations.

The second lesson involves understanding how individual choices ripple through family systems in ways that extend far beyond the person making the choices. Marcus's approach to life didn't just affect his own outcomes; it shaped his children's relationship with money, their tolerance for stress, their expectations about marriage and family life, and their assumptions about what was possible and normal in adult life.

His financial anxiety became his wife's anxiety. His crisis management lifestyle became his children's model for how adults handle challenges. His defensive communication patterns became his family's template for how to navigate conflict. The stress he created through poor planning didn't stay contained within his own experience; it radiated outward and affected everyone in his household and extended family network.

The third lesson centers on the importance of distinguishing between wanting to feel something and actually building something. Marcus spent his entire adult life making decisions based on immediate emotional needs rather than long-term practical consequences. He wanted to feel successful, so he bought things he couldn't afford. He wanted to feel generous, so he made financial commitments that jeopardized his family's security. He wanted to feel wise, so he gave advice based on his assumptions rather than his actual knowledge and experience.

This orientation toward feeling over building created a life that was emotionally chaotic and practically unsustainable. Each decision made for emotional reasons created practical consequences that had to be managed, which created new stress that drove new emotionally-based decisions. The cycle became self-perpetuating, creating constant motion without meaningful progress.

The fourth lesson involves recognizing how our bodies keep score of the stress we create through poor planning and reactive living. Marcus's health problems weren't just the inevitable consequences of aging; they were the direct result of decades spent in crisis mode, never addressing underlying problems, always managing immediate crises while creating new ones through poor decision-making.

The sleepless nights, constant worry, financial anxiety, and relationship conflicts all took a physical toll that compounded over time. What seemed like separate problems—high blood pressure, diabetes, and heart disease were actually interconnected consequences of a lifestyle that created chronic stress. The medical bills that now consumed most of his income were largely preventable costs that resulted from choices made decades earlier.

The fifth lesson highlights how patterns get transmitted across generations when they're not consciously interrupted. Marcus's children didn't choose to inherit his approach to money, relationships, and problem-solving; they absorbed these patterns by observing how he lived. His confusion became their inheritance, his stress became their normal, his reactive patterns became their default response to challenges.

Breaking these generational patterns requires first recognizing them and then making deliberate choices to do things differently. It requires developing new skills and approaches rather than just hoping that good intentions will be sufficient to create different outcomes.

The final lesson from Marcus's story involves understanding the profound loneliness that comes from living behind walls of defensiveness and external blame. The people who loved Marcus learned to avoid topics and conversations that might trigger his defensive responses. This meant they could never have the honest, direct communication that creates genuine intimacy and mutual support.

Marcus protected himself from criticism and accountability, but in doing so, he also protected himself from the very relationships that could have sustained him through difficult times. His defensive patterns created isolation at the very moments when he most needed connection and support.

Part 2: The Thinker

The Architecture of Intentional Living

David Chen stood in the main conference room of the community center that bore his family's name, watching through floor-to-ceiling windows as teenagers filed into the computer lab for their afternoon coding class. At sixty years old, his presence commanded a quiet respect that came not from authority imposed but from competence demonstrated over decades of systematic thinking and strategic action.

The community center represented something profound in Vincent's understanding of success; it was both the culmination of forty years spent building strategically and the foundation for opportunities that would extend far beyond his own lifetime. Growing rapidly within his guidelines, Vincent had established and implemented room for growth not just in his own business and family, but in the broader community that had shaped his early development.

What had begun as a small electrical contracting business operated from a rented garage had evolved through careful planning and reinvestment into a construction company that employed forty-seven people and had completed projects ranging from residential renovations to commercial complexes. But Vincent's vision had always extended beyond simply building a successful business. He understood that true success created opportunities for others rather than just accumulating benefits for himself.

Vincent was now feeling the effects of success, but in ways that would have surprised someone like Charles, who imagined that achievement led to relaxation and the absence of challenge. Instead, each milestone David reached had broadened his mental mindset for new projects, new ways to serve, and new challenges that excited rather than overwhelmed him. Success hadn't made him comfortable; it had made him more capable and more ambitious about what was possible.

The journey to this moment had required David to navigate the same kinds of challenges that had overwhelmed Marcus: economic downturns, difficult clients, family health crises, and all the normal pressures that life presents to everyone. However, David's approach to these difficulties was fundamentally different, shaped by systematic preparation rather than reactive crisis management.

He had worked day and night for decades, but this effort had been strategic rather than frantic, focused on building systems and capabilities rather than just managing immediate problems. Upon reaching this milestone, David's approach to work and life had become a model that younger entrepreneurs and community leaders actively sought to understand and emulate.

The Strategic Foundation

David's success in dealing with stressful situations hadn't come from natural talent or lucky circumstances, but from planning every step strategically in ways that equipped him mentally to cope with challenges that would have devastated someone operating in reactive mode. When problems arose—and they always did in construction, David had systems in place to address them systematically rather than emotionally.

The difference between David's stress and Marcus's stress was preparation. While Marcus experienced each challenge as a crisis that threatened to overwhelm him, David experienced challenges as problems to be solved using tools and strategies he had developed over time. This didn't mean David never felt pressure or concern, but his stress was productive rather than paralyzing because it was channeled toward systematic problem-solving rather than emotional reactivity.

When a major client declared bankruptcy owing David's company $180,000, his response demonstrated the power of strategic preparation. Rather than panicking about the cash flow impact or blaming external circumstances beyond his control, David activated the legal and financial contingency plans he had put in place for exactly this type of scenario. The loss was significant and painful, but it wasn't devastating because David had never allowed his business to become dependent on any single client or project.

His response to the crisis revealed the depth of his strategic thinking. Within twenty-four hours, David had contacted his attorney to begin collection proceedings, notified his bank to activate a pre-approved line of credit that would cover immediate cash flow needs, and called a meeting with his project managers to discuss how to reallocate resources and adjust timelines for current projects.

More importantly, David used the crisis as an opportunity to strengthen his business rather than just survive the immediate challenge. He reviewed and updated his client vetting procedures, implemented additional financial safeguards for large projects, and developed new contract terms that would provide better protection against similar situations in the future.

The Expanded Curriculum

David understood that having carefully thought-out plans came with instability from others who preferred more spontaneous approaches to business and life. Friends and business associates sometimes called him overly cautious, accused him of missing opportunities because he took time to analyze risks, or suggested that his methodical approach was slowing down his potential for rapid growth.

Some family members had initially been frustrated with David's systematic approach to major decisions, wanting him to act more quickly on what seemed like obvious choices. When opportunities arose that appeared to offer immediate benefits, they couldn't understand why David insisted on researching comparable situations, analyzing potential downsides, and developing contingency plans before moving forward.

But having his plans thought out had given David something invaluable, the mental space and emotional energy to continue learning and growing rather than spending all his resources on crisis management and damage control. While others used their time and attention to address immediate problems, David could invest his energy in understanding emerging trends in his industry, developing new capabilities that would create competitive advantages, and building the relationships that would eventually make larger projects possible.

By having his plans thought out, David's free time became available for pursuits that enhanced every other area of his life. He began to study human anatomy and mental conditioning, fascinated by research about how stress affects physical health and how systematic thinking can improve both individual performance and team dynamics. He delved into techniques of human philosophy, drawn to understand the principles that governed both personal development and community progress.

This study wasn't abstract or academic for David, it was practical knowledge that he applied immediately in his business relationships, family interactions, and community involvement. Understanding how people learned and developed made him a better employer, able to create work environments where his team members could advance their skills and build meaningful careers rather than just collecting paychecks.

Understanding how stress affected performance helped David design business processes that supported sustained high performance rather than the boom-and-bust cycles that characterized many companies in his industry. He learned to recognize the early signs of burnout in his employees and developed systems for managing workload and expectations that kept his team engaged and productive over the long term.

The Family Laboratory

David's study of human psychology and development transformed his approach to family relationships in ways that created profound benefits for everyone in his household. When his teenage daughter went through a difficult period, struggling with anxiety about academic performance and social pressures, David didn't respond with quick fixes or frustrated lectures about the importance of doing well in school.

Instead, he drew on his understanding of adolescent brain development and the psychology of stress to create supportive structures that helped his daughter develop coping skills while maintaining appropriate expectations and boundaries. He understood that her anxiety was a normal response to the pressures she was facing, but that teaching her to manage stress effectively was more important than simply reducing the stress itself.

David worked with his daughter to identify the specific factors that triggered her anxiety and helped her develop practical strategies for addressing each one. When she worried about test performance, they created study schedules that broke large assignments into manageable daily tasks. When she felt overwhelmed by social dynamics, they discussed communication strategies and perspective-taking techniques that helped her navigate relationships more effectively.

Most importantly, David modeled the kind of calm, systematic problem-solving that he wanted his daughter to learn. Rather than becoming anxious about her anxiety or trying to solve all her problems for her, he demonstrated how capable adults approach challenges with curiosity and confidence rather than panic and avoidance.

When David's son faced decisions about college and career direction, David's approach reflected his understanding that teaching decision-making frameworks was more valuable than making decisions for his children. Rather than pressuring his son toward predetermined outcomes or trying to solve his uncertainty through parental authority, David helped his son develop systematic approaches to evaluating options and making choices based on clear criteria.

They spent hours discussing the son's interests, aptitudes, and values, not to determine what he should do but to help him understand the process of making decisions that aligned with his authentic priorities rather than external expectations. David shared his own decision-making experiences, including mistakes he had made and lessons he had learned, to illustrate how conscious choice-making improved with practice and reflection.

The Partnership Model

David's wife Patricia had never experienced the financial anxiety that had characterized Marcus's marriage, not because David made more money initially, but because David included Patricia in financial planning from the beginning of their relationship. She understood their goals, knew where they stood relative to those objectives, and participated actively in decisions about how to allocate their resources toward shared priorities.

Money had become a tool that brought them together as partners working toward common objectives rather than a source of conflict that drove them apart as adversaries competing for limited resources. Their monthly financial meetings weren't occasions for argument or blame but collaborative planning sessions where they reviewed progress, adjusted strategies, and made decisions about upcoming opportunities and challenges.

Patricia's involvement in the business extended beyond just understanding the finances. David regularly sought her input on major decisions, valuing her perspective and analytical skills even though her professional background was in education rather than construction. He had learned that diverse viewpoints improved decision-making quality and that including Patricia in business planning strengthened both their marriage and their financial outcomes.

When they faced significant financial decisions, such as whether to expand the business, how to handle a major equipment purchase, or how to balance current income against long-term investment, they approached these choices as a team with shared responsibility for the outcomes, this collaborative approach created a level of trust and mutual support that made both partners more confident and capable than either could have been individually.

Their approach to parenting reflected this same collaborative partnership. Rather than defaulting to traditional role divisions or making parenting decisions in isolation, David and Patricia discussed their goals for their children and developed consistent strategies for achieving those objectives. They supported each other's parenting decisions while maintaining open communication about what was working and what needed adjustment.

The Community Architecture

The community center project required David to expand his thinking beyond his immediate family to the broader network of relationships and institutions that affected everyone's quality of life. He had spent three years researching successful community development projects in other cities, studying funding mechanisms that combined public and private resources, and building relationships with local leaders who shared his vision for what their neighborhood could become.

The process had taught David that creating lasting change in communities required the same principles that had made his business and family successful: systematic analysis, careful planning, and the patience to build something properly rather than quickly. The community center would take longer to complete and cost more than simpler alternatives, but it would serve the neighborhood for decades while creating opportunities for the kind of economic and social development that benefited everyone.

David's approach to the project reflected his understanding that true success was measured not just by what you accomplished during your own lifetime, but by what you made possible for others to build upon. The job training programs would give young people marketable skills they could use to support themselves and their families. The meeting spaces would enable community organizations to plan and coordinate services more effectively. The after-school programs would provide safe, constructive environments for children whose parents worked multiple jobs to make ends meet.

The center's computer lab, where David now stood watching teenagers learn coding skills, represented his understanding that community development had to be forward-looking rather than just addressing current needs. The young people in that lab were developing capabilities that would be increasingly valuable in an economy that demanded technological literacy, and they were building confidence in their ability to master complex skills through sustained effort.

David had insisted that the center's programs focus on developing both technical skills and the underlying habits of mind that made continued learning possible. The coding classes taught not just programming languages but systematic problem-solving approaches that would serve the students well regardless of their eventual career paths. The small business development workshops taught not just practical entrepreneurship skills but the kind of strategic thinking that could be applied to any endeavor.

The Mentorship Multiplication

As David's reputation for thoughtful leadership grew within the community, his calendar filled with requests for mentoring meetings with younger entrepreneurs who wanted to understand his approach to business development and community engagement. These conversations had become one of David's greatest sources of satisfaction, opportunities to share not just practical strategies but the underlying principles that made those strategies effective.

David's mentoring style reflected his understanding that teaching people to think systematically was more valuable than solving their immediate problems. When young business owners came to him with specific challenges, David would help them analyze the situation and develop their own solutions rather than simply telling them what to do. This approach took more time and required more patience, but it built their capacity to handle future challenges independently.

One recurring pattern in these mentoring relationships involved helping people understand the difference between working hard and working strategically. Many of the entrepreneurs David worked with were putting in long hours and tremendous effort, but they weren't seeing the results they expected because their efforts weren't guided by clear systems and measurable objectives.

David would help them step back from their day-to-day activities to examine what they were actually trying to accomplish and whether their current approaches were likely to achieve those objectives. Often, this analysis revealed that they were working very hard on activities that weren't aligned with their stated goals or weren't producing measurable progress toward their desired outcomes.

The process of helping others think more systematically about their goals and strategies reinforced David's own continued learning and development. Each mentoring conversation required him to articulate principles that he had internalized through experience, forcing him to examine his own assumptions and refine his understanding of what actually worked and why.

The Innovation Laboratory

David's study of emerging trends in construction technology and project management had positioned his company at the forefront of innovations that were transforming the industry. Rather than viewing technological change as a threat to established ways of doing business, David approached new developments as opportunities to improve quality, efficiency, and worker safety while creating competitive advantages for his company.

His systematic approach to evaluating and implementing new technologies reflected the same principles he applied to all business decisions. When new software promised to improve project scheduling and resource allocation, David didn't simply adopt it because it was new or reject it because it required change. Instead, he carefully analyzed whether it would actually improve outcomes, developed implementation plans that minimized disruption to current projects, and created training programs that helped his team develop new capabilities rather than just learn new procedures.

David's reputation for thoughtful innovation had led to consulting opportunities with other construction companies and industry organizations that wanted to understand his approach to managing technological change. These consulting projects provided additional revenue streams for his business while allowing him to contribute to the overall development of his industry.

More importantly, the consulting work kept David connected to the broader construction community and exposed him to diverse approaches and perspectives that informed his own continued learning and development. He learned as much from the companies he consulted with as they learned from him, creating mutually beneficial relationships that strengthened the entire industry ecosystem.

The Health Investment

Unlike Marcus, whose health problems had developed from decades of chronic stress and poor self-care, David's approach to physical and mental health reflected the same systematic thinking he applied to business and financial planning. He understood that maintaining his health wasn't just about feeling good in the present; it was about preserving his capacity to continue contributing to his family and community over the long term.

David's daily routine included regular exercise, not because he enjoyed working out but because he understood the connection between physical fitness and mental performance. His morning runs weren't just about maintaining cardiovascular health; they were thinking time when he could process complex problems and develop strategies for addressing upcoming challenges without the distractions of phone calls and meetings.

His approach to nutrition reflected his understanding that food was fuel for optimal performance rather than just a source of immediate pleasure. David didn't follow restrictive diets or obsess about every meal, but he made conscious choices about what and when he ate based on how different foods affected his energy and concentration throughout the day.

Most importantly, David had developed stress management strategies that allowed him to handle the inevitable pressures of business ownership and community leadership without compromising his health or family relationships. He had learned to distinguish between productive stress that motivated effective action and destructive stress that created anxiety without improving outcomes.

When David faced particularly challenging periods, major project deadlines, financial pressures, or family health concerns, he intensified his self-care practices rather than abandoning them. He understood that these were precisely the times when maintaining his physical and mental health was most important, both for making good decisions under pressure and for modeling effective stress management for his family and employees.

The Financial Architecture

David's approach to money and financial planning had evolved far beyond simple budgeting and saving into a comprehensive understanding of how financial resources could be leveraged to create opportunities and security for multiple generations. His financial planning wasn't driven by anxiety or scarcity thinking but by a clear vision of what he wanted to accomplish and how money could serve those larger purposes.

The community center project was possible not because David had inherited wealth or experienced some dramatic financial windfall but because he had consistently made financial decisions based on long-term value creation rather than short-term consumption. Every major financial choice, from business reinvestment to family spending to charitable giving, was evaluated against his overarching goals for what he wanted to build and contribute during his lifetime.

David's investment strategy reflected his understanding that building wealth was about creating systems that generated sustainable returns rather than trying to predict market movements or chase high-risk opportunities that promised quick profits. He had diversified his investments across different asset classes and time horizons, but more importantly, he had invested consistently in his own capabilities and in relationships that created ongoing value for himself and others.

His approach to business finances demonstrated the same systematic thinking. Rather than managing cash flow reactively or making financial decisions based on immediate pressures, David had developed comprehensive financial planning processes that allowed him to anticipate needs, prepare for challenges, and take advantage of opportunities when they arose.

The company's financial reserves weren't just emergency funds; they were strategic resources that allowed David to invest in new equipment, pursue larger projects, and weather economic downturns without compromising his ability to pay employees or maintain quality standards. This financial stability had become a competitive advantage that allowed his company to take on projects that other contractors couldn't handle because they lacked the resources to manage complex, long-term commitments.

The Technology Integration

David's relationship with technology reflected his broader approach to evaluating and implementing changes that could improve outcomes rather than simply adopting new tools because they were available. As construction technology evolved rapidly during the latter part of his career, David had positioned his company to benefit from innovations while avoiding the pitfalls that trapped competitors who either resisted all change or adopted every new development without strategic consideration.

His company's use of project management software, for example, wasn't just about keeping up with industry trends but about creating systems that improved communication, reduced errors, and allowed for more accurate project planning and resource allocation. David had personally invested time in understanding how these tools worked and what benefits they could provide before requiring his team to learn new systems.

The implementation process for new technologies always included comprehensive training programs that helped employees understand not just how to use new tools but why they were valuable and how they connected to the company's overall objectives. This approach created buy-in and enthusiasm rather than resistance and confusion, making technological transitions smooth and productive rather than disruptive and stressful.

David's personal use of technology demonstrated the same intentional approach. He used digital tools to enhance his learning, communication, and planning rather than as entertainment or distraction. His smartphone contained apps for financial planning, project management, and educational content, but he had consciously chosen not to engage with social media platforms or games that consumed time without creating value.

The Succession Planning

As David approached his sixtieth birthday, his thinking had naturally expanded to include questions about how to ensure that the systems and relationships he had built would continue to create value after his eventual retirement. This wasn't anxiety about mortality but strategic planning for how to transfer knowledge, responsibilities, and opportunities to the next generation of leaders in his company and community.

The community center project was partially motivated by David's understanding that creating institutional structures was more sustainable than depending on individual leadership. The center would continue serving the community regardless of who was running it, because its programs and funding were designed to be systematic rather than dependent on any single person's involvement.

Within his company, David had deliberately developed the management capabilities of his senior employees, not just giving them more responsibilities but teaching them the decision-making frameworks and strategic thinking approaches that had made the company successful. He understood that succession planning wasn't just about identifying who would take over his role, but about ensuring that the company's culture and capabilities would continue to evolve and improve.

David's approach to mentoring his potential successors reflected his understanding that leadership development required systematic attention rather than hoping that capable people would naturally emerge. He created formal development programs that combined practical experience with educational opportunities, giving rising leaders exposure to different aspects of the business while providing guidance and feedback on their decision-making and problem-solving approaches.

The financial planning for his eventual retirement had been integrated into the company's overall strategic planning for years, ensuring that the transition wouldn't create financial stress for the business or require rushed decisions about ownership transfer or management succession. David had worked with financial advisors and legal experts to develop structures that would protect the company's stability while providing for his family's long-term security.

The Generational Impact

Perhaps most significantly, David's children were developing into adults who embodied the principles and approaches they had absorbed through years of observing how their father handled challenges, made decisions, and approached relationships. Unlike Marcus's children, who had inherited patterns of anxiety and reactive thinking, David's children were entering adulthood with sophisticated frameworks for systematic problem-solving and strategic decision-making.

His daughter's approach to her career in education reflected the same kind of systematic thinking that characterized David's business development. Rather than simply hoping that teaching jobs would be available when she finished her degree, she had researched employment trends in different educational specialties, identified districts and schools that aligned with her values and interests, and developed a comprehensive plan for building the skills and experiences that would make her competitive for the positions she wanted.

More importantly, she was approaching her career with the understanding that professional development was an ongoing process rather than something that ended with graduation. She had already identified mentors in her field, joined professional organizations that would provide networking and learning opportunities, and begun developing expertise in areas that were likely to be increasingly important in education.

David's son's approach to starting his own business demonstrated the same kind of strategic thinking and systematic planning that had characterized his father's entrepreneurial journey. Rather than simply having a good idea and hoping it would succeed, he was conducting market research, developing detailed business plans, and building the financial and professional relationships that would support sustainable growth.

Both children had developed what researchers call "future orientation", the ability to think beyond immediate circumstances and make choices based on long-term consequences rather than short-term convenience or emotion. This orientation was serving them well in academic planning, relationship decisions, and personal development goals.

The Community Multiplication

The influence of David's approach extended far beyond his immediate family to the broader network of relationships and community connections that had developed around his business and civic involvement. The young people who had worked for his company over the years had absorbed lessons about professional responsibility, quality craftsmanship, and systematic problem-solving that they carried into their subsequent careers and relationships.

Many of David's former employees had started their own businesses, using principles and approaches they had learned while working for his company. This created a network of contractors and entrepreneurs who shared similar values and approaches, improving the overall quality and reliability of construction services in the community while creating opportunities for collaboration and mutual support.

The community center's programs were producing similar multiplication effects. Young people who participated in the job training programs weren't just developing technical skills; they were learning about professional behavior, systematic learning approaches, and goal-setting strategies that would serve them well regardless of their eventual career paths.

The small business development workshops were creating a cohort of local entrepreneurs who understood the importance of strategic planning, community engagement, and sustainable business practices. These new business owners were contributing to local economic development while providing employment opportunities for community members and demonstrating that success was possible through systematic effort rather than luck or exploitation.

Life Lessons from the Thinker

David Chen's journey provides a comprehensive blueprint for building success that extends beyond personal achievement to create lasting value for families and communities. His story demonstrates that strategic thinking and systematic planning aren't just about accumulating wealth or avoiding problems; they're about creating the foundation for a life that serves purposes larger than immediate personal gratification while providing security and opportunity for multiple generations.

The first lesson David teaches us is about the power of consistency over time in creating outcomes that seem impossible from any individual starting point. The community center wasn't possible because of one brilliant idea, a lucky break, or exceptional natural talent. It was the result of forty years of making good decisions consistently, building relationships systematically, and staying focused on long-term objectives even when short-term pressures suggested different priorities.

This consistency wasn't about perfectionism or never making mistakes. David had experienced failures, setbacks, and periods of uncertainty like everyone else. The difference was that he had developed systems for learning from difficulties rather than being derailed by them, and he had maintained focus on long-term value creation rather than getting distracted by short-term problems or opportunities.

The second lesson involves understanding the transformative power of preparation and systematic thinking in handling life's inevitable challenges. David's ability to remain calm and effective during crises wasn't because he was naturally more resilient than Marcus; it was because he had prepared for difficulties and created systems to address them systematically rather than reactively.

This preparation created a psychological foundation that allowed David to approach problems with curiosity and confidence rather than anxiety and defensiveness. When challenges arose, he had frameworks for analyzing them and tools for addressing them, which freed up mental and emotional energy that could be invested in learning, growing, and serving others rather than simply surviving from crisis to crisis.

The third lesson demonstrates how continuous learning creates compound benefits that extend far beyond the immediate subject matter being studied. David's investigation of human psychology didn't just make him a better businessman; it made him a better father, husband, mentor, and community leader. Skills developed in one area of life transferred naturally to others because David approached learning systematically rather than randomly.

This approach to learning was strategic rather than purely intellectual. David studied subjects that would improve his ability to create value for others and solve problems effectively. His learning was immediately applied in practical contexts, which reinforced the lessons and made them part of his automatic decision-making processes rather than just theoretical knowledge.

The fourth lesson illustrates the difference between building wealth and simply making money, and how this distinction affects both individual outcomes and community development. David didn't focus primarily on maximizing his personal income—he focused on creating value for others and building systems that generated sustainable results for everyone involved.

This approach to wealth creation meant that David's financial success was built on a foundation of genuine value rather than extraction or exploitation. His prosperity came from making others more successful rather than competing for limited resources, which created a model for economic development that benefited entire communities rather than just individual participants.

The fifth lesson shows how strategic thinking can strengthen rather than sacrifice personal relationships and family bonds. By including his wife in financial planning and teaching his children decision-making frameworks, David made his family stronger and more capable, rather than viewing family time and attention as competing with business success.

This integration of family and professional life created a household where everyone was working toward shared goals rather than competing for limited time, attention, or resources. Family relationships became sources of mutual support and collaboration rather than stress and conflict, which improved both family satisfaction and business outcomes.

The sixth lesson highlights the importance of expanding our definition of success beyond personal achievement to include contribution to community development and opportunities for others. David's community center project demonstrates how individual success can become a platform for serving others and creating possibilities that extend far beyond any single lifetime.

This expansion of purpose created meaning and satisfaction that purely personal achievement could never provide. David's sense of fulfillment came not just from what he had accomplished for himself and his family, but from what he had made possible for others and what would continue after his own involvement ended.

The final lesson from David's story teaches us that true leadership means creating systems and opportunities that enable others to succeed rather than just achieving our own goals or accumulating personal benefits. The community center will impact hundreds of families over the coming decades, creating opportunities for young people to build better futures and for established families to contribute to their community's growth and development.

This approach to leadership created a legacy that was far more sustainable and meaningful than personal achievement alone could ever be. David's influence would continue through the people he had mentored, the systems he had created, and the example he had provided for how individual capability could be channeled toward collective progress.

The Eternal Architecture

The stories of Marcus Williams and David Chen represent more than individual success or failure—they illustrate the fundamental architecture of human development and the principles that govern how families and communities either flourish or struggle across generations. These men weren't born into dramatically different circumstances or blessed with vastly different natural abilities. The profound differences in their outcomes resulted from the accumulation of daily choices made according to fundamentally different operating principles.

Marcus's approach to life was reactive and emotion-driven, focused on managing immediate problems and pursuing short-term emotional satisfaction without consideration for long-term consequences. This approach created a lifestyle that was constantly in motion but never made meaningful progress, generating stress and confusion that rippled through his family system and affected everyone he cared about.

David's approach was strategic and systems-driven, focused on building capabilities and creating value that would compound over time to benefit not just himself but everyone in his extended network of relationships. This approach required patience and delayed gratification in the short term but created opportunities and security that extended far beyond what seemed possible from his starting point.

The principles that emerged from comparing these two approaches are both simple to understand and challenging to implement consistently. Strategic thinking, systematic planning, continuous learning, and service to others create possibilities that extend far beyond what any individual can achieve alone. These principles work not because they're magical or mysterious, but because they align with fundamental realities about how human development, relationship building, and community progress actually function.

The choice between these two approaches remains available to each of us, regardless of our current circumstances, past mistakes, or inherited patterns. The principles David followed can be learned and implemented by anyone willing to embrace the patient, systematic effort required to build something lasting. The patterns Marcus fell into can be recognized and changed by anyone willing to examine their own habits honestly and make different choices going forward.

But perhaps most importantly, both stories remind us that our choices affect far more than just our own lives. The patterns we establish, the stress we create or the stability we build, the confusion we spread or the clarity we provide, all of these ripple through our families and communities in ways we may never fully understand but for which we remain fundamentally responsible.

The village that raises the child is built through individual choices that either strengthen or weaken the foundation upon which everyone depends. In choosing to build rather than merely react, to plan rather than merely hope, to serve rather than merely consume, we create the kind of communities where all children can grow into their full potential and where the bonds that matter most become truly indestructible.

The legacy we leave isn't measured in the money we accumulate or the achievements we list on our resumes, it's found in the foundation we create for others to build upon and the example we provide for what becomes possible when human potential is cultivated through sustained effort, conscious choice and commitment to purposes larger than ourselves.